FULL MUSIC HARDCOVER EDITION

G-4750C

Our Growing Years

a hymnal

GIA Publications, Inc.
Chicago

The entire liturgy section, unless otherwise noted, is from the *Book of Common Worship* © 1993, Westminster/John Knox Press. All rights reserved. The exceptions are indicated by the designations: *BCP (The Book of Common Prayer)* of the Episcopal Church; *NZPB (A New Zealand Prayer Book)* © 1989, Church of the Province of New Zealand; *SWT (A Service of the Word and Table I)* © 1972, Methodist Publishing House; and *DP (Daily Prayer)* by Eric Milner-White and George Wallace Briggs, © 1941, Oxford University Press. All rights reserved.

Biblical quotations, unless otherwise noted, are from the *New Revised Standard Version Bible* copyright © 1989, Division of Education of the National Council of the Churches of Christ in the USA. All rights reserved.

Cover illustration by Gertrude Mueller Nelson from *To Dance with God,* © 1988, Gertrude Mueller Nelson, by permission of Paulist Press.

ISBN 1-57999-032-0

1 2 3 4 5 6 7 8 9 10 11 12 13 14 15 16 17 18 19 20

PREFACE

Introduction. Hymns can be lifelong companions. In early childhood we learn "Jesus loves me." In our older years we sing, "The Lord has promised good to me, His word my hope secures; He will my shield and portion be as long as life endures," from the hymn "Amazing grace, how sweet the sound."

This hymnal was designed by a committee of residents at Westminster-Canterbury, a continuing-care retirement community in Richmond, Virginia. This committee realized that the purpose of hymns is to enable as many persons as possible to enjoy the faith which was expressed by hymn writers and composers. Thus by singing and reading hymns, we can share spiritual insights and can experience the assuring reality of God's love.

An eminent American hymnologist, Louis FitzGerald Benson (1855–1930), expressed this same idea in a lecture at Princeton Theological Seminary: "So inspiring and uplifting can the spiritual ministry of poetry and music to human lives be made that I venture to propose this task and opportunity of getting the hymnal back into the homes and hands and hearts of Christian people as one of the most rewarding that can engage us."

Since the residents of most retirement communities belong to a variety of denominations, the committee decided that the contents of this hymnal should be ecumenical in scope. Almost half of the hymns are drawn from the list of hymns selected by the Consultation on Ecumenical Hymnody.

Early in its deliberations the committee determined that the book should be light enough to be comfortably held. In addition, the texts should be clearly legible.

The liturgical resources at the beginning of the hymnal were selected to provide for ecumenical worship as well as for private devotions. Furthermore, the publisher has provided additional denominational worship materials for this hymnal, which can be placed in the pocket inside the back cover. These include Roman Catholic, Lutheran, Episcopal, and mainline Protestant supplements for the celebration of Eucharist, or Holy Communion.

The Liturgy

General Worship. The hymnbook begins with a liturgical section designed to be laity-friendly so that almost anyone will feel comfortable leading worship. Each component of the liturgy is included except for the scripture readings and the devotion or homily. There are four options for each section of the liturgy. A community may choose to use all of the (A) options for the first week of the month, (B) options for the second week, and so on, or options may be chosen at will. This allows for variation in weekly worship.

Morning and Evening Prayer. A similar structure has been designed for both the morning and evening prayer services. It is our hope that this format will encourage people to feel more comfortable in leading worship or prayer services.

Prayers. The prayers in this section represent various cultures throughout the ages of Christian faith. They were chosen for their relevance in our prayer life today.

The Psalms and Canticles

Psalms and biblical canticles are the songs found in sacred Scripture. Twenty-eight songs immediately precede the hymn section. Some are printed with full melody, but most follow the form of a refrain and verses. Several methods of performance may be employed.

The refrain, which usually summarizes the psalm, is set to an easily singable melody, often a phrase from a familiar hymn. This refrain almost always belongs to the entire congregation, and may be sung first by a soloist (cantor) to be repeated by all, or sung immediately by all after an instrumental introduction. The verses may then be recited by a worship leader, with the recurring refrain sung by the congregation, or the verses may be chanted according to one of the five tones provided in the appendix. Each of these tones is given in several keys, so that any one tone may be used with various psalms in this section.

Chanting is a form of singing in which the normal speech flow of the text governs the musical rhythm. These tones each consist of two musical phrases, which correspond to two verse lines of text. The first line of text is sung on the single pitch of the first chanting tone, followed by the mediant cadence (three notes), which begins at the dot. The second line is then chanted on the reciting note after the bar line, with the final cadence sung where the second dot occurs. The tone is repeated for each two lines of text. Often, the final pitch of either cadence will have more than one syllable. This final note is always somewhat stressed (as is the case of the downbeat of a measure in metered music). When the last word of the phrase ends on one or two weak syllables—e.g., "mountain," "heavens," "satisfied," etc.—the final pitch is sung on the accented syllable and repeated for each of the weak syllables.

The following two examples show how selected psalm verses would look if interlined with the tone, and how they would look if written as sung:

As written:

Ps. 104 Bless the Lord,   O my   soul! O Lord my God, you are ver-y great.
Ps. 23   He maketh me to lie down in green pastures: he leadeth me beside   the still waters.

As sung:

Ps. 104 Bless the Lord, O   my soul!   O Lord my God, you are ver - y great.

Ps. 23   He mak-eth me to lie down in green pas-tures: he lead-eth me be-side the still wa-ters.

One must always be careful to avoid placing a stress on a syllable that is not stressed in normal speech. The tendency to do this occurs when a weak syllable falls on the first cadence note, as is found above on both cadences of the excerpt from Psalm 23. Both "in" and "the" should not be stressed, even though they begin the cadences. Rather, the natural accents will fall on the syllable before each cadence. In performance, then, the singer would place the stresses as follows:

He maketh me to lie dówn   in green pástures: he leadeth me besíde   the still wáters.

The Hymns

Hymns have two principal uses. They can be sung and they can be read. Both purposes are equally important. Three versions of this hymnal provide formats which serve these two functions.

Full music edition. For the accompanist, this edition has the complete music score with the text interlined between the staves. Also, the many persons who enjoy singing hymns in harmony will use this edition.

Melody-only edition. This edition displays only the melody interlined with the first stanza, with the remaining stanzas given below in poetic form. This arrangement enables a person, while singing in corporate worship, to read the tune more easily and, in private, to ponder the meaning of the hymn at leisure.

Large-print edition. The preceding edition has been enlarged for the benefit of the visually impaired.

A leading hymnologist, Erik Routley (1917–1982), wrote, "When I remember how in my own youth, say thirty years back, men and women in so many branches of the church in England, my home country, would read their hymnals as eagerly and regularly as they read their Bibles, and would, if whipped off to the hospital, reach for the hymn book as well as the Bible, I simply grieve to think this particular pleasure and religious nourishment is withheld from so many or ignored by so many in these later days."

Residents are therefore urged to purchase their own copies so that the hymnal can be on their bedside tables or beside their reading chairs for private devotions and memorization. Then the books can be brought to chapel for corporate worship.

In order to find a hymn for a specific need, several means are furnished. The Table of Contents indicates the thirty broad categories of hymns. And since many hymns have several emphases, the extensive Topical Index gives further help in finding a desired hymn.

Exchanging texts and tunes. If the leader of worship wants to use a particular hymn text but knows that the tune is unfamiliar and there is not enough time or skill to teach the new tune, the Metrical Index is the means for discovering an appropriate substitute melody.

Each tune has a name, which is located just below the hymn title. Alongside the tune name are code numbers or abbreviations like 7.6.7.6.D, CMD, or SM. These symbols indicate the metrical framework of the text. In other words, these numbers and alphabetical abbreviations indicate the exact number of syllables per line or phrase.

To illustrate, consider the familiar Bishop Ken Doxology, "Praise God from whom all blessings flow." This stanza has eight syllables in each of the four lines. This formula is called Long Meter (LM) or 8.8.8.8. Here are two tunes with which the Doxology words could be sung—DUKE STREET (Jesus shall reign) or GERMANY (Where cross the crowded ways), although its traditional melody is the OLD HUNDREDTH.

Two other popular meters are the Common Meter (CM) and the Short Meter (SM). The meter of "O God, our help in ages past" is Common with 8.6.8.6 syllables in the four lines. "Blest be the tie that binds" is in Short Meter with the formula 6.6.8.6.

These three metrical pattern symbols are occasionally followed by "D" which means Doubled. For instance, a meter of 6.6.8.6.6.6.8.6 is shown as SMD or Short Meter Doubled. The text "This is my Father's world" with the tune TERRA BEATA is an example of SMD meter.

The metrical identities of the remainder of the tunes are shown by numerals. These meters are shown in rising serial order from 4 to 14. One popular meter is 8.7.8.7.D. Beethoven's HYMN TO JOY with "Joyful, joyful, we adore thee" is a well-known melody and text in this meter.

To assist you in introducing this hymnal, GIA Publications has published a manual entitled *Introducing a New Hymnal* by James R. Sydnor. Other guides written by Sydnor are *Hymns and Their Uses,* and *Hymns: A Congregational Study* (Agape).

Acknowledgments

This project was conceived by W. Ray Inscoe, Director of Pastoral Care at Westminster-Canterbury Richmond, in consultation with James R. Sydnor. Its publication was arranged by Robert J. Batastini of GIA Publications, Inc., with support from W. Thomas Cunningham, Jr., President of Westminster-Canterbury Richmond. W. Ray Inscoe chaired the editorial committee comprised of Mary Mohr, Edward Peple, Elizabeth Reynolds, Johnni Johnson Scofield, Dorothy and Mann Valentine. These committee members gave enthusiastic and knowledgeable aid to the editorial task. J. Frederick Holper, Professor at Union Theological Seminary in Virginia, was a liturgical consultant. James L. Mays, Professor Emeritus at Union Theological Seminary in Virginia, was the psalmody consultant.

Jeffry Mickus coordinated the project for GIA Publications, Inc. Engraving and typesetting was prepared by staff engravers Marc Southard and Philip Roberts. Proofreading was done by Victoria Krstansky and Clarence Reiels. The topical indexes were prepared by Robert H. Oldershaw.

The committee offers this hymnal to all persons, retirees and young people alike, so that they can have a life enriched by this treasure of hymns. This desire is expressed in a hymn of gratitude by David Mowbray for which a new tune (#65) was composed for this hymnal by Richard Proulx.

Lord of our growing years. . .
Your grace surrounds us all our days;
For all your gifts we bring our praise.

Robert J. Batastini
James Rawlings Sydnor
Editors

CONTENTS

THE LITURGY
WORSHIP
An Outline for Worship (2-17)

Gathering
Prayer before Worship
Call to Worship
Prayer of the Day or Opening Prayer
Hymn of Praise, Psalm, or Spiritual
Confession and Pardon
The Peace
Canticle, Psalm, Hymn, or Spiritual
The Word
Prayer for Illumination
First Reading
Psalm (45-64)
Second Reading
Anthem, Hymn, Psalm, Canticle, or Spiritual
Gospel Reading
Sermon
Affirmation of Faith
Concluding Prayers
Prayers of the People
Lord's Prayer
Hymn, Spiritual, Canticle, or Psalm
Charge and Benediction

Gathering

Prayers for Use Before Worship

The following prayers may be used by worshipers as they prepare for the service.

A. Eternal God,
you have called us to be members of one body.
Join us with those
who in all times and places have praised your name,
that, with one heart and mind,
we may show the unity of your church,
and bring honor to our Lord and Savior,
Jesus Christ. **Amen.**

B. Everlasting God,
in whom we live and move and have our being:
You have made us for yourself,
so that our hearts are restless
until they rest in you.
Give us purity of heart and strength of purpose,
that no selfish passion may hinder us from knowing your will,
no weakness keep us from doing it;
that in your light we may see light clearly,
and in your service find perfect freedom;
through Jesus Christ our Lord,
who lives and reigns with you and the Holy Spirit,
one God, now and for ever. **Amen.**

C. Almighty God,
you pour out the spirit of grace and supplication
on all who desire it.
Deliver us from cold hearts and wandering thoughts,
that with steady minds and burning zeal
we may worship you
in spirit and in truth;
through Jesus Christ our Lord. **Amen.**

BCP

D. God of grace,
you have given us minds to know you,
hearts to love you,
and voices to sing your praise.
Fill us with your Spirit,
that we may celebrate your glory
and worship you in spirit and in truth;
through Jesus Christ our Lord. **Amen.**

In preparation for worship, the people may wish to meditate on the law or the summary of the law.

The Ten Commandments

God spoke all these words, saying,
I am the Lord your God, you shall have no other gods before me.
You shall not make for yourself an idol, whether in the form of anything that is in heaven above or that is on the earth beneath, or that is in the water under the earth.
You shall not bow down to them or worship them.
You shall not make wrongful use of the name of the Lord your God.
Remember the Sabbath day, and keep it holy.
Honor your father and your mother.
You shall not murder.
You shall not commit adultery.
You shall not steal.
You shall not bear false witness against your neighbor.
You shall not covet your neighbor's house;
you shall not covet your neighbor's wife, or anything that belongs to your neighbor.

Ex. 20:1-17

Summary of the Law

Our Lord Jesus said:
You shall love the Lord your God with all your heart,
and with all your soul, and with all your mind.
This is the greatest and first commandment.
And a second is like it: You shall love your neighbor as yourself.
On these two commandments hang all the law and the prophets.

Matt. 22:37-4

Call to Worship

A. Our help is in the name of the Lord,
who made heaven and earth.

Ps. 124:8

B. This is the day that the Lord has made;
let us rejoice and be glad in it.

Ps. 118:24

C. O come, let us sing to the Lord
and shout with joy to the rock of our salvation!
Let us come into God's presence with thanksgiving,
singing joyful songs of praise.

Ps. 95:1, 2

D. Cry out with joy to the Lord, all the earth.
Worship the Lord with gladness.
Come into God's presence with singing!
For the Lord is a gracious God,
whose mercy is everlasting;
and whose faithfulness endures to all generations.

Ps. 100:1, 2, 5

Opening Prayer

A. Almighty God,
to whom all hearts are open, all desires known,
and from whom no secrets are hid:
Cleanse the thoughts of our hearts
by the inspiration of your Holy Spirit,
that we may perfectly love you
and worthily magnify your holy name;
through Christ our Lord. **Amen.**

BCP

B. God of all glory,
on this first day you began creation,
bringing light out of darkness.
On this first day you began your new creation,
raising Jesus Christ out of the darkness of death.
On this Lord's Day grant that we,
the people you create by water and the Spirit,
may be joined with all your works
in praising you for your great glory.
Through Jesus Christ,
in union with the Holy Spirit,
we praise you now and for ever. **Amen.**

C. O God, light of the hearts that see you,
life of the souls that love you,
strength of the thoughts that seek you:
to turn from you is to fall,
to turn to you is to rise,
to abide in you is to stand fast for ever.
Although we are unworthy to approach you,
or to ask anything at all of you,
grant us your grace and blessing
for the sake of Jesus Christ our Redeemer. **Amen.**

D. O God, you are infinite,
eternal and unchangeable,
glorious in holiness,
full of love and compassion,
abundant in grace and truth.
Your works everywhere praise you,
and your glory is revealed
in Jesus Christ our Savior.
Therefore we praise you, blessed and holy Trinity,
one God, for ever and ever. **Amen.**

Hymn of Praise

Confession

Call to Confession

A. If we say we have no sin,
we deceive ourselves,
and the truth is not in us.
But if we confess our sins,
God who is faithful and just
will forgive us our sins
and cleanse us from all unrighteousness.
In humility and faith
let us confess our sin to God.

1 John 1:8, 9

B. The proof of God's amazing love is this:
While we were sinners
Christ died for us.
Because we have faith in him,
we dare to approach God with confidence.
In faith and penitence,
let us confess our sin before God and one another.

Rom. 5:8; Heb. 4:16

C. Remember that our Lord Jesus can sympathize with us in our weaknesses,
since in every respect he was tempted as we are,
yet without sin.
Let us then with boldness approach the throne of grace,
that we may receive mercy
and find grace to help in time of need.
Let us confess our sins
against God and our neighbor.

See Heb. 4:14-16

D. This is the covenant
which I will make with the house of Israel,
says the Lord:
I will put my law within them,
and I will write it upon their hearts;
and I will be their God,
and they shall be my people.
I will forgive their evil deeds,
and I will remember their sin no more.
In penitence and faith,
let us confess our sins to almighty God.

Jer. 31:33, 34

Confession of Sin

A. Merciful God,
we confess that we have sinned against you in thought, word, and deed,
by what we have done, and by what we have left undone.
We have not loved you with our whole heart and mind and strength.
We have not loved our neighbors as ourselves.
In your mercy forgive what we have been,
help us amend what we are, and direct what we shall be,
so that we may delight in your will and walk in your ways,
to the glory of your holy name. **Amen.**

B. Holy and merciful God,
in your presence we confess our sinfulness, our shortcomings,
and our offenses against you.
You alone know how often we have sinned in wandering from your ways,
in wasting your gifts, in forgetting your love.
Have mercy on us, O Lord,
for we are ashamed and sorry for all we have done to displease you.
Forgive our sins, and help us to live in your light,
and walk in your ways, for the sake of Jesus Christ our Savior. **Amen.**

C. Eternal God, our judge and redeemer,
we confess that we have tried to hide from you,
for we have done wrong.
We have lived for ourselves, and apart from you.
We have turned from our neighbors and refused to bear the burdens of others.
We have ignored the pain of the world
and passed by the hungry, the poor and the oppressed.
In your great mercy forgive our sins and free us from selfishness,
that we may choose your will and obey your commandments;
through Jesus Christ our Savior. **Amen.**

D. Merciful God,
you pardon all who truly repent and turn to you.
We humbly confess our sins and ask your mercy.
We have not loved you with a pure heart,
nor have we loved our neighbor as ourselves.
We have not done justice, loved kindness,
or walked humbly with you, our God.
Have mercy on us, O God, in your loving-kindness.
In your great compassion, cleanse us from our sin.
Create in us a clean heart, O God, and renew a right spirit within us.
Do not cast us from your presence, or take your Holy Spirit from us.
Restore to us the joy of your salvation and sustain us with your bountiful Spirit. **Amen.**

Declaration of Forgiveness

A. The mercy of the Lord
is from everlasting to everlasting.
I declare to you, in the name of Jesus Christ,
we are forgiven.
May the God of mercy,
who forgives you all your sins,
strengthen you in all goodness,
and by the power of the Holy Spirit
keep you in eternal life. **Amen.**

B. Hear the good news!
The saying is sure and worthy of full acceptance,
that Christ Jesus came into the world to save sinners.
He himself bore our sins
in his body on the cross,
that we might be dead to sin,
and alive to all that is good.
I declare to you in the name of Jesus Christ,
you are forgiven. **Amen.**

1 Tim. 1:15; 1 Peter 2:24

C. Hear the good news!
Who is in a position to condemn?
Only Christ,
and Christ died for us,
Christ rose for us,
Christ reigns in power for us,
Christ prays for us.
Anyone who is in Christ
is a new creation.
The old life has gone;
a new life has begun.
Know that you are forgiven
and be at peace. **Amen.**

Rom. 8:34; 2 Cor. 5:17

D. Hear the good news!
In baptism you were buried with Christ.
In baptism also you were raised to life with him,
through faith in the power of God
who raised Christ from the dead.
Anyone who is in Christ is a new creation.
The old life has gone;
a new life has begun.
I declare to you in the name of Jesus Christ,
you are forgiven. **Amen.**

Col. 2:12; 2 Cor. 5:17

The Peace

Since God has forgiven us in Christ,
let us forgive one another.

The peace of our Lord Jesus Christ be with you all.
And also with you.

John 20:19, 21, 26

People may turn and briefly greet their neighbor.

Hymn

The Word

Prayer for Illumination

Let us pray.

A. Lord, open our hearts and minds
by the power of your Holy Spirit,
that as the scriptures are read
and your Word is proclaimed,
we may hear with joy what you say to us today. **Amen.**

SWT

B. Prepare our hearts, O God,
to accept your Word.
Silence in us any voice but your own,
that, hearing, we may also obey your will;
through Jesus Christ our Lord. **Amen.**

C. O God,
by your Spirit tell us what we need to hear,
and show us what we ought to do,
to obey Jesus Christ our Savior. **Amen.**

D. O Lord our God,
your Word is a lamp to our feet
and a light to our path.
Give us grace to receive your truth in faith and love,
that we may be obedient to your will
and live always for your glory;
through Jesus Christ our Savior. **Amen.**

First Reading

Psalm

Second Reading

Hymn of Meditation

Gospel Reading

Sermon or Devotion

Affirmation of Faith

Let us confess the faith of our baptism, as we say:

Apostles' Creed

I believe in God the Father Almighty, Maker of heaven and earth;
And in Jesus Christ His only Son our Lord;
who was conceived by the Holy Ghost, born of the Virgin Mary,
suffered under Pontius Pilate, was crucified, dead, and buried;
He descended into hell; the third day He rose again from the dead;
He ascended into heaven,
and sitteth on the right hand of God the Father Almighty;
from thence He shall come to judge the quick and the dead.
I believe in the Holy Ghost; the holy catholic Church;
the communion of saints; the forgiveness of sins;
the resurrection of the body; and the life everlasting. **Amen.**

Nicene Creed

I believe in one God, the Father Almighty,
Maker of heaven and earth, and of all things visible and invisible;
And in one Lord Jesus Christ, the only-begotten Son of God,
begotten of His Father before all worlds;
God of God; Light of Light; Very God of Very God;
Begotten, not made; Being of one substance with the Father,
by whom all things were made;
Who for us men, and for our salvation, came down from heaven;
And was incarnate by the Holy Ghost of the Virgin Mary, and was made man;
And was crucified also for us under Pontius Pilate.
He suffered and was buried;
And the third day He rose again according to the Scriptures;
And ascended into heaven; And sitteth on the right hand of the Father,
And He shall come again with glory to judge both the quick and the dead;
Whose kingdom shall have no end.
And I believe in the Holy Ghost; The Lord and Giver of Life;
Who proceedeth from the Father and the Son;
Who with the Father and the Son together is worshipped and glorified;
Who spake by the prophets. And I believe one holy Catholic and Apostolic Church.
I acknowledge one Baptism for the remission of sins.
And I look for the Resurrection of the dead; And the Life of the world to come. **Amen.**

Concluding Prayers

Prayers of the People

A. Almighty God,
in Jesus Christ you taught us to pray,
and to offer our petitions to you in his name.
Guide us by your Holy Spirit,
that our prayers for others may serve your will
and show your steadfast love;
through the same Jesus Christ our Lord.   **Amen.**

Let us pray for the **world.**
Silent prayer.
God our creator,
you made all things in your wisdom,
and in your love you save us.
We pray for the whole creation.
Overthrow evil powers, right what is wrong,
feed and satisfy those who thirst for justice,
so that all your children may freely enjoy the earth you have made,
and joyfully sing your praises;
through Jesus Christ our Lord.   **Amen.**

Let us pray for the **church.**
Silent prayer.
Gracious God,
you have called us to be the church of Jesus Christ.
Keep us one in faith and service,
breaking bread together,
and proclaiming the good news to the world,
that all may believe you are love,
turn to your ways,
and live in the light of your truth;
through Jesus Christ our Lord.   **Amen.**

Let us pray for **peace.**
Silent prayer.
Eternal God,
you sent us a Savior, Christ Jesus,
to break down the walls of hostility that divide us.
Send peace on earth,
and put down greed, pride, and anger,
which turn nation against nation and race against race.
Speed the day when wars will end
and the whole world accepts your rule;
through Jesus Christ our Lord.   **Amen.**

Let us pray for **enemies.**
Silent prayer.
O God, whom we cannot love unless we love our neighbors,
remove hate and prejudice from us and from all people,
so that your children may be reconciled
with those we fear, resent, or threaten;
and live together in your peace;
through Jesus Christ our Lord.   **Amen.**

Let us pray for those who **govern** us.
Silent prayer.
Mighty God, sovereign over the nations,
direct those who make, administer, and judge our laws;
the President of the United States
and others in authority among us (especially N., N.);
that, guided by your wisdom,
they may lead us in the way of righteousness;
through Jesus Christ our Lord.   **Amen.**

Let us pray for **world leaders.**
Silent prayer.
Eternal Ruler, hope of all the earth,
give vision to those who serve the United Nations,
and to those who govern all countries;
that, with goodwill and justice,
they may take down barriers,
and draw together one new world in peace;
through Jesus Christ our Lord.   **Amen.**

Let us pray for the **sick.**
Silent prayer.
Merciful God, you bear the pain of the world.
Look with compassion on those who are sick (especially on N., N.);
cheer them by your word,
and bring healing as a sign of your grace;
through Jesus Christ our Lord.   **Amen.**

Let us pray for those who **sorrow.**
Silent prayer.
God of comfort, stand with those who sorrow (especially N., N.);
that they may be sure that neither death nor life,
nor things present nor things to come,
shall separate them from your love;
through Jesus Christ our Lord.   **Amen.**

Let us pray for **friends** and **families.**
Silent prayer.
God of compassion,
bless us and those we love,
our friends and families;
that, drawing close to you,
we may be drawn closer to each other;
through Jesus Christ our Lord.   **Amen.**

B. Gracious God,
because we are not strong enough to pray as we should,
you provide Christ Jesus and the Holy Spirit to intercede for us in power.
In this confidence we ask you to accept our prayers.
God of mercy,
hear our prayer.

Let us pray for the **church.**
Silent prayer.
Faithful God, you formed your church from the despised of the earth
and showed them mercy,
that they might proclaim your salvation to all.
Strengthen those whom you choose today,
that they may faithfully endure all trials
by which you conform your church to the cross of Christ.
God of mercy,
hear our prayer.

Let us pray for **creation.**
Silent prayer.
Creator of all, you entrusted the earth to the human race,
yet we disrupt its peace with violence
and corrupt its purity with our greed.
Prevent your people from ravaging creation,
that coming generations may inherit lands brimming with life.
God of mercy,
hear our prayer.

Let us pray for the **world.**
Silent prayer.
Sovereign God, you hold both the history of nations
and the humble life of villages in your care.
Preserve the people of every nation from tyrants,
heal them of disease,
and protect them in time of upheaval and disaster,
that all may enter the kingdom that cannot be shaken.
God of mercy,
hear our prayer.

Let us pray for **peace.**
Silent prayer.
Judge of the nations,
you created humanity for salvation, not destruction,
and sent your Son to guide us into the way of peace.
Enable people of every race and nation
to accept each other as sisters and brothers,
your children, on whom you lavish honor and favor.
God of mercy,
hear our prayer.

Let us pray for those who **govern** us.
Silent prayer.
God Most High,
in Jesus of Nazareth you show us the authority that pleases you:
for he rules not by power or might, but serves in obedience to your will.
We pray for all in authority over us:
for our President, N., for Congress,
for our Governor, N., and our state legislature, (and N., N.).
Deliver them from vain ambitions
that they may govern in wisdom and justice.
God of mercy,
hear our prayer.

Let us pray for this **community.**
Silent prayer.
Merciful God, since Jesus longed to protect Jerusalem
as a hen gathers her young under her wings,
we ask you to guard and strengthen all who live and work here.
Deliver your people from jealousy and contempt
that they may show mercy to all their neighbors.
God of mercy,
hear our prayer.

Let us pray for all **families**
and those who **live alone.**
Silent prayer.
Holy God, from whom every family on earth takes its name:
Strengthen parents to be responsible and loving
that their children may know security and joy.
Lead children to honor parents by compassion and forgiveness.
May all people discover your parental care
by the respect and love given them by others.
God of mercy,
hear our prayer.

Let us pray for all who suffer any **sorrow** or **trial.**
Silent prayer.
Compassionate God,
your Son gives rest to those weary with heavy burdens.
Heal the sick in body, mind, and spirit.
Lift up the depressed.
Befriend those who grieve.
Comfort the anxious.
Stand with all victims of abuse and other crime.
Awaken those who damage themselves and others
through the use of any drug.
Fill all people with your Holy Spirit
that they may bear each other's burdens
and so fulfill the law of Christ.
God of mercy,
hear our prayer.

Let us give thanks for the lives of the **departed**
who now have rest in God.
Silent prayer.
Eternal God,
your love is stronger than death,
and your passion more fierce than the grave.
We rejoice in the lives of those
whom you have drawn into your eternal embrace.
Keep us in joyful communion with them
until we join the saints of every people and nation,
gathered before your throne in ceaseless praise.
God of glory,
you see how all creation groans in labor as it awaits redemption.
As we work for and await your new creation,
we trust that you will answer our prayers with grace,
and fulfill your promise
that all things work together for good for those who love you;
through Jesus Christ our Lord.   **Amen.**

C. As God's people, called to love one another,
let us pray for the needs of the church,
the whole human family,
and all the world, saying: Hear our prayer.
That churches of all traditions
may discover their unity in Christ
and exercise their gifts in service of all,
we pray to you, O God:
hear our prayer.

That the earth may be freed
from war, famine and disease,
and the air, soil and waters cleansed of poison,
we pray to you, O God:
hear our prayer.

That those who govern and maintain peace in every land
may exercise their powers in obedience to your commands,
we pray to you, O God:
hear our prayer.

That you will strengthen this nation to pursue just priorities
so that the races may be reconciled;
the young, educated; the old, cared for;
the hungry, filled; the homeless, housed;
and the sick, comforted and healed,
we pray to you, O God:
hear our prayer.

That you will preserve all who live and work
in this city (town, village, community)
in peace and safety,
we pray to you, O God:
hear our prayer.

That you will comfort and empower
those who face any difficulty or trial:
the sick (especially N., N.),
the disabled, the poor, the oppressed,
those who grieve and those in prison,
we pray to you, O God:
hear our prayer.

That you will accept our thanksgiving
for all faithful servants of Christ now at rest,
who, with us, await a new heaven and a new earth,
your everlasting kingdom,
we pray to you, O God:
hear our prayer.

Merciful God, as a potter fashions a vessel from humble clay,
you form us into a new creation.
Shape us, day by day,
through the cross of Christ your Son,
until we pray as continually as we breathe
and all our acts are prayer;
through Jesus Christ
and in the mystery of the Holy Spirit, we pray. **Amen.**

The Lord's Prayer

As our Savior Christ has taught us, we are bold to pray:

Our Father, who art in heaven,
hallowed be thy name,
thy kingdom come,
thy will be done,
on earth as it is in heaven.
Give us this day our daily bread;
and forgive us our debts,
as we forgive our debtors;
and lead us not into temptation,
but deliver us from evil.
For thine is the kingdom,
and the power, and the glory,
for ever. Amen.

Hymn

Charge

A. Go out into the world in peace.
Love the Lord your God with all your heart,
with all your soul, with all your mind;
and love your neighbor as yourself.

Matt. 22:37-40

B. Whatever you do, in word or deed,
do everything in the name of the Lord Jesus, giving thanks to God through him.

Col. 3:17

C. Be watchful, stand firm in your faith,
be courageous and strong.
Let all that you do be done in love.

1 Cor. 16:13, 14

D. God has shown you what is good.
What does the Lord require of you but to do justice,
and to love kindness, and to walk humbly with your God?

Micah 6:8

Blessing

A. The grace of the Lord Jesus Christ,
the love of God,
and the communion of the Holy Spirit
be with you all.
Alleluia! **Amen.**

2 Cor. 13:13

B. The Lord bless you and keep you.
The Lord be kind and gracious to you.
The Lord look upon you with favor
and give you peace.
Alleluia! **Amen.**

See Num. 6:24-26

C. The peace of God,
which passes all understanding,
keep your hearts and minds
in the knowledge and love of God,
and of God's Son, Jesus Christ our Lord;
and the blessing of God almighty,
the Father, the Son, and the Holy Spirit,
remain with you always. **Amen.**

See Phil. 4:7

D. May the God of hope
fill you with all joy and peace in believing,
so that you may abound in hope
by the power of the Holy Spirit.
Alleluia! **Amen.**

Rom. 15:13

DAILY PRAYER

MORNING PRAYER

An Outline of Morning Prayer (18-25)

Opening Sentences
Morning Psalm or Morning Hymn
Psalm(s)
Psalm (45-64)
Silent Prayer
[Psalm Prayer]
Scripture Reading
Silent Reflection
[A Brief Interpretation of the Reading, or a Nonbiblical Reading]
Canticle
Canticle of Zechariah or Other Canticle   (37-44)
Prayers of Thanksgiving and Intercession
Thanksgivings and Intercessions
Concluding Prayer
Lord's Prayer
[Hymn or Spiritual]
Dismissal
[Sign of Peace]

When a person is worshipping alone, or in a family group, or when circumstances call for an abbreviated order, the following is suggested:
Psalm (45-64)
Scripture Reading
Silent Reflection
Prayers of Thanksgiving and Intercession

Opening Sentences

All may stand.

O Lord, open my lips.
And my mouth shall proclaim your praise.

And one of the following:
Sunday
The Lord's unfailing love and mercy never cease,
fresh as the morning and sure as the sunrise.

Lam. 3:22-23

Monday
You created the day and the night, O God;
you set the sun and the moon in their places;
you set the limits of the earth;
you made summer and winter.

Ps. 74:16, 17

Tuesday
I pray to you, O Lord;
you hear my voice in the morning;
at sunrise I offer my prayer
and wait for your answer.

Ps. 5:2b-3

Wednesday
O depth of wealth, wisdom, and knowledge of God!
How unsearchable are God's judgments,
how untraceable are God's ways!
The source, guide, and goal of all that is,
to God be glory for ever!   **Amen.**

Rom. 11:33, 36

Thursday
Alleluia!
For the Lord our God the Almighty reigns.
Let us rejoice and exult and give God the glory.

Rev. 19:6, 7

Friday
Through Jesus let us continually offer up a sacrifice of praise to God,
the fruit of lips that acknowledge God's name.

Heb. 13:15

Saturday
You are worthy, our Lord and God,
to receive glory and honor and power
for you created all things,
and by your will they existed
and were created.

Rev. 4:11

Morning Psalm or Morning Hymn

One of the morning psalms (95:1-7; 100; 63:1-8; 51:1-12) or a morning hymn may be sung or spoken.

Psalms

Scripture Reading

At the conclusion of the reading of scripture, the reader may say:

The Word of the Lord.
Thanks be to God.

Silence may follow for reflection on the meaning of the scripture.
The scripture may be briefly interpreted, or a devotion may be read.

Canticle

The Canticle of Zechariah or another canticle may be sung or spoken. (37-44)
All may stand.

Prayers of Thanksgiving and Intercession

Satisfy us with your love in the morning,
and we will live this day in joy and praise.

One of the following, or other prayers of thanksgiving and intercession, may be spoken:

Sunday
Mighty God of mercy, we thank you for the resurrection dawn bringing the glory of our risen Lord who makes every day new. Especially we thank you for
  the beauty of your creation . . .
  the new creation in Christ and all gifts of healing and forgiveness . . .
  the sustaining love of family and friends . . .
  the fellowship of faith in your church. . . .
Merciful God of might, renew this weary world, heal the hurts of all your children, and bring about your peace for all in Christ Jesus, the living Lord. Especially we pray for
  those who govern nations of the world . . .
  the people in countries ravaged by strife or warfare . . .
  all who work for peace and international harmony . . .
  all who strive to save the earth from destruction . . .
  the church of Jesus Christ in every land. . . .

Monday
We praise you, God our creator, for your handiwork in shaping and sustaining your wondrous creation. Especially we thank you for
  the miracle of life and the wonder of living . . .
  particular blessings coming to us in this day . . .
  the resources of the earth . . .

gifts of creative vision and skillful craft . . .

the treasure stored in every human life. . . .

We dare to pray for others, God our Savior, claiming your love in Jesus Christ for the whole world, committing ourselves to care for those around us in his name. Especially we pray for

those who work for the benefit of others . . .

those who cannot work today . . .

those who teach and those who learn . . .

people who are poor . . .

the church in Europe. . . .

Tuesday

Eternal God, we rejoice this morning in the gift of life, which we have received by your grace, and the new life you give in Jesus Christ. Especially we thank you for

the love of our families . . .

the affection of our friends . . .

strength and abilities to serve your purpose today . . .

this community in which we live . . .

opportunities to give as we have received. . . .

God of grace, we offer our prayers for the needs of others and commit ourselves to serve them even as we have been served in Jesus Christ. Especially we pray for

those closest to us, families, friends, neighbors . . .

refugees and homeless men, women and children . . .

the outcast and persecuted . . .

those from whom we are estranged . . .

the church in Africa. . . .

Wednesday

God of all mercies, we praise you that you have brought us to this new day, brightening our lives with the dawn of promise and hope in Jesus Christ. Especially we thank you for

the warmth of sunlight, the wetness of rain and snow, and all that nourishes the earth . . .

the presence and power of your Spirit . . .

the support and encouragement we receive from others . . .

those who provide for public safety and well-being . . .

the mission of the church around the world. . . .

Merciful God, strengthen us in prayer that we may lift up the brokenness of this world for your healing, and share in the saving love of Jesus Christ. Especially we pray for

those in positions of authority over others . . .

the lonely and forgotten . . .

children without families or homes . . .

agents of caring and relief . . .

the church in Asia and the Middle East. . . .

Thursday

Loving God, as the rising sun chases away the night, so you have scattered the power of death in the rising of Jesus Christ, and you bring us all blessings in him. Especially we thank you for

>   the community of faith in our church . . .

>   those with whom we work or share common concerns . . .

>   the diversity of your children . . .

>   indications of your love at work in the world . . .

>   those who work for reconciliation. . . .

Mighty God, with the dawn of your love you reveal your victory over all that would destroy or harm, and you brighten the lives of all who need you. Especially we pray for

>   families suffering separation . . .

>   people different from ourselves . . .

>   those isolated by sickness or sorrow . . .

>   the victims of violence or warfare . . .

>   the church in the Pacific region. . . .

Friday

Eternal God, we praise you for your mighty love given in Christ's sacrifice on the cross, and the new life we have received by his resurrection. Especially we thank you for

>   the presence of Christ in our weakness and suffering . . .

>   the ministry of Word and Sacrament . . .

>   all who work to help and heal . . .

>   sacrifices made for our benefit . . .

>   opportunities for our generous giving. . . .

God of grace, let our concern for others reflect Christ's self-giving love, not only in our prayers, but also in our practice. Especially we pray for

>   those subjected to tyranny and oppression . . .

>   wounded and injured people . . .

>   those who face death . . .

>   those who may be our enemies . . .

>   the church in Latin America. . . .

Saturday

Great and wonderful God, we praise and thank you for the gift of renewal in Jesus Christ. Especially we thank you for

>   opportunities for rest and recreation . . .

>   the regenerating gifts of the Holy Spirit . . .

>   activities shared by young and old . . .

>   fun and laughter . . .

>   every service that proclaims your love. . . .

You make all things new, O God, and we offer our prayers for the renewal of the world and the healing of its wounds. Especially we pray for

>   those who have no leisure . . .

>   people enslaved by addictions . . .

those who entertain and enlighten . . .
those confronted with temptation . . .
the church in North America. . . .

*Individual prayers of thanksgiving and intercession may be offered.
There may be silent prayer.*

The leader then says one of the following prayers, or a similar prayer.
Sunday
Eternal God,
our beginning and our end,
be our starting point and our haven,
and accompany us in this day's journey.
Use our hands
to do the work of your creation,
and use our lives
to bring others the new life you give this world
in Jesus Christ, Redeemer of all. **Amen.**

Monday
As you cause the sun to rise, O God,
bring the light of Christ to dawn in our souls
and dispel all darkness.
Give us grace to reflect Christ's glory;
and let his love show in our deeds,
his peace shine in our words,
and his healing in our touch,
that all may give him praise, now and for ever. **Amen.**

Tuesday
Eternal God,
your touch makes this world holy.
Open our eyes to see your hand at work
in the splendor of creation,
and in the beauty of human life.
Help us to cherish the gifts that surround us,
to share your blessings with our sisters and brothers,
and to experience the joy of life in your presence.
We ask this through Christ our Lord. **Amen.**

Wednesday

Eternal God,
you never fail to give us each day all that we ever need,
and even more.
Give us such joy in living
and such peace in serving Christ,
that we may gratefully make use of all your blessings,
and joyfully seek our risen Lord
in everyone we meet.
In Jesus Christ we pray.   **Amen.**

Thursday

O God,
you are the well-spring of life.
Pour into our hearts the living water of your grace,
that we may be refreshed to live this day in joy,
confident of your presence
and empowered by your peace,
in Jesus Christ our Lord.   **Amen.**

NZPB, alt.

Friday

Eternal God,
you call us to ventures
of which we cannot see the ending,
by paths as yet untrodden,
through perils unknown.
Give us faith to go out with courage,
not knowing where we go,
but only that your hand is leading us
and your love supporting us;
through Jesus Christ our Lord.   **Amen.**

DP, alt.

Saturday

God our creator,
yours is the morning and yours is the evening.
Let Christ the sun of righteousness
shine for ever in our hearts
and draw us to that light
where you live in radiant glory.
We ask this for the sake of Jesus Christ our Redeemer.   **Amen.**

NZPB, alt.

The Lord's Prayer

Now let us pray the prayer Jesus taught his disciples to pray saying:

Our Father, who art in heaven,
hallowed be thy name,
thy kingdom come,
thy will be done,
on earth as it is in heaven.
Give us this day our daily bread;
and forgive us our debts,
as we forgive our debtors;
and lead us not into temptation,
but deliver us from evil.
For thine is the kingdom,
and the power, and the glory,
for ever.   Amen.

[Hymn or Spiritual]

Dismissal

The leader dismisses the people using one of the following:

A. The grace of God be with us all, now and always.
Amen.
Bless the Lord.
The Lord's name be praised.

1 Tim. 6:21

B. May the God of hope fill us with all joy and peace
through the power of the Holy Spirit.
Amen.
Bless the Lord.
The Lord's name be praised.

Rom. 15:13

C. To God be honor and glory for ever and ever.
Amen.
Bless the Lord.
The Lord's name be praised.

1 Tim. 1:17

D. May we continue to grow in the grace and knowledge
of Jesus Christ, our Lord and Savior.
Amen.
Bless the Lord.
The Lord's name be praised.

2 Peter 3:18

A sign of peace may be exchanged by all.

EVENING PRAYER

An Outline of Evening Prayer (26-32)

Opening Sentences
Evening Hymn
Psalm(s)
Psalm (45-64)
Silent Prayer
[Psalm Prayer]
Scripture Reading
Silent Reflection
[A Brief Interpretation of the Reading, or a Nonbiblical Reading]
Canticle
Canticle of Mary or Other Canticle (37-44)
Prayers of Thanksgiving and Intercession
Concluding Prayer
Lord's Prayer
[Hymn or Spiritual]
Dismissal
[Sign of Peace]

When a person is worshipping alone, or in a family group, or when circumstances call for an abbreviated order, the following is suggested:
Psalm (45-64)
Scripture Reading
Silent Reflection
Prayers of Thanksgiving and Intercession

Opening Sentences

All may stand.

A. Our help is in the name of the Lord,
who made heaven and earth.

Ps. 24:34

B. O God, come to our assistance.
O Lord, hasten to help us.

See Ps. 70:1

C. Light and peace in Jesus Christ our Lord.
Thanks be to God.

And one of the following prayers is spoken:

Sunday

God reveals deep and mysterious things, and knows what is hidden in darkness.
God is surrounded by light. To you, O God, we give thanks and praise.

Dan. 2:22-23

Monday

I could ask the darkness to hide me or the light around me to become night,
but even darkness is not dark for you, and the night is as bright as the day;
for darkness is as light with you.

Ps. 139:11-12

Tuesday

The city of God has no need of sun or moon, for the glory of God is its light,
and its lamp is the Lamb.
By its light shall the nations walk, and the rulers of earth shall bring their treasures into it.

Rev. 21:23-24

Wednesday

In the city of God, night shall be no more; they need no light of lamp or sun,
for the Lord God will be their light, and they will reign for ever and ever.

Rev. 22:5

Thursday

God will come, and there shall be continuous day, for at evening time there shall be light.
God is light; in God there is no darkness at all.

Zech. 14:5c, 7, and 1 John 1:5

Friday

God who said, "Out of darkness the light shall shine!" is the same God who made light
shine in our hearts to bring us the knowledge of God's glory shining in the face of Christ.

2 Cor. 4:6

Saturday

You are my lamp, O Lord. My God lightens my darkness.
This God is my strong refuge and has made my way safe.

2 Sam. 22:29, 33

Evening Hymn

An evening hymn is sung or read.

All may be seated.

Psalm(s)

One or more psalms are sung or spoken. (45-64)
Silence for reflection follows each psalm.
A psalm prayer may follow the silence.

Scripture Reading

At the conclusion of the reading of scripture the reader may say:

The Word of the Lord.
Thanks be to God.

Silence follows for reflection on the meaning of the scripture.
The scripture may be briefly interpreted, or a nonbiblical reading may be read.

Canticle

The Canticle of Mary (Magnificat) or Phos Hilaron or another canticle may be sung or
spoken. (37-44)
All may stand.

Prayers of Thanksgiving and Intercession

The following prayers may be used:

Let my prayer rise before you as incense,
the lifting of my hands as an evening sacrifice.

Ps. 141:2

Or

To you, O Lord, I lift my soul.
O God, in you I trust.

Ps. 25:1-2

One of the following, or other prayers of thanksgiving and intercession, are spoken:

Sunday
We lift our voices in prayers of praise, holy God, for you have lifted us to new life in Jesus
Christ, and your blessings come in generous measure. Especially we thank you for
>   the privilege of worship and service in this congregation . . .
>   the good news of the gospel of Jesus Christ for us . . .
>   food and drink to share in the Lord's name . . .
>   our calling to discipleship. . . .
We hold up before you human needs, God of compassion, for you have come to us in
Jesus Christ and shared our life so we may share his resurrection. Especially we pray for
>   the healing of those who are sick . . .
>   the comfort of the dying . . .
>   the renewal of those who despair . . .
>   the Spirit's power in the church. . . .

Monday

We rejoice in your generous goodness, O God, and celebrate your lavish gifts to us this day, for you have shown your love in giving Jesus Christ for the salvation of the world. Especially we give thanks for

> the labors of those who have served us today . . .
>
> friends with whom we have shared . . .
>
> those whom we love and have loved us . . .
>
> opportunities for our work to help others . . .
>
> all beauty that delights us. . . .

Gracious God, we know you are close to all in need, and by our prayers for others we come closer to you. We are bold to claim for others your promises of new life in Jesus Christ, as we claim them for ourselves. Especially we pray for

> those in dangerous occupations . . .
>
> physicians and nurses . . .
>
> those who are ill or confined to nursing homes . . .
>
> those who mourn . . .
>
> the Roman Catholic Church. . . .

Tuesday

Eternal God, we thank you for being with us today, and for every sign of your truth and love in Jesus Christ. Especially we thank you for

> the gift of peace in Christ . . .
>
> reconciliation in our relationships . . .
>
> each new insight into your love . . .
>
> energy and courage to share your love . . .
>
> the ministries of the church. . . .

Gracious God, we remember in our own hearts the needs of others, that we may reach up to claim your love for them, and reach out to give your love in the name of Christ. Especially we pray for

> racial harmony and justice . . .
>
> those imprisoned . . .
>
> strangers we have met today . . .
>
> friends who are bereaved . . .
>
> Orthodox and Coptic churches. . . .

Wednesday

Give us your peace, O God, that we may rejoice in your goodness to us and to all your children, and be thankful for your love revealed in Jesus Christ. Especially we thank you for

people who reveal your truth and righteousness . . .

courage to be bold disciples . . .

those who show hospitality . . .

surprises that have blessed us . . .

the unity of the church of Jesus Christ. . . .

Give us your peace, O God, that we may be confident of your care for us and all your children, as we remember the needs of others. Especially we pray for

friends and relatives who are far away . . .

neighbors in special need . . .

those who suffer hunger and thirst . . .

those who work at night while others sleep . . .

Episcopal and Methodist churches. . . .

Thursday

We give you our praise and thanks, O God, for all gifts of love we have received from you, and for your persistent mercy in Jesus Christ. Especially we thank you for

work we have accomplished pleasing to you . . .

the faithful witness of Christian people . . .

the example of righteousness we see in parents and teachers . . .

the innocence and openness we see in children . . .

all works of Christian compassion. . . .

We give you our cares and concerns, O God, because we know you are kind and care for your children in every circumstance. Especially we pray for

those who struggle with doubt and despair . . .

people afflicted with disease . . .

those called to special ministries . . .

people neglected or abused . . .

Baptist, Disciples of Christ, and other free churches. . . .

Friday

Merciful God, we praise you that you give strength for every weakness, forgiveness for our failures, and new beginnings in Jesus Christ. Especially we thank you for

the guidance of your spirit through this day . . .

signs of new life and hope . . .

people who have helped us . . .

those who struggle for justice . . .

expressions of love unexpected or undeserved. . . .

Almighty God, you know all needs before we speak our prayers, yet you welcome our concerns for others in Jesus Christ. Especially we pray for

those who keep watch over the sick and dying . . .

those who weep with the grieving . . .

those who are without faith and cannot accept your love . . .

the aged who are lonely, distressed or weak . . .

Reformed, Presbyterian, and Lutheran churches. . . .

Saturday

God of glory, we praise you for your presence in our lives, and for all goodness that you shower upon your children in Jesus Christ. Especially we thank you for

> promises kept and hope for tomorrow . . .
>
> the enjoyment of friends . . .
>
> the wonders of your creation . . .
>
> love from our parents, our sisters and brothers, our spouses and children . . .
>
> pleasures of living. . . .

God of grace, we are one with all your children, for we are sisters and brothers of Jesus Christ, and we offer our prayers for all whom we love. Especially we pray for

> those we too often forget . . .
>
> people who have lost hope . . .
>
> victims of tragedy and disaster . . .
>
> those who suffer mental anguish . . .
>
> ecumenical councils and church agencies. . . .

Individual prayers of thanksgiving and intercession may be offered.
There may be silent prayer.

The leader then says one of the following prayers, or a similar prayer.

Sunday

As you have made this day, O God, you also make the night.
Give light for our comfort.
Come upon us with quietness and still our souls, that we may listen for the whisper of your Spirit and be attentive to your nearness in our dreams.
Empower us to rise again in new life to proclaim your praise,
and show Christ to the world, for he reigns for ever and ever. **Amen.**

Monday

Great God, you are one God,
and you bring together what is scattered and mend what is broken.
Unite us with the scattered peoples of the earth that we may be one family of your children.
Bind up all our wounds, and heal us in spirit,
that we may be renewed as disciples of Jesus Christ, our Master and Savior. **Amen.**

Tuesday

God of all who fear you, make us one with all your saints and with any who are in need.
Teach us to befriend the weak, and welcome the outcast,
that we may serve the Lord Jesus Christ and live to offer him glory.
In his holy name we pray. **Amen.**

Wednesday

God our shepherd, you have brought us through this day to a time of reflection and rest.
Calm our souls, and refresh us with your peace.
Keep us close to Christ and draw us closer to one another in the bonds of his wondrous love.
We pray through Christ our Lord. **Amen.**

Thursday

To you, O God we give up the burdens of this day, trusting your love and mercy.
To you, O God, we surrender ourselves, trusting our risen Lord to lead us always
in the way of peace, today, tomorrow, and for ever. **Amen.**

Friday

Protect your people, O God, and keep us safe
until the coming of your new dawn and the establishment of your righteous rule.
By your Holy Spirit, stir up within us a longing for the light of your new day,
and guide us by the radiance of Jesus Christ your Son, our risen Lord. **Amen.**

NZPB, alt.

Saturday

Abide with us, O Lord, for evening comes and the day is almost over.
Abide with us, for the days are hastening on and we hasten with them.
Abide with us and with all your faithful people,
until the daystar rises and the morning light appears,
and we shall abide with you for ever. **Amen.**

The Lord's Prayer

Now let us pray the prayer Jesus taught his disciples to pray saying:

Our Father, who art in heaven,
hallowed be thy name,
thy kingdom come,
thy will be done,
on earth as it is in heaven.
Give us this day our daily bread;
and forgive us our debts,
as we forgive our debtors;
and lead us not into temptation,
but deliver us from evil.
For thine is the kingdom,
and the power, and the glory,
for ever. Amen.

[Hymn or Spiritual]

Dismissal

The leader dismisses the people using one of the following:

A. May the grace of the Lord Jesus Christ be with us all.
Amen.
Bless the Lord.
The Lord's name be praised.

Phil. 4:23

B. May the Lord, who is our peace,
give us peace at all times and in every way.
Amen.
Bless the Lord.
The Lord's name be praised.

2 Thess. 3:16

C. May the peace of God, which surpasses all understanding,
guard our hearts and minds in Christ Jesus.
Amen.
Bless the Lord.
The Lord's name be praised.

Phil. 4:7

A sign of peace may be exchanged by all.

SPECIAL PRAYERS

Lord, Open Our Eyes

Lord, open our eyes, that we may see you in our brothers and sisters.
Lord, open our ears, that we may hear the cries of the hungry, the cold,
the frightened, the oppressed.
Lord, open our hearts, that we may love each other as you love us.
Renew in us your spirit, Lord, free us and make us one.

Mother Teresa, 1910-1997

Teach Us to Pray

Lord, teach us to pray. Some of us are not skilled in the art of prayer. As we draw near to
thee in thought, our spirits long for thy Spirit, and reach out for thee, longing to feel thee
near. We know not how to express the deepest emotions that lie hidden in our hearts.

In these moments, we have no polished phrases with which to impress one another, no
finely molded, delicately turned clauses to present to thee. Nor would we be confined to con-
ventional petitions and repeat our prayers like the unwinding of a much-exposed film. We
know, Father, that we are praying most when we are saying least. We know that we are closest to thee when we have left behind the things that have held us captive so long.

We would not be ignorant in prayer and, like children, make want lists for thee. Rather,
we pray that thou wilt give unto us only what we really need. We would not make our prayers
the importuning of thee, an omnipotent God, to do what we want thee to do. Rather, give us
the vision, the courage, that shall enlarge our horizons and stretch our faith to the adventure
of seeking thy loving will for our lives.

We thank thee that thou art hearing us even now. We thank thee for the grace of prayer.
We thank thee for thyself.

Peter Marshall, 1902-1944

Unity of Faiths

O God, we are one with you. You have made us one with you. You have taught us that if we are open to one another, you dwell in us. Help us to preserve this openness and to fight for it with all our hearts. Help us to realize that there can be no understanding where there is mutual rejection. O God, in accepting one another wholeheartedly, fully, completely, we accept you, and we thank you, and we adore you, and we love you with our whole being, because our being is in your being, our spirit is rooted in your spirit. Fill us then with love, and let us be bound together with love as we go our diverse ways, united in this one spirit which makes you present in the world, and which makes you witness to the ultimate reality that is love. Love has overcome. Love is victorious.

Thomas Merton, 1915-1968

Comfort Prayer

O Lord God, great is the misery that has come upon me.
My cares overwhelm me: I am at a loss. O God, comfort and help me.
Give me strength to bear what you send, and do not let fear rule over me.
As a loving Father, take care of my loved ones, my wife and my children.
O merciful God, forgive all the sins I have committed
Against you and against my fellow men.
I put my trust in your grace, and commit my life wholly into your hands.
Do with me as is best for you, for that will be best for me too.
Whether I live or die, I am with you, and you are with me.
Lord, I wait for your salvation and for your kingdom.

Dietrich Bonhoeffer, 1906-1945

In Personal Crisis

God of life, there are days when the burdens we carry are heavy on our shoulders and weigh us down, when the road seems dreary and endless, the skies gray and threatening, when our lives have no music in them, and our hearts are lonely, and our souls have lost their courage. Flood the path with light, turn our eyes to where the skies are full of promise; tune our hearts to brave music; give us the sense of comradeship with heroes and saints of every age; and so quicken our spirits that we may be able to encourage the souls of all who journey with us on the road of life, to your honor and glory. Amen.

Attr. to Augustine of Hippo, 354-430

The Serenity Prayer

God, give us grace to accept with serenity the things that cannot be changed, courage to change the things that should be changed, and the wisdom to distinguish the one from the other. Amen.

Reinhold Niebuhr, 1892-1971

Give Me Strength

Lord God, you know all things. You know how much I long to be chaste, that I may give my whole self, body and soul, to you. And you know how I struggle to abstain from meat and strong drink, that my mind may be pure for you. I desire never to go against your will; so whenever I fail to keep your commands, I am overcome with sorrow. Now, blessed Jesus, make your will known to me at all times, and give me the strength to obey it.

Margey Kempe, 1373-1432

Seed of Love

What a good friend you are, Lord! You are so patient, willing to wait as long as necessary for me to turn to you. You rejoice at the times when I love you, but you do not hold against me the times when I ignore you. Your patience is beyond my understanding. Even when I pray, my mind fills with worldly concerns and vain daydreams. Yet you are happy if I give only a single second of honest prayer, turning that second into a seed of love. O Lord, I enjoy your friendship so much, why is it not possible for me to think of you constantly?

Teresa of Ávila, 1515-1582

For Personal Devotion

Lord, make me an instrument of your peace. Where there is hatred, let me sow love: where there is injury, pardon: where there is doubt, faith: where there is despair, hope: where there is darkness, light: where there is sadness, joy.

O Divine Master, grant that I may not seek so much to be consoled as to console, to be understood as to understand, to be loved as to love. For it is in giving that we receive, it is in pardoning that we are pardoned, and it is in dying that we are born to eternal life. Amen.

Attr. to Francis of Assisi, 1181-1226

For the Bereaved

O merciful God, you teach us in your Holy Word that you do not willingly afflict or grieve your children. Look with pity on the sorrows of (N., N.) your servant, for whom we pray. Remember him/her, O Lord, in mercy. Strength him/her in patience, comfort him/her with the memory of your goodness, let your presence shine on him/her, and give him/her peace. Through Jesus Christ our Lord. Amen.

BCP

For the Lonely

God of comfort, companion of the lonely, be with those who by neglect or willful separation are left alone. Fill empty places with present love, and long times of solitude with lively thoughts of you. Encourage us to visit lonely men and women, so they may be cheered by the Spirit of Jesus Christ, who walked among us as a friend, and is our Lord for ever. Amen.

For Families

Eternal God, our creator, you set us to live in families. We commend to your care all the homes where your people live. Keep them, we pray, free from bitterness, from the thirst for personal victory, and from pride in self. Fill them with faith, virtue, knowledge, moderation, patience and godliness. Knit together in enduring affection those who have become one in marriage. Let children and parents have full respect for one another: and light the fire of kindliness among us all, that we may show affection for each other; through Jesus Christ our Lord. Amen.

BCP

For Children

Great God, guard the laughter of children. Bring them safely through injury and illness, so they may live the promises you give. Do not let us be so preoccupied with our purposes that we fail to hear their voices, or pay attention to their special vision of the truth; but keep us with them, ready to listen and to love, even as in Jesus Christ you have loved us, your grown-up wayward children. Amen.

For the Aged

O Lord God, look with mercy on all whose increasing years bring them isolation, distress or weakness. Provide for them homes of dignity and peace; give them understanding helpers and the willingness to accept help; and, as their strength diminishes, increase their faith and their assurance of your love. We pray in the name of Jesus Christ our Lord.　Amen.

BCP

For the Sick

O God, the strength of the weak and the comfort of sufferers, mercifully hear our prayers and grant to your servant N. the help of your power, that his/her sickness may be turned into health and our sorrow into joy; through Jesus Christ.　Amen.

BCP

During an Illness

You are medicine for me when I am sick.
You are my strength when I need help.
You are life itself when I fear death.
You are the way when I long for heaven.
You are the light when all is dark.
You are my food when I need nourishment!　Amen.

Ambrose of Milan, 340-397

For Healing

Mighty and merciful God, you sent Jesus Christ to heal broken lives. We praise you that today you send healing in doctors and nurses, and bless us with technology in medicine. We claim your promises of wholeness as we pray for those who are ill in body or mind, who long for your healing touch.

Make the weak strong, the sick healthy, the broken whole, and confirm those who serve them as agents of your love. Then all shall be renewed in vigor to point to the risen Christ who conquered death that we might live eternally.　Amen.

For Social Justice

Yes, Jesus, I want to be on your right side or your left side, not for any selfish reason. I want to be on your right or your best side, not in terms of some political kingdom or ambition, but I just want to be there in love and in justice and in truth and in commitments to others, so we can make of this old world a new world.　Amen.

Martin Luther King, Jr., 1929-1968

For Faithfulness

Give me, O Lord, a steadfast heart, which no unworthy affection may drag downward; give me an unconquered heart, which no tribulation can wear out; give me an upright heart, which no unworthy purpose may tempt aside.

Bestow on me also, O Lord my God, understanding to know you, diligence to seek you, wisdom to find you, and a faithfulness that may finally embrace you; through Jesus Christ our Lord.　Amen.

Thomas Aquinas, c.1225-1274

37   Canticle of Praise to God

Psalm 95:1-7; 96:9, 13

William Boyce

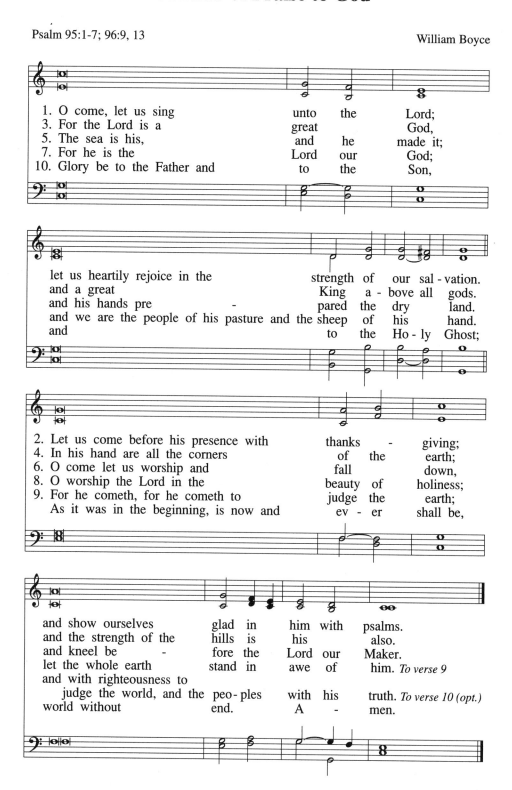

1. O come, let us sing unto the Lord;
3. For the Lord is a great God,
5. The sea is his, and he made it;
7. For he is the Lord our God;
10. Glory be to the Father and to the Son,

let us heartily rejoice in the strength of our sal - vation.
and a great King a - bove all gods.
and his hands pre - pared the dry land.
and we are the people of his pasture and the sheep of his hand.
and to the Ho - ly Ghost;

2. Let us come before his presence with thanks - giving;
4. In his hand are all the corners of the earth;
6. O come let us worship and fall down,
8. O worship the Lord in the beauty of holiness;
9. For he cometh, for he cometh to judge the earth;
   As it was in the beginning, is now and ev - er shall be,

and show ourselves glad in him with psalms.
and the strength of the hills is his also.
and kneel be - fore the Lord our Maker.
let the whole earth stand in awe of him. *To verse 9*
and with righteousness to
   judge the world, and the peo-ples with his truth. *To verse 10 (opt.)*
world without end. A - men.

Canticle of God's Glory

Luke 2:14; John 1:29; ICET, rev. ELLC   Alexander Peloquin (1972)

Response

Glo-ry to God in the high-est, and peace to God's peo-ple on earth.

R

**Glory to God in the highest,
    and peace to God's people on earth.
    Lord God, heavenly King,
    almighty God and Father,
    we worship you, we give you thanks,
    we praise you for your glory. R**

**Lord Jesus Christ, only Son of the Father,
    Lord God, Lamb of God,
    you take away the sin of the world:
    have mercy on us;
    you are seated at the right hand of the Father:
    receive our prayer. R**

**For you alone are the Holy One,
    you alone are the Lord,
    you alone are the Most High,
    Jesus Christ,
    with the Holy Spirit,
    in the glory of God the Father. Amen. R**

39 Canticle of Thanksgiving

Psalm 100; Response, Edward H. Plumptre

Arthur H. Messiter

Response

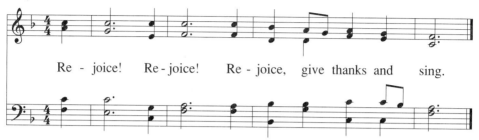

Re - joice! Re - joice! Re - joice, give thanks and sing.

R

Make a joyful noise unto the Lord, all ye lands.
Serve the Lord with gladness;
come before his presence with singing.
Know ye that the Lord, he is God;
it is he that hath made us, and not we ourselves;
we are his people, and the sheep of his pasture.
Enter into his gates with thanksgiving,
and into his courts with praise;
be thankful unto him, and bless his name.
For the Lord is good;
his mercy is everlasting;
and his truth endureth to all generations. R

Canticle of Eventide

40

Phos Hilaron, Greek, c. 200
Tr. by William G. Storey, c. 1970

Plainsong, Mode IV
Harm. by C. Winfred Douglas, 1943, alt.

1. O ra - diant Light, O Sun di - vine,
2. O Son of God, the source of life,
3. Lord Je - sus Christ, as day - light fades,

Of God the Fa - ther's death - less face,
Praise is your due by night and day.
As shine the lights of ev - en - tide,

O im - age of the Light sub - lime,
Our hap - py lips must raise the strain
We praise the Fa - ther with the Son,

That fills the heav - n'ly dwell - ing place.
Of your es - teemed and splen - did name.
The Spir - it blest and with them one.   A - men.

41   **Canticle of Mary**

Luke 1:46b-55, ICET, rev. ELLC
Response, Joachim Neander

LOBE DEN HERREN (99)

Response

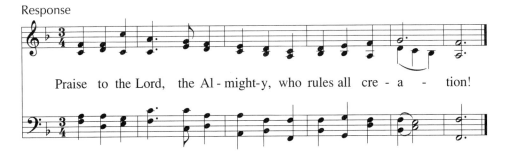

Praise to the Lord, the Al - might-y, who rules all cre - a - tion!

R

My soul proclaims the greatness of the Lord,
my spirit rejoices in God my Savior,
    who has looked with favor on me, a lowly servant.
From this day all generations shall call me blessed:
the Almighty has done great things for me
    and holy is the name of the Lord,
    whose mercy is on those who fear God
    from generation to generation.
The arm of the Lord is strong.
    and has scattered the proud in their conceit.
God has cast down the mighty from their thrones
    and lifted up the lowly.
God has filled the hungry with good things
    and sent the rich empty away.
God has come to the aid of Israel, the chosen servant,
    remembering the promise of mercy,
    the promise made to our forebears,
    to Abraham and his children for ever. R

Canticle of Simeon

Luke 2:29-32, ICET, rev. ELLC

LASST UNS ERFREUEN (83)

Response

Let all things their re - deem - er bless: Al - le - lu - ia!

Al - le - lu - ia! Al - le - lu - ia!

R

Lord, now let your servant go in peace;
    your word has been fulfilled:
    my own eyes have seen the salvation
    which you have prepared in the presence of all people,
    a light to reveal you to the nations
    and the glory of your people Israel. R

43   Canticle of Zechariah

Luke 1:68-79; ICET, rev. ELLC
Response, James Montgomery (1821)

ELLACOMBE (117)

Response

Hail to the Lord's A-noint-ed, great Da-vid's great-er Son.

R

Blessed be the Lord, the God of Israel,
    who has come to set the chosen people free.
The Lord has raised up for us
    a mighty Savior from the house of David.
Through the holy prophets, God promised of old
    to save us from our enemies,
    from the hands of all who hate us;
to show mercy to our forebears
    and to remember the holy covenant.
This was the oath God swore to our father Abraham:
to set us free from the hands of our enemies,
    free to worship without fear,
    holy and righteous in the Lord's sight,
    all the days of our life. R

And you, child, shall be called the prophet of the Most High,
    for you will go before the Lord to prepare the way,
to give God's people knowledge of salvation
    by the forgiveness of their sins.
In the tender compassion of our God
    the dawn from on high shall break upon us,
to shine on those who dwell in darkness and the shadow of death,
    and to guide our feet into the way of peace. R

Canticle of Light and Darkness

44

Isaiah 9:2; 59:9-10; Psalm 139:11-12;
Daniel 2:20, 22; 1 John 1:5, adapt. by Alan Luff

ADESTE FIDELES (133)

Response

O come, let us a - dore him, Christ, the Lord!

R

We look for light but find darkness,
    for brightness, but walk in gloom.
    We grope like those who have no eyes;
    we stumble at noon as in the twilight. R

If I say, "Let only darkness cover me,
    and the light about me be night,"
    even the darkness is not dark to you,
    the night is bright as the day,
    for darkness is as light with you. R

Blessed be your name, O God, for ever.
    You reveal deep and mysterious things;
    you are light and in you is no darkness.
    Our darkness is passing away
    and already the true light is shining. R

45
Psalm 8

MIT FREUDEN ZART (110)

Response

Sing praise to God who reigns a - bove,

The God of all cre - a - tion.

R

1   O Lord, our Lord,
   how majestic is your name in all the earth!
2   Your glory is chanted above the heavens
   by the mouth of babes and infants:
   you have set up a defense against your foes,
   to still the enemy and the avenger.   R

3   When I look at your heavens, the work of your fingers,
   the moon and the stars which you have established;
4   what are human beings that you are mindful of them,
   and mortals that you care for them?
5   Yet you have made them little less than God,
   and crowned them with glory and honor.   R

6   You have given them dominion over the works of your hands;
   you have put all things under their feet,
7   all sheep and oxen,
   and also the beasts of the field,
8   the birds of the air, and the fish of the sea,
   whatever passes along the paths of the seas.
9   O Lord, our Lord,
   how majestic is your name in all the earth!   R

Psalm 16:5-11

Response   HYMN TO JOY (92)

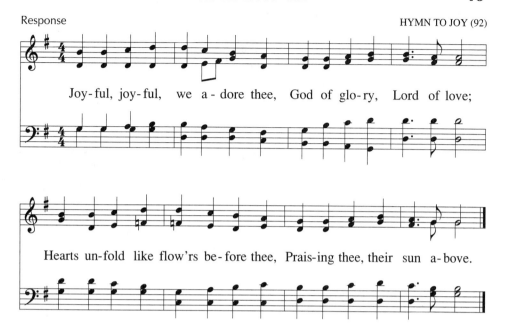

Joy-ful, joy-ful, we a-dore thee, God of glo-ry, Lord of love;

Hearts un-fold like flow'rs be-fore thee, Prais-ing thee, their sun a-bove.

R

5   The Lord is my chosen portion and my cup;
        you hold my lot.

6   **The lines have fallen for me in pleasant places;**
        I have a glorious heritage.

7   I bless the Lord who gives me counsel;
        even at night my heart instructs me.

8   **I have set the Lord always before me;**
        the Lord is at my right hand;
        I shall not be moved.   R

9   Therefore my heart is glad, and my soul rejoices;
        my body also dwells secure.

10   **For you do not give me up to Sheol,**
        or let your godly one see the pit.

11   You show me the path of life;
        in your presence there is fullness of joy,
        in your right hand are pleasures for evermore.   R

47 Psalm 19

Response LEONI (96)

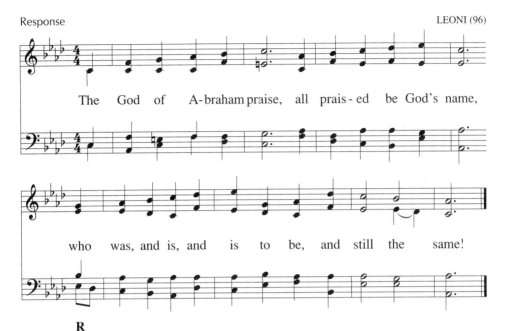

The God of A-braham praise, all prais-ed be God's name,

who was, and is, and is to be, and still the same!

R

1   The heavens are telling the glory of God;
  and the firmament proclaims God's handiwork.
2   **Day to day pours forth speech,**
  and night to night declares knowledge.
3   There is no speech, nor are there words;
  their voice is not heard;
4   **yet their voice goes out through all the earth,**
  and their words to the end of the world.
 In them God has set a tent for the sun,
5   which comes forth like a bridegroom leaving his chamber,
  and runs its course with joy like a strong man.
6   **Its rising is from the end of the heavens,**
  and its circuit to the end of them;
  and there is nothing hid from its heat.   R

7   The law of the Lord is perfect,
  reviving the soul;
the testimony of the Lord is sure,
  making wise the simple;
8   the precepts of the Lord are right,
  rejoicing the heart;
the commandment of the Lord is pure,
  enlightening the eyes;

9   the fear of the Lord is clean,
       enduring for ever;
   the ordinances of the Lord are true,
      and righteous altogether.

10   More to be desired are they than gold,
       even much fine gold;
   sweeter also than honey
      and drippings of the honeycomb. R

11   Moreover by them is your servant warned;
      in keeping them there is great reward.
12   **But who can understand one's own errors?**
      Clear me from hidden faults.
13   Also keep your servant from the insolent;
      let them not have dominion over me!
   Then I shall be blameless,
      and innocent of great transgression.
14   **Let the words of my mouth / and the meditation of my heart**
      be acceptable in your sight,
       O Lord, my rock and my redeemer. R

48   **Psalm 22:1-18, 25-31**

Response   PASSION CHORALE (168)

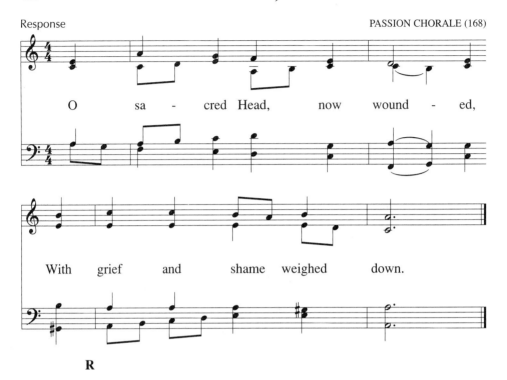

O   sa - cred Head,   now   wound - ed,

With grief and shame weighed down.

R

1   My God, my God, why have you forsaken me?
        Why are you so far from helping me,
        from the words of my groaning?
2   O my God, I cry by day, but you do not answer;
        and by night, but find no rest.
3   Yet you, the praise of Israel,
        are enthroned in holiness.
4   **In you our forbears trusted;**
        they trusted and you delivered them.
5   To you they cried, and were saved;
        in you they trusted, and were not disappointed.   R

6   But I am a worm, and not human;
        scorned by others, and despised by the people.
7   All who see me mock at me,
        they make mouths at me, they wag their heads;
8   "He committed his cause to the Lord;
        let the Lord deliver him.
        Let the Lord rescue him,
        for the Lord delights in him!"
9   **Yet it was you who took me from the womb;**
        you kept me safe upon my mother's breast.

10   Upon you I was cast from my birth,
          and since my mother bore me, you have been my God.
11   **Do not be far from me,**
          for trouble is near
          and there is none to help.   R

12   Many bulls encompass me,
          strong bulls of Bashan surround me;
13   **they open wide their mouths at me,**
          like a ravening and roaring lion.
14   I am poured out like water
          and all my bones are out of joint;
      my heart is like wax,
          it is melted within my breast;
15   my mouth is dried up like a potsherd,
          and my tongue cleaves to my jaws;
          you lay me in the dust of death.
16   Indeed, dogs surround me;
          a company of evildoers encircles me;
          they have pierced my hands and feet—
17   I can count all my bones—
          they stare and gloat over me;
18   they divide my garments among them,
          and for my raiment, they cast lots.   R

25   From you comes my praise in the great congregation;
          my vows I will pay before those who worship the Lord.
26   The poor shall eat and be satisfied;
          those who seek the Lord shall praise the Lord!
          May your hearts live for ever!
27   All the ends of the earth shall remember
          and turn to the Lord;
      and all the families of the nations
          shall worship before the Lord.
28   For dominion belongs to the Lord
          who rules over the nations.
29   **All who sleep in the earth**
          shall bow down to the Lord.
      All who go down to the dust shall bow before the Lord,
          and I shall live for God.
30   **Posterity shall serve the Lord;**
          each generation shall tell of the Lord,
31   and proclaim his deliverance to a people yet unborn.
          Surely the Lord has done it.   R

49   Psalm 23

Response   Joseph Gelineau

My shep-herd is the Lord, noth-ing in-deed shall I want.

R

1 The Lord is my shepherd;
   I shall not want.
2 **He maketh me to lie down in green pastures:**
   he leadeth me beside the still waters.
3 He restoreth my soul:
   he leadeth me in the paths of righteousness for his name's sake.
4 **Yea, though I walk through the valley of the shadow of death,**
      I will fear no evil:
      For thou art with me;
      thy rod and thy staff they comfort me.   R

5 Thou preparest a table before me
      in the presence of mine enemies:
   thou anointest my head with oil;
      my cup runneth over.
6 **Surely goodness and mercy shall follow me**
      all the days of my life:
   and I will dwell in the house of the Lord for ever.   R

Psalm 24

Response   TRURO (123)

Lift up your heads, O might - y gates;

the Sav - ior of the world is here.

R

1   The earth is the Lord's and the fullness thereof,
     the world and those who dwell therein;
2   for God has founded it upon the seas,
     and established it upon the rivers.
3   Who shall ascend the hill of the Lord?
     And who shall stand in God's holy place?
4   Those who have clean hands and pure hearts,
     who do not lift up their souls to what is false,
     and do not swear deceitfully.
5   They will receive blessing from the Lord,
     and vindication from the God of their salvation.
6   Such is the generation of those who seek the Lord,
     who seek the face of the God of Jacob. R

7   Lift up your heads, O gates!
     and be lifted up, O ancient doors!
     that the Ruler of glory may come in.
8   **Who is the Ruler of glory?**
     The Lord, strong and mighty,
     the Lord, mighty in battle!
9   **Lift up your heads, O gates!**
     and be lifted up, O ancient doors!
     that the Ruler of glory may come in.
10   Who is this Ruler of glory?
     The Lord of hosts,
     the Lord is the Ruler of glory! R

51   Psalm 27

Response   NUN DANKET ALLE GOTT (358)

Sing praise to God our rock, in whom we take our ref - uge.

R

1   The Lord is my light and my salvation;
        whom shall I fear?
    The Lord is the stronghold of my life;
        of whom shall I be afraid?
2   When evildoers assail me,
        to devour my flesh,
    my adversaries and foes
        shall stumble and fall.
3   **Though a host encamp against me,**
        my heart shall not fear;
    though war arise against me,
        yet I will be confident.
4   One thing I asked of the Lord,
        that will I seek after:
    that I may dwell in the house of the Lord
        all the days of my life,
    to behold the beauty of the Lord,
        and to inquire in the Lord's temple.   R

5   The Lord will hide me in his shelter
        in the day of trouble,
    will conceal me under the cover of his tent,
        and will set me high upon a rock.
6   **And now my head shall be lifted up**
        above my enemies round about me;
    and I will offer sacrifices in the Lord's tent
        with shouts of joy;
    I will sing and make melody to the Lord.   R

7   Hear, O Lord, when I cry aloud,
  be gracious to me and answer me!
8   **"Come," my heart said, "seek the Lord's face."**
  Your face, O Lord, I seek.
9   Hide not your face from me.
  Turn not your servant away in anger,
  for you have been my help.
10   **Cast me not off, forsake me not,**
  O God of my salvation!
  If my father and mother should forsake me,
  the Lord would take me up. R

11   Teach me your way, O Lord;
  and lead me on a level path
  because of my enemies.
12   **Give me not up to the will of my adversaries;**
  for false witnesses have risen against me,
  and they breathe out violence.
13   I believe that I shall see the goodness of the Lord
  in the land of the living!
14   **Wait for the Lord;**
  be strong, and let your heart take courage.
  Wait for the Lord! R

52   Psalm 46

Response   EIN' FESTE BURG (330)

A   might - y   for - tress   is   our   God,

a   bul - wark   nev - er   fail - ing.

R

1   God is our refuge and strength,
        a very present help in trouble.
2   **Therefore we will not fear though the earth should change,**
        though the mountains shake in the heart of the sea;
3   though its waters roar and foam,
        though the mountains tremble with its tumult.
4   **There is a river whose streams make glad the city of God,**
        the holy habitation of the Most High.
5   God is in the midst of the city which shall not be moved;
        God will help it at the dawn of the day.
6   **The nations rage, the kingdoms totter;**
        God's voice resounds, the earth melts.
7   The Lord of hosts is with us;
        the God of Jacob is our refuge.   R

8   Come, behold the works of the Lord,
        who has wrought desolations in the earth;
9   **who makes wars cease to the end of the earth,**
        breaks the bow, shatters the spear,
        and burns the shields with fire!
10   "Be still, and know that I am God.
        I am exalted among the nations,
        I am exalted in the earth!"
11   **The Lord of hosts is with us;**
        the God of Jacob is our refuge.   R

Psalm 51:1-17

Response

AUS TIEFER NOT (152)

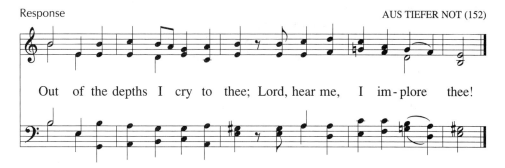

Out of the depths I cry to thee; Lord, hear me, I im-plore thee!

R

1 Have mercy on me, O God,
    according to your steadfast love;
according to your abundant mercy
    blot out my transgressions.
2 Wash me thoroughly from my iniquity,
    and cleanse me from my sin!
3 **For I know my transgressions,**
    and my sin is ever before me.
4 Against you, you only, have I sinned,
    and done that which is evil in your sight,
so that you are justified in your sentence
    and blameless in your judgment.
5 **Behold, I was born into iniquity,**
    and I have been sinful since my mother conceived me. R

6 Behold, you desire truth in the inward being,
    therefore teach me wisdom in my secret heart.
7 **Purge me with hyssop, and I shall be clean;**
    wash me, and I shall be whiter than snow;
8 Make me hear with joy and gladness;
    let the bones which you have broken rejoice.
9 **Hide your face from my sins,**
    and blot out all my iniquities. R

10   Create in me a clean heart, O God,
        and put a new and right spirit within me.

11   **Cast me not away from your presence,**
        and take not your holy Spirit from me.

12   Restore to me the joy of your salvation,
        and sustain in me a willing spirit.

13   **Then I will teach transgressors your ways,**
        and sinners will return to you.

14   Deliver me from death, O God, God of my salvation,
        and my tongue will sing aloud of your deliverance.

15   **O Lord, open my lips,**
        and my mouth shall show forth your praise.

16   For you have no delight in sacrifice;
        were I to give a burnt offering, you would not be pleased.

17   **The sacrifice acceptable to God is a broken spirit;**
        a broken and contrite heart, O God, you will not despise.   R

Psalm 62:5-12

Come, thou Fount of ev-'ry bless-ing, Tune my heart to sing thy grace.

R

5   For God alone my soul waits in silence,
        for my hope is from God,
6   **who alone is my rock and my salvation,**
        my fortress; I shall not be shaken.
7   On God rests my deliverance and my honor;
        my mighty rock, my refuge is God.
8   **Trust in God at all times, O people;**
        pour out your heart before God who is a refuge for us. R

9   Those of low estate are but a breath,
        those of high estate are a delusion;
     in the balances they go up;
        they are together lighter than a breath.
10   **Put no confidence in extortion,**
        set no vain hopes on robbery;
        if riches increase, set not your heart on them.
11   Once God has spoken,
        twice have I heard this:
        power belongs to God;
12   **and to you, O Lord, belongs steadfast love,**
        for you repay all according to their work. R

55   Psalm 90

Response   ST. ANNE (314)

O God, our help in a - ges past, Our

hope for years to come, Our shel - ter from the

storm - y blast, And our e - ter - nal home.

R

1   Lord, you have been our dwelling place
        in all generations.
2   **Before the mountains were brought forth,**
        or ever you had formed the earth and the world,
        from everlasting to everlasting you are God.
3   You turn us back to the dust,
        and say, "Turn back, O mortal ones!"
4   **For a thousand years in your sight**
        are but as yesterday when it is past,
        or as a watch in the night.
5   You sweep them away; they are like a dream,
        like grass which is renewed in the morning:
6   **in the morning it flourishes and is renewed;**
        in the evening it fades and withers.   R

7 For we are consumed by your anger;
    by your wrath we are overwhelmed.
8 **You have set our iniquities before you,**
    our secret sins in the light of your countenance.
9 For all our days pass away under your wrath,
    our years come to an end like a sigh.
10 **The years of our life are threescore and ten,**
    or even by reason of strength fourscore;
    yet their span is but toil and trouble;
    they are soon gone, and we fly away.
11 Who considers the power of your anger,
    the awesomeness of your wrath?
12 **So teach us to number our days**
    that we may receive a heart of wisdom.   R

13 Return, O Lord! How long?
    Have pity on your servants!
14 **Satisfy us in the morning with your steadfast love,**
    that we may rejoice and be glad all our days.
15 Make us glad as many days as you have afflicted us,
    and as many years as we have seen evil.
16 **Let your work be manifest to your servants,**
    and your glorious power to their children.
17 Let the favor of the Lord our God be upon us,
    and establish the work of our hands;
    yes, establish the work of our hands.   R

56   Psalm 96

Response   ANTIOCH (145)

Joy   to   the world! the Lord is   come: Let earth re-ceive her King.

R

1   O sing to the Lord a new song;
         sing to the Lord, all the earth!
2   **Sing to the Lord, bless God's name;**
         proclaim God's salvation from day to day.
3   Declare the Lord's glory among the nations,
         the Lord's marvelous works among all the peoples!
4   **For great is the Lord and greatly to be praised,**
         to be feared above all gods.
5   For all the gods of the peoples are idols;
         but the Lord made the heavens.
6   **Honor and majesty are before the Lord**
         in whose sanctuary are strength and beauty.   R

7   Ascribe to the Lord, O families of the peoples,
         ascribe to the Lord glory and strength!
8   **Ascribe to the Lord the glory of his name!**
         Bring an offering, and come into the courts of the Lord!
9   Worship the Lord in holy splendor;
         tremble before the Lord, all the earth!   R

10   Say among the nations, "The Lord reigns!
         The Lord has established the world,
         it shall never be moved.
         The Lord will judge the peoples with equity."
11   Let the heavens be glad, and let the earth rejoice;
         let the sea roar, and all that fills it;
12   let the field exult, and everything in it!
     Then shall all the trees of the wood sing for joy
13   **before the Lord, who comes to judge the earth.**
     The Lord will judge the world with righteousness,
         and the peoples with his truth.   R

Psalm 100

Response

OLD HUNDREDTH (84)

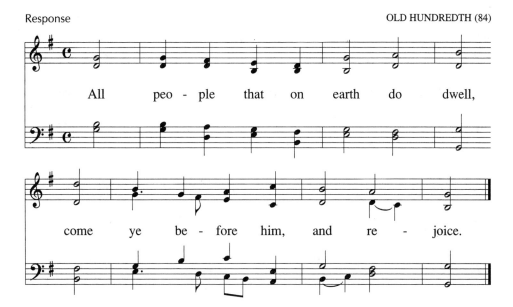

All peo - ple that on earth do dwell,

come ye be - fore him, and re - joice.

R

1 Make a joyful noise to the Lord, all the lands!
2 **Serve the Lord with gladness!**
   Come into God's presence with singing!
3 Know that the Lord, who made us, is God.
   We are the Lord's;
   we are the people of God,
   the sheep of God's pasture.
4 Enter God's gates with thanksgiving,
   and God's courts with praise!
   Give thanks and bless God's name!
5 For the Lord is good;
   God's steadfast love endures for ever;
   God's faithfulness to all generations. R

58   **Psalm 103:1-18**

Response   LAUDA ANIMA (100)

Praise, my soul, the King of heav - en;

Glo - rious in his faith - ful - ness.

R

¹ Bless the Lord, O my soul!
and all that is within me,
bless God's holy name!

² **Bless the Lord, O my soul,**
and forget not all God's benefits,

³ who forgives all your iniquity,
who heals all your diseases,

⁴ **who redeems your life from the pit,**
who crowns you with steadfast love and mercy,

⁵ **who satisfies you with good as long as you live**
so that your youth is renewed like the eagle's. R

⁶ The Lord, who works vindication
and justice for all who are oppressed,

⁷ has made known God's ways to Moses,
God's acts to the people of Israel.

⁸ **The Lord is merciful and gracious,**
slow to anger and abounding in steadfast love.

⁹ The Lord will not always chide,
nor harbor anger for ever.

¹⁰ **The Lord does not deal with us according to our sins,**
nor repay us according to our iniquities.

¹¹ For as the heavens are high above the earth,
so great is the Lord's steadfast love toward the faithful;

12   **as far as the east is from the west,**
        so far does the Lord remove our transgressions from us.
13   As a father shows compassion to his children,
        so the Lord shows compassion to the faithful.
14   **For the Lord knows our frame,**
        and remembers that we are dust. R

15   As for mortals, their days are like grass;
        they flourish like a flower of the field;
16   for the wind passes over it, and it is gone,
        and its place knows it no more.
17   **But the steadfast love of the Lord**
        is from everlasting to everlasting upon the faithful,
   and the righteousness of the Lord to children's children,
18   **to those who keep his covenant**
        and remember to do his commandments. R

59   Psalm 104:1-13, 24-35

Response   LOBE DEN HERREN (99)

Praise to the Lord, the Al-might-y, who rules all cre - a - tion!

R

1   Bless the Lord, O my soul!
      O Lord my God, you are very great!
   You are clothed with honor and majesty,
2   and cover yourself with light as with a garment;
      you have stretched out the heavens like a tent,
3   **and have laid the beams of your chambers on the waters;**
   you make the clouds your chariot,
      and ride on the wings of the wind;
4   **you make the winds your messengers,**
      fire and flame your ministers.
5   You set the earth on its foundations,
      so that it should never be shaken.
6   **You covered it with the deep as with a garment;**
      the waters stood above the mountains.
7   At your rebuke they fled;
      at the sound of your thunder they took to flight.
8   They rose up to the mountains, ran down to the valleys,
      to the place which you appointed for them.
9   **You set a bound which they should not pass,**
      so that they might not again cover the earth. R

10   You make springs gush forth in the valleys;
      they flow between the hills;
11   **they give drink to every beast of the field;**
      the wild asses quench their thirst.
12   Above the springs the birds of the air have their nests;
      they sing among the branches.
13   **From your lofty place you water the mountains;**
      with the fruit of your work the earth is satisfied. R

24   O Lord, how manifold are your works!
        In wisdom you have made them all;
        the earth is full of your creatures.

25   Yonder is the sea, great and wide,
        creeping things innumerable are there,
        living things both small and great.

26   There go the ships,
        and Leviathan whom you formed to play in it.

27   **These all look to you,**
        to give them their food in due season.

28   When you give to them, they gather it;
        when you open your hand, they are filled with good things.

29   When you hide your face, they are dismayed;
        when you take away their breath, they die
        and return to their dust.

30   When you send forth your spirit, they are created;
        and you renew the face of the ground.

31   May the glory of the Lord endure for ever,
        may the Lord rejoice in his works,

32   **who looks on the earth and it trembles,**
        who touches the mountains and they smoke.

33   I will sing to the Lord as long as I live;
        I will sing praise to my God while I have being.

34   May my meditation be pleasing to the Lord
        in whom I rejoice.

35   **Let sinners be consumed from the earth,**
        and let the wicked be no more!
    Bless the Lord, O my soul!
        O praise the Lord! R

60 Psalm 116

Response

LASST UNS ERFREUEN (83)

Let all things their re - deem - er bless: Al - le - lu - ia!

Al - le - lu - ia! Al - le - lu - ia!

R

1 I love the Lord, who has heard
    my voice and my supplications,

2 and has inclined his ear to me
    whenever I called.

3 **The snares of death encompassed me;**
    the pangs of Sheol laid hold on me;
    I suffered distress and anguish.

4 Then I called on the name of the Lord:
    "O Lord, I beseech you, save my life!" R

5 Gracious is the Lord, and righteous;
    our God is merciful.

6 **The Lord preserves the simple;**
    when I was brought low, the Lord saved me.

7 Return, O my soul, to your rest;
    for the Lord has dealt bountifully with you.

8 For you have delivered my soul from death,
    my eyes from tears,
    my feet from stumbling;

9 **I walk before the Lord**
    in the land of the living.

10   I kept my faith, even when I said,
         "I am greatly afflicted."
11   **I said in my consternation,**
         "All humans are a vain hope." R

12   What shall I return to the Lord
         for all my benefits?
13   **I will lift up the cup of salvation**
         and call on the name of the Lord,
14   I will pay my vows to the Lord,
         in the presence of all his people.
15   **Precious in the sight of the Lord**
         is the death of his faithful ones.
16   O Lord, I am your servant;
         I am your servant, the child of your handmaid.
         You have loosed my bonds.
17   **I will offer to you the sacrifice of thanksgiving**
         and call on the name of the Lord.
18   I will pay my vows to the Lord,
         in the presence of all his people,
19   **in the courts of the house of the Lord,**
         in your midst, O Jerusalem.
         O praise the Lord! R

61　　　　Psalm 118:14-29

Response　　　　　　　　　　　　　　　　　　FOREST GREEN (77)

The Lord has done great things for us, and we are filled with joy.

R

14　The Lord is my strength and my power;
　　　the Lord has become my salvation.
15　**There are joyous songs of victory**
　　　in the tents of the righteous:
　　　"The right hand of the Lord does valiantly,
16　　　the right hand of the Lord is exalted,
　　　the right hand of the Lord does valiantly!"
17　I shall not die, but I shall live,
　　　and recount the deeds of the Lord.
18　**The Lord has chastened me sorely,**
　　　but has not given me over to death.
19　Open to me the gates of righteousness,
　　　that I may enter through them
　　　and give thanks to the Lord.
20　**This is the gate of the Lord;**
　　　the righteous shall enter through it.　R

21　I thank you that you have answered me
　　　and have become my salvation.
22　**The stone which the builders rejected**
　　　has become the cornerstone.
23　This is the Lord's doing;
　　　it is marvelous in our eyes.
24　**This is the day which the Lord has made;**
　　　let us rejoice and be glad in it.　R

25 Save us, we beseech you, O Lord!
O Lord, we beseech you, give us success!
26 Blessed is the one who comes in the name of the Lord!
We bless you from the house of the Lord.
27 The Lord is God,
who has given us light.
Lead the festal procession with branches,
up to the horns of the altar!
28 You are my God, and I will give thanks to you;
you are my God, I will extol you.
29 **O give thanks to the Lord, who is good;**
for God's steadfast love endures for ever!   R

62 Psalm 121

Response

DUNDEE (104)

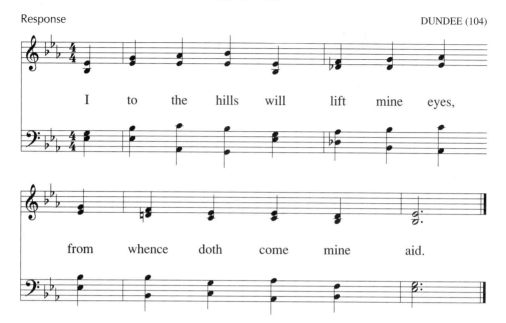

I to the hills will lift mine eyes,

from whence doth come mine aid.

R

1 I lift up my eyes to the hills.
 From whence does my help come?
2 **My help comes from the Lord,**
 who made heaven and earth.
3 The Lord will not let your foot be moved,
 the Lord who keeps you will not slumber.
4 **Behold, the One who keeps Israel**
 will neither slumber nor sleep.
5 The Lord is your keeper;
 the Lord is your shade
 on your right hand.
6 The sun shall not smite you by day,
 nor the moon by night.
7 The Lord will keep you from all evil,
 and will keep your life.
8 **The Lord will keep**
 your going out and your coming in
 from this time forth and for evermore. R

Psalm 130

Response   AMAZING GRACE (261)

The Lord has prom - ised good to me, His word my hope se - cures; He will my shield and por - tion be As long as life en - dures.

R

¹ Out of the depths I cry to you, O Lord!
²   Lord, hear my voice!
Let your ears be attentive
     to the voice of my supplications!
³ If you, O Lord, should mark iniquities,
     Lord, who could stand?
⁴ **But there is forgiveness with you,**
     that you may be worshipped.
⁵ I wait for the Lord, my soul waits,
     in the Lord's word I hope;
⁶ **my soul waits for the Lord**
     more than those who watch for the morning,
     more than those who watch for the morning.
⁷ O Israel, hope in the Lord!
     For with the Lord there is steadfast love,
     with the Lord is plenteous redemption.
⁸ **And the Lord will redeem Israel**
     from all iniquities.   R

64   **Psalm 139**

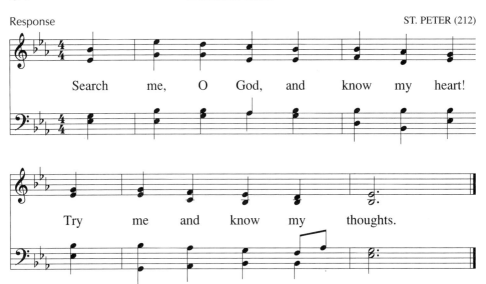

Response

Search me, O God, and know my heart!

Try me and know my thoughts.

R

1   O Lord, you have searched me
        and you have known me!
2   **You know when I sit down and when I rise up;**
        you discern my thoughts from afar.
3   You search out my path and my lying down,
        and are acquainted with all my ways.
4   **Even before a word is on my tongue, O Lord,**
        you know it altogether.
5   You pursue me behind and before,
        and lay your hand upon me.
6   **Such knowledge is too wonderful for me;**
        it is high, I cannot attain it.   R

7   Whither shall I go from your spirit?
        Or whither shall I flee from your presence?
8   If I ascend to heaven, you are there!
        If I make my bed in Sheol, you are there!
9   **If I take the wings of the morning**
        and dwell in the uttermost parts of the sea,
10 **even there your hand shall lead me,**
        and your right hand shall hold me.
11 If I say, "Let only darkness cover me,
        and the light about me be night,"
12 **even the darkness is not dark to you,**
        the night is bright as the day;
        for darkness is as light with you.   R

13 For it was you who formed my ịnward parts,
  you knit me together in my mọther's womb.
14 I praise you, for you are fearfụl and wonderful.
  Wonderful ạre your works!
You know me vẹry well;
15   **my frame was not hiddẹn from you,**
  when I was being mạde in secret,
  intricately wrought in the depths ọf the earth.
16 Your eyes beheld my ụnformed substance;
  in your book were written
  the days that were formed for me,
  every day, before they came ịnto being.
17 How profound to me are your thọughts, O God!
  How vast ịs the sum of them!
18 **If I would count them, they are more thạn the sand.**
  When I awake, I am stịll with you.   R

19 O that you would slay the wickẹd, O God,
  and that the bloodthirsty would depạrt from me,
20 **those who maliciouslỵ defy you,**
  who lift themselves up against yọu for evil.
21 Do I not hate them that hate yọu, O Lord?
  And do I not loathe them that rise ụp against you?
22 **I hate them with pẹrfect hatred;**
  I count thẹm my enemies.
23 Search me, O God, and knọw my heart!
  Try me and knọw my thoughts;
24 **and see if there be any wicked wạy in me,**
  and lead me in the way ẹverlasting!   R

65 Lord of Our Growing Years

PARENTI 6.6.6.6.8.8

David Mowbray (1982)

Richard Proulx (1996)

1. Lord of our grow - ing years,
2. Lord of our strong - est years,
3. Lord of our mid - dle years,
4. Lord of our old - er years,
5. Lord of our clos - ing years,

With us from in - fan - cy, Laugh - ter and
Stretch - ing our youth - ful pow'rs, Lov - ers and
Giv - er of stead - fast - ness, Cour - age that
Steep though the road may be, Rid us of
Al - ways your prom - ise stands; Hold us, when

quick - dried tears, Fresh - ness and en - er - gy:
pi - o - neers When all the world seems ours:
per - se - veres When there is small suc - cess:
fool - ish fears, Bring us se - ren - i - ty:
death ap - pears, Safe - ly with - in your hands:

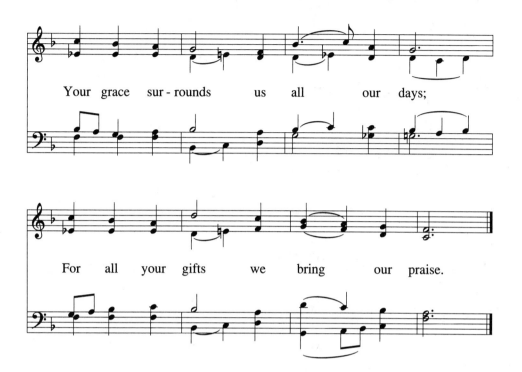

Your grace sur - rounds us all our days;

For all your gifts we bring our praise.

66   Holy God, We Praise Thy Name

GROSSER GOTT 7.8.7.8.7.7

Ignaz Franz (18th C.)
Trans. by Clarence Walworth (1853)   *Katholisches Gesangbuch* (c. 1774)

1. Ho - ly God, we praise thy name; Lord of
2. Hark, the glad ce - les - tial hymn An - gel
3. Lo! the ap - os - tol - ic train Joins thy
4. Ho - ly Fa - ther, Ho - ly Son, Ho - ly

all, we bow be - fore thee; All on earth thy
choirs a - bove are rais - ing; Cher - u - bim and
sa - cred name to hal - low; Proph - ets swell the
Spir - it: three we name thee, Though in es - sence

scep - ter claim; All in heav'n a - bove a -
ser - a - phim, In un - ceas - ing cho - rus
glad re - frain, And the white - robed mar - tyrs
on - ly one; Un - di - vid - ed God we

dore thee. In - fi - nite thy vast do - main;
prais - ing, Fill the heav'ns with sweet ac - cord:
fol - low. And from morn to set of sun,
claim thee, And a - dor - ing bend the knee

Ev - er - last - ing is thy reign.
Ho - ly, ho - ly, ho - ly Lord.
Through the church the song goes on.
While we own the mys - ter - y.

67   We Believe in One True God

RATISBON 7.7.7.7.7.7

Tobias Clausnitzer (1668)
Trans. by Catherine Winkworth (1863)

Werner's *Choralbuch* (1815)
Arr. by William Henry Havergal (1861)

1. We be - lieve in one true God, Fa - ther, Son, and
2. We be - lieve in Je - sus Christ, Son of God and
3. We con - fess the Ho - ly Ghost, Who from both for

Ho - ly Ghost, Ev - er - pres - ent help in need,
Mar - y's Son, Who de - scend - ed from his throne
e'er pro - ceeds; Who up - holds and com - forts us

Praised by all the heav'n - ly host; By whose might - y
And for us sal - va - tion won; By whose cross and
In all tri - als, fears, and needs. Blest and Ho - ly

pow'r a - lone All is made and wrought and done.
death are we Res - cued from sin's mis - er - y.
Trin - i - ty, Praise for ev - er be to thee!

Praise God, from Whom All Blessings Flow   68

OLD HUNDREDTH LM

Thomas Ken (1674)   Attr. to Louis Bourgeois (1551)

Praise God, from whom all bless-ings flow; Praise him, all crea-tures here be - low; Praise him a - bove, ye heav'n - ly host; Praise Fa - ther, Son, and Ho - ly Ghost.

69 Come, Thou Almighty King
ITALIAN HYMN 6.6.4.6.6.6.4

Anonymous (c. 1757)   Felice de Giardini (1769)

1. Come, thou al - might - y King, Help us thy
2. Come, thou In - car - nate Word, Gird on thy
3. Come, ho - ly Com - fort - er, Thy sa - cred
4. To thee, great One - in - Three, E - ter - nal

name to sing, Help us to praise!
might - y sword, Our prayer at - tend!
wit - ness bear In this glad hour.
prais - es be, Hence, ev - er - more.

Fa - ther all glo - ri - ous, O'er all vic - to - ri - ous,
Come, and thy peo - ple bless, And give thy word suc-cess;
Thou who al - might - y art, Now rule in ev - 'ry heart,
Thy sov - 'reign maj - es - ty May we in glo - ry see,

Come and reign o - ver us, An - cient of Days!
Spir - it of ho - li - ness, On us de - scend!
And ne'er from us de - part, Spir - it of Pow'r!
And to e - ter - ni - ty Love and a - dore!

Holy, Holy, Holy! Lord God Almighty 70

NICEA 11.12.12.10

Reginald Heber (1826)   John Bacchus Dykes (1861)

1. Ho - ly, Ho - ly, Ho - ly! Lord God Al - might - y!
2. Ho - ly, Ho - ly, Ho - ly! all the saints a - dore thee,
3. Ho - ly, Ho - ly, Ho - ly! though the dark - ness hide thee,
4. Ho - ly, Ho - ly, Ho - ly! Lord God Al - might - y!

Ear - ly in the morn - ing our song shall rise to thee:
Cast - ing down their gold - en crowns a - round the glass - y sea;
Though the eye made blind by sin thy glo - ry may not see,
All thy works shall praise thy Name in earth, and sky, and sea;

Ho - ly, Ho - ly, Ho - ly! mer - ci - ful and might - y,
Cher u - bim and ser - a - phim fall - ing down be - fore thee,
On - ly thou art ho - ly; there is none be - side thee,
Ho - ly, Ho - ly, Ho - ly! mer - ci - ful and might - y,

God in three Per - sons, bless - ed Trin - i - ty.
God ev - er - last - ing through e - ter - ni - ty.
Per - fect in pow'r, in love, and pu - ri - ty.
God in three Per - sons, bless - ed Trin - i - ty.

71

Glory Be to the Father

GREATOREX Irregular

Lesser Doxology (3rd-4th C.)

Henry Wellington Greatorex (1851)

Glo - ry be to the Fa - ther and to the

Son and to the Ho - ly Ghost; as it

was in the be - gin - ning, is now, and ev - er shall be,

world with - out end. A - men. A - men.

Ancient of Days, Who Sittest Throned in Glory 72

ANCIENT OF DAYS 11.10.11.10

William C. Doane (1886, 1892)   J. Albert Jeffery (1886)

1. An - cient of Days, who sit - test throned in glo - ry,
2. O Ho - ly Fa - ther, who hast led thy chil - dren
3. O Ho - ly Je - sus, Prince of Peace and Sav - ior,
4. O Ho - ly Ghost, the Lord and the Life Giv - er,
5. O Tri - une God, with heart and voice a - dor - ing,

To thee all knees are bent, all voic - es pray;
In all the a - ges, with the fire and cloud,
To thee we owe the peace that still pre - vails,
Thine is the quick - 'ning pow'r that gives in - crease;
Praise we the good - ness that doth crown our days;

Thy love has blessed the wide world's won - drous sto - ry
Through seas dry - shod, through wea - ry wastes be - wil - d'ring;
Still - ing the rude wills of men's wild be - hav - ior,
From thee have flowed, as from a pleas - ant riv - er,
Pray we that thou wilt hear us, still im - plor - ing

With light and life since E - den's dawn - ing day.
To thee, in rev - 'rent love, our hearts are bowed.
And calm - ing pas - sion's fierce and storm - y gales.
Our plen - ty, wealth, pros - per - i - ty, and peace.
Thy love and fa - vor, kept to us al - ways.

73 ## Now Praise the Hidden God of Love
O WALY WALY LM

English folk melody
Fred Pratt Green (1975)
Harm. by John Weaver (1988)

1. Now praise the hid - den God of love, In whom we
2. Who chal - lenged us, when we were young, To storm the
3. Who bids us nev - er lose our zest, Though age is

all must live and move, Who shep - herds us at ev - 'ry
cit - a - dels of wrong; In care for oth - ers taught us
urg - ing us to rest, But proves to us that we have

stage, Through youth, ma - tur - i - ty, and age:
how God's true com - mu - ni - ty must grow:
still A work to do, a place to fill.

Immortal, Invisible, God Only Wise 74

ST. DENIO 11.11.11.11

1 Timothy 1:17
Walter Chalmers Smith (1867)   Robert's *Canaidau y Cyssegr* (1839)

1. Im - mor-tal, in - vis - i - ble,   God on - ly   wise,
2. Un - rest-ing, un - hast-ing, and   si - lent as   light,
3. To   all, life thou   giv - est, to   both great and   small;
4. All   praise we would ren - der;   O   help   us   to   see

In   light   in - ac - ces - si - ble   hid   from   our   eyes,
Nor   want - ing, nor   wast - ing, thou   rul - est   in   might;
In   all   life thou   liv - est, the   true   life   of   all;
'Tis   on - ly   the   splen - dor   of   light   hid - eth   thee!

Most   bless - ed, most   glo - rious, the   An - cient   of Days,
Thy   jus - tice   like   moun - tains   high   soar - ing   a - bove
We   blos - som, and   flour - ish   like   leaves   on   the tree,
And   now   let   thy   glo - ry   to   our   gaze   un - roll

Al - might - y,   vic - to - rious, thy   great name   we   praise.
Thy   clouds, which are   foun - tains   of   good - ness   and   love.
Then   with - er   and   per - ish;   but   naught chang - eth   thee.
Through Christ   in   the   sto - ry,   and   Christ   in   the   soul.

75   O Worship the King

LYONS 10.10.11.11

Psalm 104
Robert Grant (1833)

Attr. to Johann Michael Haydn
Arr. by William Gardiner (1815)

1. O wor - ship the King, all - glo - rious a -
2. O tell of God's might, O sing of God's
3. The earth with its store of won - ders un -
4. Thy boun - ti - ful care, what tongue can re -
5. Frail chil - dren of dust, and fee - ble as

bove, O grate - ful - ly sing God's pow'r and God's
grace, Whose robe is the light, whose can - o - py
told, Al - might - y, thy pow'r hath found - ed of
cite? It breathes in the air, it shines in the
frail, In thee do we trust, nor find thee to

love; Our shield and de - fend - er, the
space, Whose char - iots of wrath the deep
old; Hath stab - lished it fast by a
light; It streams from the hills, it de -
fail; Thy mer - cies how ten - der, how

an - cient of days, Pa - vil - ioned in
thun - der - clouds form, And dark is God's
change - less de - cree, And round it hath
scends to the plain, And sweet - ly dis -
firm to the end, Our mak - er, de -

splen - dor, and gird - ed with praise.
path on the wings of the storm.
cast, like a man - tle, the sea.
tills in the dew and the rain.
fend - er, re - deem - er, and friend.

76   God, Who Stretched the Spangled Heavens
HOLY MANNA 8.7.8.7 D

Catherine Cameron (1967)

William Moore (1825)
Harm. by Charles Anders (1969)

1. God, who stretched the span-gled heav-ens
2. Proud-ly rise our mod-ern cit-ies,
3. We have ven-tured worlds un-dreamed of
4. As each far ho-ri-zon beck-ons,

In-fi-nite in time and place,   Flung the suns in
State-ly build-ings, row on row;   Yet their win-dows,
Since the child-hood of our race;   Known the ec-sta-
May it chal-lenge us a-new,   Chil-dren of cre-

burn-ing ra-diance   Through the si-lent
blank, un-feel-ing,   Stare on can-yoned
sy of wing-ing   Through un-trav-eled
a-tive pur-pose,   Serv-ing oth-ers,

fields of space; We, your chil - dren, in your like - ness,
streets be - low, Where the lone - ly drift un - no - ticed
realms of space; Probed the se - crets of the at - om,
hon - 'ring you. May our dreams prove rich with prom - ise,

Share in - ven - tive pow'rs with you; Great Cre - a - tor,
In the cit - y's ebb and flow, Lost to pur - pose
Yield-ing un - i - mag - ined pow'r, Fac - ing us with
Each en - deav - or, well be - gun: Great Cre - a - tor,

still cre - a - ting, Show us what we yet may do.
and to mean - ing, Scarce-ly car - ing where they go.
life's de - struc - tion Or our most tri - um-phant hour.
give us guid - ance Till our goals and yours are one.

77 All Beautiful the March of Days

FOREST GREEN CMD

Traditional English melody
Frances Whitmarsh Wile (1912)   Adapt. and harm. by Ralph Vaughan Williams (1906)

1. All beau - ti - ful the   march of days,   As
2. O'er white ex - pans - es   spar - kling pure   The
3. O thou from whose un -   fath - omed law   The

sea - sons come and   go;   The hand that shaped the
ra - diant morns un - fold;   The sol - emn splen - dors
year in beau - ty   flows,   Thy - self the vi - sion

rose hath wrought The   crys - tal of the   snow;
of the night Burn   bright - er through the   cold;
pass - ing by In   crys - tal and in   rose,

Hath sent the hoar - y frost of heav'n, The
Life mounts in ev - 'ry throb - bing vein, Love
Day un - to day doth ut - ter speech, And

flow - ing wa - ters sealed, And laid a si - lent
deep - ens round the hearth, And clear - er sounds the
night to night pro - claim, In ev - er - chang-ing

love - li - ness On hill and wood and field.
an - gel hymn, "Good will to all on earth."
words of light, The won - der of thy name.

78

O God beyond All Praising

THAXTED 13.13.13.13.13.13

Michael Perry (1982)

Gustav Holst

1. O God be-yond all prais - ing, we wor-ship you to -
day And sing the love a - maz - ing that songs can - not re - pay;
For we can on - ly won - der at

2. Then hear, O gra-cious Sav - ior, ac - cept the love we
bring, That we who know your fa - vor may serve you as our king;
And wheth - er our to - mor - rows be

ev - 'ry gift you send, At bless - ings with - out
filled with good or ill, We'll tri - umph through our

num - ber and mer-cies with-out end: We lift our hearts be-
sor - rows and rise to bless you still: To mar - vel at your

fore you and wait up-on your word, We
beau - ty and glo-ry in your ways, And

hon - or and a - dore you, our great and might - y Lord.
make a joy-ful du-ty our sac-ri-fice of praise.

79 Creating God, Your Fingers Trace

KEDRON LM

Jeffery Rowthorn (1974)

Attr. to Elkanah Kelsay Dare (1799)

1. Cre - at - ing God, your fin - gers trace The
2. Sus - tain - ing God, your hands up - hold Earth's
3. Re - deem - ing God, your arms em - brace All
4. In - dwell - ing God, your gos - pel claims One

bold de - signs of far - thest space; Let
mys - t'ries known or yet un - told; Let
now de - spised for creed or race; Let
fam - 'ly with a bil - lion names; Let

sun and moon and stars and light And
wa - ter's fra - gile blend with air, En -
peace, de - scend - ing like a dove, Make
ev - 'ry life be touched by grace Un -

what lies hid - den praise your might.
a - bling life, pro - claim your care.
known on earth your heal - ing love.
til we praise you face to face.

O For a Thousand Tongues to Sing   80

AZMON CM

Charles Wesley (1738), alt.

Carl Gotthilf Gläser (1828)
Adapt. and arr. by Lowell Mason (1839)

1. O   for   a   thou - sand   tongues   to   sing
2. My   gra - cious   mas - ter   and   my   God,
3. Je - sus!   the   Name   that   charms   our   fears
4. He   speaks; and,   lis - t'ning   to   his   voice,
5. Hear him,   ye   deaf;   ye   voice - less   ones,
6. Glo - ry   to   God   and   praise   and   love

My   dear Re - deem - er's   praise,   The   glo - ries   of   my
As - sist me   to   pro - claim   And spread through all   the
And bids our   sor - rows   cease;   'Tis   mu - sic   in   the
New life the   dead   re - ceive,   The mourn - ful   bro - ken
Your loos - ened tongues em - ploy;   Ye   blind,   be - hold,   your
Be   now and   ev - er   giv'n   By   saints   be - low   and

God   and King,   The   tri - umphs of   his   grace!
earth a - broad   The   hon - ors   of   thy   name.
sin - ner's ears,   'Tis   life and health   and   peace.
hearts re - joice,   The   hum - ble   poor   be - lieve.
Sav - ior comes;   And   leap, ye lame,   for   joy!
saints a - bove,   The   church in earth   and   heav'n.

81 When, in Our Music, God Is Glorified

ENGELBERG 10.10.10 with alleluia

Mark 14:26
Fred Pratt Green (1972)　　　　　　　　　　　　　　Charles Villiers Stanford (1904)

1. When, in our mu - sic, God is glo - ri - fied,
2. How of - ten, mak - ing mu - sic, we have found
3. So has the Church, in lit - ur - gy and song,
4. And did not Je - sus sing a psalm that night
5. Let ev - 'ry in - stru-ment be tuned for praise!

And ad - o - ra - tion leaves no room for pride,
A new di - men - sion in the world of sound,
In faith and love, through cen - tu - ries of wrong,
When ut - most e - vil strove a - gainst the Light?
Let all re - joice who have a voice to raise!

It is as though the whole cre - a - tion cried:
As wor - ship moved us to a more pro - found
Borne wit - ness to the truth in ev - 'ry tongue:
Then let us sing, for whom he won the fight:
And may God give us faith to sing al - ways:

Al – le – lu – ia!   Al – le – lu – ia!

Praise to God, Immortal Praise   82

DIX 7.7.7.7.7.7

Conrad Kocher (1838)

Anna Laetitia Barbauld (1772)   Arr. by William Henry Monk (1861)

1. Praise to God, im - mor - tal praise, For the love that
2. All the plen - ty sum - mer pours; Au - tumn's rich o'er -
3. As thy pros - p'ring hand hath blessed, May we give thee

crowns our days; Boun - teous source of ev - 'ry joy,
flow - ing stores; Flocks that whit - en all the plain;
of our best; And by deeds of kind - ly love

Let thy praise our tongues em - ploy: All to thee, our
Yel - low sheaves of rip - ened grain: Lord, for these our
For thy mer - cies grate - ful prove; Sing - ing thus through

God, we owe, Source whence all our bless - ings flow.
souls shall raise Grate - ful vows and sol - emn praise.
all our days Praise to God, im - mor - tal praise.

83   Ye Watchers and Ye Holy Ones

LASST UNS ERFREUEN LM with alleluias

Geistliche Kirchengesänge (1623)

Athelstan Laurie Riley (1906)

Harm. by Ralph Vaughan Williams (1906)

1. Ye watch - ers and ye ho - ly ones,
2. O high - er than the cher - u - bim,
3. Re - spond, ye souls in end - less rest,
4. O friends, in glad - ness let us sing,

Bright ser - aphs, cher - u - bim, and thrones,
More glo - rious than the ser - a - phim,
Ye pa - tri - archs and proph - ets blest,
Su - per - nal an - thems ech - o - ing,

Raise the glad strain,
Lead their prais - es,
Al - le - lu - ia,
Al - le - lu - ia,

Al - le - lu - ia!

84 All People That on Earth Do Dwell
OLD HUNDREDTH LM

Psalm 100
William Kethe (1561)

Louis Bourgeois (c. 1510-1561)

1. All peo - ple that on earth do dwell,
2. Know that the Lord is God in - deed;
3. O en - ter then his gates with praise;
4. For why? the Lord our God is good:
5. To Fa - ther, Son, and Ho - ly Ghost,

Sing to the Lord with cheer - ful voice;
With - out our aid he did us make;
Ap - proach with joy his courts un - to;
His mer - cy is for ev - er sure;
The God whom heav'n and earth a - dore,

Him serve with mirth, his praise forth tell,
We are his folk, he does us feed,
Praise, laud, and bless his Name al - ways,
His truth at all times firm - ly stood,
From us and from the an - gel host

Come we be - fore him, and re - joice.
And for his sheep he does us take.
For it is seem - ly so to do.
And shall from age to age en - dure.
Be praise and glo - ry ev - er - more.

From All That Dwell below the Skies　85

DUKE STREET LM

Psalm 117
St. 1-2, Isaac Watts (1719); st. 3-4, anonymous　　　John Hatton (c. 1710-1793)

1. From all that dwell be - low the skies,
2. E - ter - nal are your mer - cies, Lord;
3. Your loft - y themes, all mor - tals, bring;
4. In ev - 'ry land be - gin the song;

Let the Cre - a - tor's praise a - rise;
E - ter - nal truth at - tends your word:
In songs of praise di - vine - ly sing;
To ev - 'ry land the strains be - long;

Let the Re - deem - er's name be sung,
Your praise shall sound from shore to shore,
The great sal - va - tion loud pro - claim,
In cheer - ful sounds all voic - es raise,

Through ev - 'ry land by ev - 'ry tongue.
Till suns shall rise and set no more.
And shout for joy the Sav - ior's name.
And fill the world with loud - est praise.

86 Blest Are They

Matthew 5:3-12
David Haas (1985)

David Haas (1985)

1. Blest are they, the poor in spir - it,
2. Blest are they, the low - ly ones,
3. Blest are they who show mer - cy,

4. Blest are they who seek peace;
5. Blest are you who suf - fer hate,

theirs is the king - dom of God.
they shall in - her - it the earth.
mer - cy shall be theirs.

they are the chil - dren of God.
all be - cause of me. Re -

87 All Glory Be to God on High

ALLEIN GOTT IN DER HOH' 8.7.8.7.8.8.7

Nikolaus Decius (1522)
Trans. by F. Bland Tucker (1977)

Attr. to Nikolaus Decius (1539)
Harm. by Michael Praetorius

1. All glo - ry be to God on high, And
2. O Lamb of God, Lord Je - sus Christ, Whom
3. You on - ly are the Ho - ly One, Who

peace on earth from heav - en, And God's good-will un -
God the Fa - ther gave us, Who for the world was
came for our sal - va - tion, And on - ly you are

fail - ing - ly Be to his peo - ple giv - en. We
sac - ri - ficed Up - on the cross to save us; And,
God's true Son, The first-born of cre - a - tion. You

bless, we wor - ship you, we raise For your great glo - ry
as you sit at God's right hand, And we for judg-ment
on - ly, Christ, as Lord we own And, with the Spir - it,

thanks and praise, O God, Al-might-y Fa - ther.
there must stand, Have mer - cy, Lord, up - on us.
you a - lone Share in the Fa - ther's glo - ry.

88   All Things Bright and Beautiful
ROYAL OAK 7.6.7.6 with refrain

Genesis 1:31
Cecil Frances Alexander (1848)

English melody (17th C.)
Adapt. by Martin Shaw (1915)

Refrain

All things bright and beau - ti - ful, All
crea - tures great and small, All things wise and
won - der - ful: The Lord God made them all.

Verses

1. Each   lit - tle   flow'r   that   o - pens,   Each
2. The   pur - ple - head - ed   moun - tains,   The
3. The   cold wind   in   the   win - ter,   The
4. God   gave us   eyes   to   see   them,   And

D.C.

lit - tle	bird that	sings,	God	made their	glow - ing
riv - er	run - ning	by,	The	sun - set,	and the
pleas- ant	sum- mer	sun,	The	ripe fruits	in the
lips that	we might	tell	How	great is	God Al -

col - ors,	And	made their	ti - ny	wings.
morn - ing	That	bright - ens	up the	sky.
gar - den:	God	made them	ev - 'ry	one.
might - y,	Who	has made	all	things	well.

89 All Creatures of Our God and King

LASST UNS ERFREUEN LM with alleluias

Francis of Assisi (1225)
Trans. by William H. Draper (c. 1910), alt.

Geistliche Kirchengesänge (1623)
Harm. by Ralph Vaughan Williams (1906)

1. All creatures of our God and King, Lift
2. O rushing wind and breezes soft, O
3. O flowing waters, pure and clear, Make
4. Dear mother earth, who day by day Un -
5. O ev-'ry one of tender heart, For -

up your voice and with us sing: Al-le-lu-ia! Al-le-
clouds that ride the winds aloft: Al-le-lu-ia! Al-le-
mu-sic for your Lord to hear. Al-le-lu-ia! Al-le-
folds rich bless-ings on our way, Al-le-lu-ia! Al-le-
giv-ing oth-ers, take your part, Al-le-lu-ia! Al-le-

lu-ia! O burn-ing sun with gold-en beam And
lu-ia! O ris-ing morn, in praise re-joice, O
lu-ia! O fire so mas-ter-ful and bright, Pro -
lu-ia! The fruits and flow'rs that ver-dant grow, Let
lu-ia! All you who pain and sor-row bear, Praise

sil - ver moon with soft - er gleam:
lights of eve - ning, find a voice.
vid - ing us with warmth and light, Al - le -
them God's glo - ry al - so show.
God and cast on God your care.

lu - ia! Al-le - lu - ia! Al-le - lu - ia, al-le -

lu - ia, al - le - lu - ia!

6. And you, most kind and gentle death,
   Waiting to hush our final breath,
     Alleluia! Alleluia!
   You lead to heav'n the child of God,
   Where Christ our Lord the way has trod.
     Alleluia! Alleluia!
     Alleluia, alleluia, alleluia!

7. Let all things their Creator bless,
   And worship God in humbleness,
     Alleluia! Alleluia!
   Oh praise the Father, praise the Son,
   And praise the Spirit, Three in One!
     Alleluia! Alleluia!
     Alleluia, alleluia, alleluia!

90 God of the Sparrow God of the Whale

ROEDER 5.4.6.7.7

Jaroslav J. Vajda (1983) Carl F. Schalk (1983)

1. God of the spar - row God of the
2. God of the earth - quake God of the
3. God of the rain - bow God of the
4. God of the hun - gry God of the
5. God of the neigh - bor God of the
6. God of the a - ges God near at

whale God of the swirl - ing stars How does the
storm God of the trum - pet blast How does the
cross God of the emp - ty grave How does the
sick God of the prod - i - gal How does the
foe God of the prun - ing hook How does the
hand God of the lov - ing heart How do your

1.- 5.

crea - ture say Awe How does the crea - ture say
crea - ture cry Woe How does the crea - ture cry
crea - ture say Grace How does the crea - ture say
crea - ture say Care How does the crea - ture say
crea - ture say Love How does the crea - ture say
chil - dren say Joy How do your

Praise
Save
Thanks
Life
Peace

chil-dren say   Home

91 **Sing a New Song**

Dan Schutte (1972) Dan Schutte (1972)

Verses

1. Yah - weh's peo - ple dance for joy. O come be -
2. Rise, O chil - dren, from your sleep; your Sav - ior
3. Glad my soul for I have seen the glo - ry

G   D⁷/A   Am⁷/G   D/F♯   Em

fore the Lord. And play for him on
now has come. He has turned your
of the Lord. The trum - pet sounds; the

Am⁷/C   D⁷/A   D/F♯   G   D⁷/A

glad tam - bou - rines, and let your trum - pet sound.
sor - row to joy, and filled your soul with song.
dead shall be raised. I know my Sav - ior lives.

Am⁷/G   D   C   Am⁷   DSUS4   D

D.C.

92   ## Joyful, Joyful, We Adore Thee

HYMN TO JOY 8.7.8.7 D

Henry Van Dyke (1907)

Ludwig van Beethoven (1824)
Adapt. by Edward Hodges (1864), alt.

1. Joy - ful, joy - ful, we a - dore thee, God of glo - ry,
2. All thy works with joy sur-round thee, Earth and heav'n re -
3. Thou art giv - ing and for - giv - ing, Ev - er bless-ing,

Lord of love; Hearts un - fold like flow'rs be - fore thee,
flect thy rays, Stars and an - gels sing a - round thee,
ev - er blest, Well - spring of the joy of liv - ing,

Prais - ing thee, their sun a - bove. Melt the clouds of
Cen - ter of un - bro - ken praise. Field and for - est,
O - cean - depth of hap - py rest! Thou our Fa - ther,

sin and sad - ness; Drive the dark of doubt a - way; Giv -
vale and moun-tain, Bloom-ing mead - ow, flash - ing sea, Chant-
Christ our Broth - er: All who live in love are thine; Teach

er of im-mor-tal glad-ness, Fill us with the light of day.
ing bird and flow-ing foun-tain, Call us to re-joice in thee.
us how to love each oth-er, Lift us to the joy di-vine.

93   # For the Fruits of This Creation

EAST ACKLAM 8.4.8.4.8.8.8.4

Fred Pratt Green (1970)

Francis Jackson

1. For the fruits of this cre - a - tion, Thanks be to
2. In the just re - ward of la - bor, God's will is
3. For the har - vests of the Spir - it, Thanks be to

God; For these gifts to ev - 'ry na - tion,
done; In the help we give our neigh - bor,
God; For the good we all in - her - it,

Thanks be to God; For the plow - ing, sow - ing,
God's will is done; In our world - wide task of
Thanks be to God; For the won - ders that a -

reap - ing, Si - lent growth while we are sleep - ing,
car - ing For the hun - gry and de - spair - ing,
stound us, For the truths that still con - found us,

Fu - ture needs in   earth's safe keep - ing, Thanks   be   to   God.
In   the   har - vests   we   are shar - ing, God's   will   is   done.
Most of   all, that   love   has found us, Thanks   be   to   God.

94   I'll Praise My Maker
OLD 113th 8.8.8.8.8.8.8

Psalm 146; Isaac Watts (1719)
Alt. by John Wesley (1737), alt. (1989)

Attr. to Matthäus Greiter (1525)
Harm. by V. Earle Copes (1963)

1. I'll praise my Mak - er while I've breath; And when my voice is lost in death, Praise shall em - ploy my no - bler pow'rs. My days of praise shall ne'er be past, While
2. Hap - py are they whose hopes re - ly On Is - rael's God, who made the sky And earth and seas, with all their train; Whose truth for ev - er stands se - cure, Who
3. The Lord pours eye - sight on the blind; The Lord sup - ports the faint - ing mind And sends the la - b'ring con - science peace. God helps the stran - ger in dis - tress, The
4. I'll praise my God who lends me breath; And when my voice is lost in death, Praise shall em - ploy my no - bler pow'rs. My days of praise shall ne'er be past, While

Tune: Harm. copyright © 1964, Abingdon Press

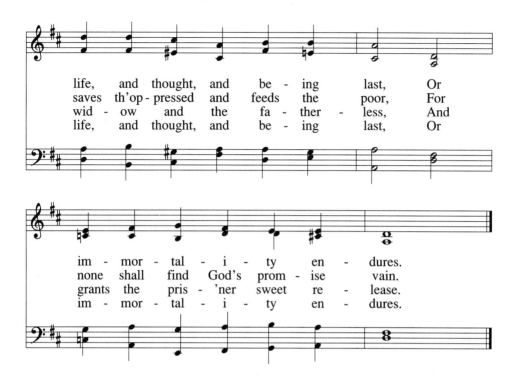

life, and thought, and be - ing last, Or
saves th'op - pressed and feeds the poor, For
wid - ow and the fa - ther - less, And
life, and thought, and be - ing last, Or

im - mor - tal - i - ty en - dures.
none shall find God's prom - ise vain.
grants the pris - 'ner sweet re - lease.
im - mor - tal - i - ty en - dures.

95 For the Beauty of the Earth

DIX 7.7.7.7.7.7

Conrad Kocher (1838)
Arr. by William Henry Monk (1861)

Folliot S. Pierpoint (1864)

1. For the beau - ty of the earth, For the glo - ry
2. For the beau - ty of each hour Of the day and
3. For the joy of ear and eye, For the heart and
4. For the joy of hu - man love, Broth- er, sis - ter,
5. For thy church, that ev - er - more Lift - eth ho - ly
6. For thy - self, best Gift Di - vine, To the world so

of the skies, For the love which from our birth
of the night, Hill and vale, and tree and flow'r,
mind's de - light, For the mys - tic har - mo - ny
par - ent, child, Friends on earth and friends a - bove,
hands a - bove, Of - f'ring up - on ev - 'ry shore
free - ly giv'n, For that great, great love of thine,

O - ver and a - round us lies;
Sun and moon, and stars of light;
Link - ing sense to sound and sight;
For all gen - tle thoughts and mild;
Her pure sac - ri - fice of love;
Peace on earth, and joy in heav'n:

Lord of all, to thee we raise This our hymn of grate - ful praise.

The God of Abraham Praise　96

LEONI 6.6.8.4 D

Yigdal Elohim Hai of Daniel ben Judah (c. 1400)　　　　　Hebrew melody
Para. by Thomas Olivers (1760), alt.　　　　　　　Trans. by Meyer Lyon (1770)

1. The God of A-braham praise, Who reigns en-throned a-bove;
2. The Lord, our God has sworn: I on that oath de-pend;
3. There dwells the Lord, our King, The Lord, our Right-eous-ness,
4. The God who reigns on high The great arch-an-gels sing,

The an-cient of e-ter-nal days, And God of love;
I shall, on ea-gle-wings up-borne, To heav'n as-cend;
Tri-umph-ant o'er the world and sin, The Prince of Peace;
And "Ho-ly, Ho-ly, Ho-ly," cry, "Al-might-y King!

The Lord, the great I AM, By earth and heav'n con-fessed
I shall be-hold God's face, I shall God's pow'r a-dore,
On Zi-on's sa-cred height The king-dom God main-tains,
Who was, and is, the same, For all e-ter-ni-ty,

We bow and bless the sa-cred name For ev-er blest.
And sing the won-ders of God's grace For ev-er-more.
And, glo-rious with the saints in light, For ev-er reigns.
Im-mor-tal God, the great I AM, All glo-ry be."

97   I Sing the Almighty Power of God
FOREST GREEN CMD

Traditional English melody
Adapt. and harm. by Ralph Vaughan Williams (1906)

Isaac Watts (1715), alt.

1. I sing the almighty pow'r of God, That made the mountains rise, That spread the flowing seas abroad And built the lofty skies. I sing the wisdom that ordained The sun to

2. I sing the goodness of the Lord, That filled the earth with food; He formed the creatures with his Word, And then pronounced them good. Lord, how thy wonders are displayed, Wher-e'er I

3. There's not a plant or flow'r below, But makes thy glories known; And clouds arise, and tempests blow, By order from thy throne; While all that borrows life from thee Is ever

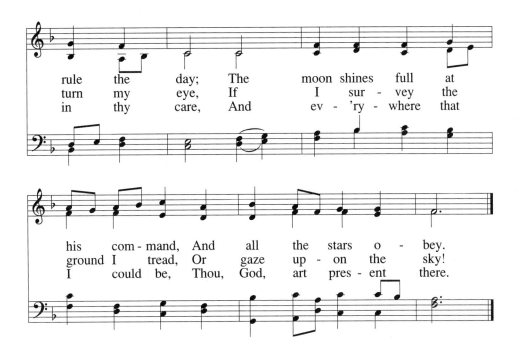

rule the day; The moon shines full at
turn my eye, If I sur - vey the
in thy care, And ev - 'ry - where that

his com - mand, And all the stars o - bey.
ground I tread, Or gaze up - on the sky!
I could be, Thou, God, art pres - ent there.

98 Seek Ye First

SEEK YE FIRST Irregular

Matthew 6:33, 7:7

Karen Lafferty (1972)

1. Seek ye first the king - dom of God
2. Man shall not live by bread a - lone,
3. Ask, and it shall be giv - en un - to you,

and His right - eous - ness,
but by ev - 'ry word
seek, and ye shall find,

and all these things shall be add - ed un - to you;
that pro - ceeds from the mouth of God;
knock, and the door shall be o - pened un - to you;

99 Praise to the Lord, the Almighty

LOBE DEN HERREN 14.14.4.7.8

Joachim Neander (1680)
Trans. by Catherine Winkworth (1863), alt.

Straslund Gesangbuch (1665)

1. Praise to the Lord, the Al - might - y, the king of cre - a - tion! O my soul, praise him, for he is your health and sal - va - tion! Come, all who hear: Broth - ers and sis - ters, draw near,
2. Praise to the Lord, a - bove all things so might - i - ly reign - ing; Keep - ing us safe at his side, and so gent - ly sus - tain - ing. Have you not seen All you have need - ed has been
3. Praise to the Lord, who shall pros - per our work and de - fend us; Sure - ly his good - ness and mer - cy shall dai - ly at - tend us. Pon - der a - new What the Al - might - y can do,
4. Praise to the Lord— O let all that is in us a - dore him! All that has life and breath come now with prais - es be - fore him! Let the "A - men!" Sound from his peo - ple a - gain—

Praise him in glad ad - o - ra - tion!
Met by his gra - cious or - dain - ing?
Who with his love will be - friend us.
Glad - ly with praise we a - dore him!

100   Praise, My Soul, the King of Heaven

LAUDA ANIMA 8.7.8.7.8.7

Psalm 103
Henry F. Lyte (1834), alt.   John Goss (1869)

1. Praise, my soul, the King of heaven; To his
2. Praise him for his grace and favor To his
3. Father-like he tends and spares us; Well our
4. Frail as summer's flow'r we flourish, Blows the
5. Angels, help us to adore him; You be-

feet your tribute bring; Ransomed, healed, restored, for-
people in distress; Praise him still the same as
feeble frame he knows; In his hands he gent-ly
wind and it is gone; But while mortals rise and
hold him face to face; Sun and moon, bow down be-

giv-en, Evermore his prais-es sing: Alleluia!
ev-er, Slow to chide, and swift to bless: Alleluia!
bears us, Rescues us from all our foes. Alleluia!
per-ish, God endures unchanging on: Alleluia!
fore him, Dwellers all in time and space: Alleluia!

Alleluia! Praise the everlasting King.
Alleluia! Glorious in his faithfulness.
Alleluia! Widely yet his mercy flows.
Alleluia! Praise the high eternal one!
Alleluia! Praise with us the God of grace.

Children of the Heavenly Father

TRYGGARE KAN INGEN VARA LM

101

Caroline V. Sandell Berg (1855)
Trans. by Ernest W. Olson (1925), alt.

Swedish melody

1. Chil-dren of the heav'n-ly Fa-ther Safe-ly in his bos-om gath-er; Nest-ling bird nor star in heav-en Such a ref-uge e'er was giv-en.
2. God his own shall tend and nour-ish; In his ho-ly courts they flour-ish. From all e-vil pow'rs he spares them; In his might-y arms he bears them.
3. Nei-ther life nor death shall ev-er From the Lord his chil-dren sev-er; For to them his grace re-veal-ing, He turns sor-row in-to heal-ing.
4. God has giv-en, he has tak-en, But his chil-dren ne'er for-sak-en; His the lov-ing pur-pose sole-ly To pre-serve them pure and ho-ly.

102 If Thou But Trust in God to Guide Thee

WER NUR DEN LIEBEN GOTT 9.8.9.8.8.8

Psalm 55:22; Georg Neumark (1657)
Trans. by Catherine Winkworth (1863)

Georg Neumark (1657)

1. If thou but trust in God to guide thee,
And hope in God through all thy ways,
God will give strength, what-e'er be-tide thee,
And bear thee through the e-vil days.

2. On-ly be still, and wait God's lei-sure
In cheer-ful hope, with heart con-tent
To take what-e'er thy Mak-er's pleas-ure
And all-dis-cern-ing love hath sent;

3. Sing, pray, and keep God's ways un-swerv-ing;
So do thine own part faith-ful-ly,
And trust God's word; though un-de-serv-ing,
Thou yet shalt find it true for thee.

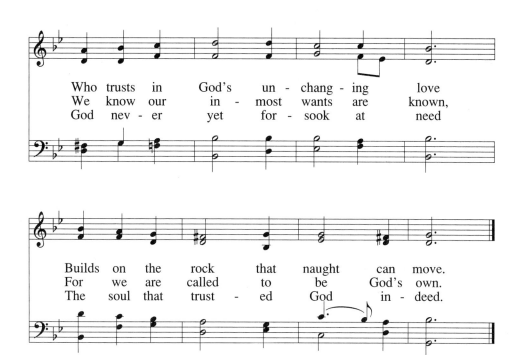

Who trusts in God's un - chang - ing love
We know our in - most wants are known,
God nev - er yet for - sook at need

Builds on the rock that naught can move.
For we are called to be God's own.
The soul that trust - ed God in - deed.

103   The Lord's My Shepherd

BROTHER JAMES' AIR 8.6.8.6.8.6

Psalm 23
Scottish Psalter (1650)

J. L. Macbeth Bain
Harm. by Gordon Jacob (1934), alt.

1. The Lord's my shep-herd; I'll not want. He makes me down to
2. My soul he doth re-store a-gain, And me to walk doth
3. Yea, though I walk in death's dark vale, Yet will I fear no
4. My ta-ble thou hast fur-nish-ed In pres-ence of my
5. Good-ness and mer-cy all my life Shall sure-ly fol-low

lie In pas-tures green; he lead-eth me The
make With-in the paths of right-eous-ness E'en
ill; For thou art with me, and thy rod And
foes; My head thou dost with oil a-noint, And
me, And in God's house for ev-er-more My

qui-et wa-ters by; He lead-eth me, he
for his own name's sake; With-in the paths of
staff me com-fort still; For thou art with me,
my cup o-ver-flows; My head thou dost with
dwell-ing place shall be; And in God's house for

lead-eth me The qui-et wa-ters by.
right-eous-ness, E'en for his own name's sake.
and thy rod And staff me com-fort still.
oil a-noint, And my cup o-ver-flows.
ev-er-more My dwell-ing place shall be.

God Moves in a Mysterious Way   104

DUNDEE CM

Scottish Psalter (1615)
William Cowper (1774)   Harm. by Thomas Ravenscroft (1621)

1. God moves in a mys - te - rious way His won - ders to per - form. He plants his foot - steps in the sea And rides up - on the storm.
2. Deep in un - fath - om - a - ble mines Of nev - er - fail - ing skill, He treas - ures up his bright de - signs And works his sov - 'reign will.
3. You fear - ful saints, fresh cour - age take; The clouds you so much dread Are big with mer - cy and shall break In bless - ings on your head.
4. His pur - pos - es will rip - en fast, Un - fold - ing ev - 'ry hour. The bud may have a bit - ter taste, But sweet will be the flow'r.
5. Blind un - be - lief is sure to err And scan his work in vain. God is his own in - ter - pret - er, And he will make it plain.

105 He Leadeth Me: O Blessed Thought

HE LEADETH ME LM with refrain

Psalm 23
Joseph H. Gilmore (1862)

William B. Bradbury (1864)

1. He lead - eth me: O bless - ed thought! O
2. Some - times mid scenes of deep - est gloom, Some -
3. Lord, I would place my hand in thine, Nor
4. And when my task on earth is done, When

words with heav'n - ly com - fort fraught! What - e'er I do, wher-
times where E - den's bow - ers bloom, By wa - ters still, o'er
ev - er mur - mur nor re - pine; Con - tent, what - ev - er
by thy grace the vic - t'ry's won, E'en death's cold wave I

e'er I be, Still 'tis God's hand that lead - eth me.
troub - led sea, Still 'tis his hand that lead - eth me.
lot I see, Since 'tis my God that lead - eth me.
will not flee, Since God through Jor - dan lead - eth me.

He lead - eth me, he lead - eth me, By

his own hand he lead-eth me; His faith-ful fol-low'r

I would be, For by his hand he lead - eth me.

106 **On Eagle's Wings**

Psalm 91
Michael Joncas (1979)

Michael Joncas (1979)

guard you in all of your ways; up - on their hands they will

bear you up, lest you dash your foot a - gainst a stone.

And hold you, hold you in the

palm of his hand.

Providence

107 The King of Love My Shepherd Is
ST. COLUMBA 8.7.8.7

Psalm 23
Henry Williams Baker (1868)

Irish melody
Harm. by A. Gregory Murray, OSB

1. The King of love my shep-herd is, Whose good-ness
2. Where streams of liv - ing wa - ter flow My ran - somed
3. Con - fused and fool - ish oft I strayed, But yet in
4. In death's dark vale I fear no ill With you, dear

fails me nev - er; I noth - ing lack if
soul he's lead - ing, And where the ver - dant
love he sought me; And on his shoul - der
Lord, be - side me, Your rod and staff my

I am his, And he is mine for ev - er.
pas - tures grow With food ce - les - tial feed - ing.
gent - ly laid, And home, re - joic - ing, brought me.
com - fort still, Your cross be - fore to guide me.

5. You spread a table in my sight;
Your saving grace bestowing;
And O what transport of delight
From your pure chalice flowing!

6. As so through all the length of days
Your goodness fails me never;
Good Shepherd, may I sing your praise
Within your house for ever.

The Care the Eagle Gives Her Young   108

ST. ANNE CM

Psalm 90
Isaac Watts (1719)

Attr. to William Croft (1708)
Harm. by William Henry Monk (1861)

1. The care the ea - gle gives her young, Safe
2. As when the time to ven - ture comes, She
3. And if we flut - ter help - less - ly, As

in her loft - y nest, Is like the ten - der
stirs them out to flight, So we are pressed to
fledg - ling ea - gles fall, Be - neath us lift God's

love of God For us made man - i - fest.
bold - ly try, To strive for dar - ing height.
might - y wings To bear us, one and all.

109 # Glory and Praise to Our God

Daniel L. Schutte (1976)

Daniel L. Schutte (1976)
Acc. by Sr. Theophane Hytrek, OSF, alt.

Refrain

Glo-ry and praise to our God, who a - lone gives light to our days. Man - y are the bless-ings he bears to those who trust in his ways.

Verses 1-3

1. We, the daugh-ters and sons of him who built the
2. In his wis-dom he strength-ens us, like gold that's
3. Ev - 'ry mo - ment of ev - 'ry day our God is

110   Sing Praise to God Who Reigns Above

MIT FREUDEN ZART 8.7.8.7.8.8.7

Deuteronomy 32:3
Johann J. Schütz (1675)
Trans. by Frances E. Cox (1864)   Bohemian Brethren's *Kirchengesange* (1566)

1. Sing   praise   to   God   who   reigns   a - bove,   The
2. What   God's   al - might - y   pow'r   has   made,   His
3. Then   all   my   glad - some   way   a - long,   I
4. Let   all   who name   Christ's   ho - ly   name,   Give

God   of   all   cre - a - tion,   The
gra - cious   mer - cy   keep - ing;   By
sing   a - loud   your   prais - es,   That
God   all   praise   and   glo - ry;   All

God   of   pow'r,   the   God   of   love,   The
morn - ing   glow   or   eve - ning   shade   His
all   may   hear   the   grate - ful   song   My
you   who   own   his   pow'r,   pro - claim   A -

God   of   our   sal - va - tion;   With
watch - ful   eye   ne'er   sleep - ing;   With -
voice   un - wea - ried   rais - es;   Be
loud   the   won - drous   sto - ry!   Cast

heal-ing balm my soul he fills, And
in the king - dom of his might, Lo!
joy - ful in the Lord, my heart, Both
each false i - dol from its throne, The

ev - 'ry faith - less mur - mur stills: To
all is just and all is right: To
soul and bod - y sing your part: To
Lord is God, and he a - lone: To

God all praise and glo - ry.
God all praise and glo - ry.
God all praise and glo - ry.
God all praise and glo - ry.

111   Guide Me, O Thou Great Jehovah

CWM RHONDDA 8.7.8.7.8.7.7

William Williams (1745)
Trans. by Peter Williams and William Williams (1771), alt.

John Hughes (1907)

1. Guide me, O thou great Je - ho - vah,
Pil - grim through this bar - ren land; I am weak, but
thou art might - y; Hold me with thy
pow'r - ful hand; Bread of heav - en,

2. O - pen now the crys - tal foun - tain,
Whence the heal - ing stream doth flow; Let the fire and
cloud - y pil - lar Lead me all my
jour - ney through; Strong de - liv - 'rer,

3. When I tread the verge of Jor - dan,
Bid my anx - ious fears sub - side; Death of death, and
hell's de - struc - tion, Land me safe on
Ca - naan's side; Songs of prais - es,

bread   of heav - en, Feed   me now and ev - er -
strong de - liv - 'rer, Be   thou still my strength and
songs   of prais - es, I   will ev - er give to

more,   Feed me now and ev - er - more.
shield,   Be thou still my strength and shield.
thee,   I will ev - er give to thee.

112 There's a Wideness in God's Mercy
IN BABILONE 8.7.8.7 D

Dutch melody
Frederick William Faber (1854), alt.   Arr. by Julius Röntgen (1906)

1. There's a   wide-ness   in   God's mer - cy   Like the wide-ness
2. For   the   love   of   God is   broad - er   Than the meas - ures
3. Troub - led   souls, why   will you   scat - ter   Like a   crowd of

of   the   sea;   There's   a   kind - ness   in   God's jus - tice
of   our   mind,   And   the   heart   of   the   E - ter - nal
fright - ened sheep?   Fool - ish hearts, why   will   you   wan - der

Which   is   more   than   lib - er - ty.   There   is   plen - ti -
Is   most won - der - ful - ly   kind.   If   our   love   were
From   a   love   so   true   and   deep?   There   is   wel - come

ful   re - demp - tion   In   the   blood   that   has   been   shed;
but   more   sim - ple   We   should take   him   at   his   word,
for   the   sin - ner   And   more   grac - es   for   the   good;

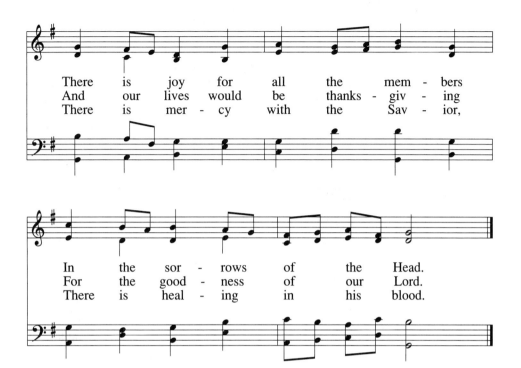

There is joy for all the mem - bers
And our lives would be thanks - giv - ing
There is mer - cy with the Sav - ior,

In the sor - rows of the Head.
For the good - ness of our Lord.
There is heal - ing in his blood.

113   Great Is Thy Faithfulness

FAITHFULNESS 11.10.11.10 with refrain

Lamentations 3:22-23
Thomas O. Chisholm (1923)

William M. Runyan (1923)

1. Great is thy faith-ful-ness, O God my Fa-ther;
2. Sum-mer and win-ter and spring-time and har-vest,
3. Par-don for sin and a peace that en-dur-eth,

There is no shad-ow of turn-ing with thee;
Sun, moon, and stars in their cours-es a - bove
Thine own dear pres-ence to cheer and to guide;

Thou chang-est not, thy com-pas-sions, they fail not;
Join with all na - ture in man-i-fold wit-ness
Strength for to - day and bright hope for to-mor-row,

As thou hast been, thou for ev-er wilt be.
To thy great faith - ful-ness, mer-cy, and love.
Bless-ings all mine, with ten thou-sand be - side!

114   This Is My Father's World

TERRA BEATA SMD

Maltbie D. Babcock (1901), alt.
St. 2 rev. by Mary Babcock Crawford (1972)

English melody
Adapt. by Franklin L. Sheppard (1915)

1. This is my Fa-ther's world, And to my lis-t'ning ears All na-ture sings and round me rings The mu-sic of the spheres. This is my Fa-ther's world; I rest me in the thought Of rocks and trees, of

2. This is our Fa-ther's world: O let us not for-get That though the wrong is great and strong, God is the rul-er yet. He trusts us with his world, To keep it clean and fair— All earth and trees, all

3. This is my Fa-ther's world: He shines in all that's fair; In rus-tling grass I hear him pass— He speaks to me ev-'ry-where. This is my Fa-ther's world: Why should my heart be sad? The Lord is King, let

skies and seas— His hand the won - ders wrought.
skies and seas, All crea - tures ev - 'ry - where.
heav - en ring! God reigns; let earth be glad.

115 He's Got the Whole World in His Hands

WHOLE WORLD Irregular

African-American spiritual African-American spiritual

2. He's got the wind and the rain in his hands. *Sing three times.*
   He's got the whole world in his hands.

3. He's got the little tiny baby in his hands...
   He's got the whole world in his hands.

4. He's got you and me, brother, in his hands...
   He's got the whole world in his hands.

5. He's got you and me, sister, in his hands...
   He's got the whole world in his hands.

6. He's got everybody here in his hands...
   He's got the whole world in his hands.

On Jordan's Bank   116

WINCHESTER NEW LM

Charles Coffin (1736)
Trans. by John Chandler (1837)

Musikalisches Handbuch (1690)
Harm. by William Henry Monk (1847), alt.

1. On Jor - dan's bank the Bap - tist's cry An -
2. Then cleansed be ev - 'ry heart from sin; Make
3. For you are our sal - va - tion, Lord, Our
4. To heal the sick stretch out your hand, And
5. All praise the Son e - ter - nal - ly, Whose

noun - ces that the Lord is nigh; A - wake and heark - en,
straight the way of God with - in, And let each heart pre -
ref - uge, and our great re - ward; With - out your grace we
bid the fall - en sin - ner stand; Shine forth, and let your
ad - vent sets his peo - ple free; Whom with the Fa - ther

for he brings Glad tid - ings of the King of kings.
pare a home Where such a might - y guest may come.
waste a - way Like flow'rs that with - er and de - cay.
light re - store Earth's own true love - li - ness once more.
we a - dore And Spir - it blest for ev - er - more.

117 Hail to the Lord's Anointed

ELLACOMBE 7.6.7.6 D

Psalm 72
James Montgomery (1821)

Gesangbuch der Herzogl, Wirtermberg (1784), alt.
Harm. by William Henry Monk (1868)

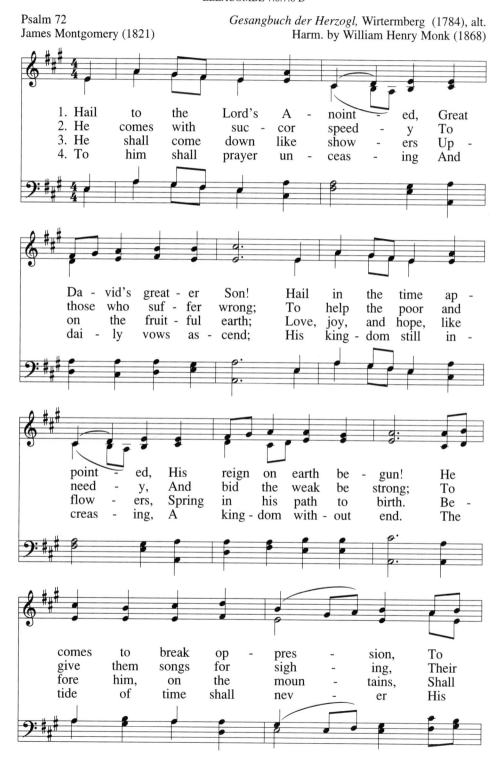

1. Hail to the Lord's A - noint - ed, Great Da - vid's great - er Son! Hail in the time ap - point - ed, His reign on earth be - gun! He comes to break op - pres - sion, To
2. He comes with suc - cor speed - y To those who suf - fer wrong; To help the poor and need - y, And bid the weak be strong; To give them songs for sigh - ing, Their
3. He shall come down like show - ers Up - on the fruit - ful earth; Love, joy, and hope, like flow - ers, Spring in his path to birth. Be - fore him, on the mou - tains, Shall
4. To him shall prayer un - ceas - ing And dai - ly vows as - cend; His king - dom still in - creas - ing, A king - dom with - out end. The tide of time shall nev - er His

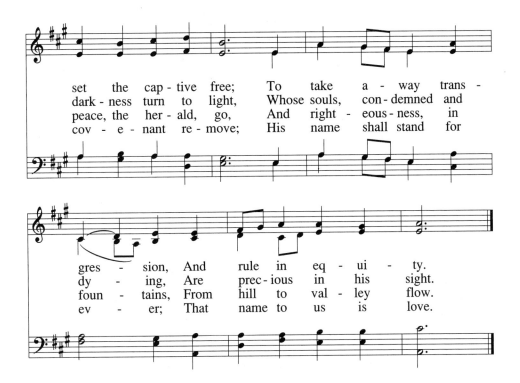

set the cap - tive free; To take a - way trans -
dark - ness turn to light, Whose souls, con - demned and
peace, the her - ald, go, And right - eous - ness, in
cov - e - nant re - move; His name shall stand for

gres - sion, And rule in eq - ui - ty.
dy - ing, Are prec - ious in his sight.
foun - tains, From hill to val - ley flow.
ev - er; That name to us is love.

118 Savior of the Nations, Come

NUN KOMM DER HEIDEN HEILAND 7.7.7.7

Attr. to St. Ambrose (4th C.)
Sts. 1-3a trans. by William Reynolds (1851)
Sts. 3b-5 trans. by Martin L. Seltz (1969), alt.   *Geystliche gesangk Buchleyn* (1524)

1. Sav - ior of the na - tions, come; Show the glo - ry
2. Not by hu - man flesh and blood, By the Spir - it
3. Won - drous birth! O won - drous child Of the Vir - gin
4. God Cre - a - tor is his source, Back to God he
5. Now your low - ly man - ger bright Hal - lows night with

of the Son! Mar - vel now, O heav'n and earth,
of our God Was the word of God made flesh—
un - de - filed! Might - y God and man in one,
runs his course, Down to death and hell de - scends,
new - born light; Let no night this light sub - due,

That our Lord chose such a birth.
Wom - an's off - spring, pure and fresh.
Ea - ger now his race to run!
God's high throne he re - as - cends.
Let our faith shine ev - er new.

Lo, How a Rose E'er Blooming

119

ES IST EIN' ROS' ENTSPRUNGEN 7.6.7.6.6.7.6

Isaiah 11:1, sts. 1-2 (15th C.)
Trans. by Theodore Baker (1894)
St. 3, *The Hymnal 1940*

Geistliche Kirchengesang (1599)
Harm. by Michael Praetorius (1609)

1. Lo, how a Rose e'er bloom-ing From ten-der stem hath
2. I - sa - iah 'twas for - told it, The Rose I have in
3. O Flow'r, whose fra-grance ten - der With sweet-ness fills the

sprung! Of Jes-se's lin-eage com-ing As seers of old have
mind, With Mar-y we be-hold it, The Vir-gin Moth - er
air, Dis - pel in glo-rious splen-dor The dark-ness ev - 'ry-

sung. It came, a blos-som bright, A - mid the cold of
kind. To show God's love a - right, She bore to us a
where; True man, yet ver - y God, From sin and death now

win - ter, When half spent was the night.
Sav - ior, When half spent was the night.
save us, And share our ev - 'ry load.

120 Tell Out, My Soul, the Greatness of the Lord

WOODLANDS 10.10.10.10

Luke 1:46b-55
Timothy Dudley-Smith (1961)

Walter Greatorex (1919)

1. Tell out, my soul, the great-ness of the Lord! Un-num-bered bless-ings give my spir - it voice; Ten - der to me the prom - ise of his word; In God my
2. Tell out, my soul, the great-ness of his name! Make known his might, the deeds his arm has done; His mer - cy sure, from age to age the same; His
3. Tell out, my soul, the great-ness of his might! Pow'rs and do - min - ions lay their glo - ry by; Proud hearts and stub - born wills are put to flight, The
4. Tell out, my soul, the glo - ries of his word! Firm is his prom - ise, and his mer - cy sure. Tell out, my soul, the great-ness of the Lord To

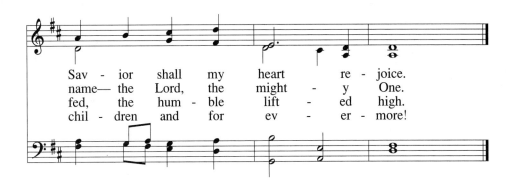

Sav - ior shall my heart re - joice.
name— the Lord, the might - y One.
fed, the hum - ble lift - ed high.
chil - dren and for ev - er - more!

121 O Come, O Come, Emmanuel

VENI EMMANUEL LM with refrain

Latin (9th C.)

Processionale (15th C.)
Adapt. by Thomas Helmore (1854)

1. O come, O come, Emman - u - el, And
2. O come, O Wis - dom from on high, Who
3. O come, O come, great Lord of might, Who
4. O come, O Branch of Jes - se's stem, Un -
5. O come, O Key of Da - vid, come And

ran - som cap - tive Is - ra - el That
or - dered all things might - i - ly; To
to your tribes on Si - nai's height In
to your own and res - cue them! From
o - pen wide our heav'n - ly home. Make

mourns in lone - ly ex - ile here
us the path of knowl - edge show
an - cient times did give the law
depths of hell your peo - ple save,
safe for us the heav'n - ward road

Un - til the Son of God ap - pear.
And teach us in its ways to go.
In cloud and maj - es - ty and awe.
And give them vic - t'ry o'er the grave.
And bar the way to death's a - bode.

Re - joice! Re - joice! Em - man - u - el shall

come to you, O Is - ra - el.

6. O come, O Bright and Morning Star,
   And bring us comfort from afar!
   Dispel the shadows of the night
   And turn our darkness into light.

7. O come, O King of nations, bind
   In one the hearts of all mankind.
   Bid all our sad divisions cease
   And be yourself our King of Peace.

122 Come, Thou Long-expected Jesus

STUTTGART 8.7.8.7

Psalmodia Sacra (1715)

Charles Wesley (1744)

Adapt. and harm. by William Henry Havergal, alt.

1. Come, thou long - ex - pect - ed Je - sus,
2. Is - rael's strength and con - so - la - tion,
3. Born thy peo - ple to de - liv - er,
4. By thine own e - ter - nal Spir - it

Born to set thy peo - ple free; From our fears and
Hope of all the earth thou art: Dear de - sire of
Born a child, and yet a king, Born to reign in
Rule in all our hearts a - lone; By thine all - suf -

sins re - lease us, Let us find our rest in thee.
ev - 'ry na - tion, Joy of ev - 'ry long - ing heart.
us for ev - er, Now thy gra - cious king - dom bring.
fi - cient mer - it Raise us to thy glo - rious throne.

Lift Up Your Heads, O Mighty Gates   123

TRURO LM

Based on Psalm 24; Georg Weissel (1642)
Trans. by Catherine Winkworth (1855)

Williams' *Psalmodia Evangelica* (1789)

1. Lift up your heads, O might - y gates;
2. O blest the land, the cit - y blest,
3. Fling wide the por - tals of your heart;
4. Come, Sav - ior, come with us a - bide;

Be - hold the King of glo - ry waits!
Where Christ the rul - er is con - fest!
Make it a tem - ple, set a - part
Our hearts to you we o - pen wide:

The King of kings is draw - ing near;
O hap - py hearts and hap - py homes
From earth - ly use for heav'n's em - ploy,
Your Ho - ly Spir - it guide us on,

The Sav - ior of the world is here.
To whom this King of tri - umph comes!
A - dorned with prayer and love and joy.
Un - til our glo - rious goal is won.

124   Wake, O Wake, and Sleep No Longer

WACHET AUF 8.9.8.8.9.8.6.6.4.4.4.8

Philipp Nicolai (1599)
Trans. and adapt. by Christopher Idle (1982)

Philipp Nicolai (1599)
Harm. by Johann Sebastian Bach (1731)

1. Wake, O wake, and sleep no long - er, For he who calls you is no stran - ger: A - wake, God's own Je - ru - sa - lem! Hear, the mid - night bells are chim - ing The sig - nal for his roy - al com -

2. Zi - on hears the sound of sing - ing; Her heart is thrilled with sud - den long - ing: She stirs, and wakes, and stands pre - pared. Christ, her friend, and lord, and lov - er, Her star and sun and strong re - deem -

3. Glo - ry, glo - ry, sing the an - gels, While mu - sic sounds from strings and cym - bals; All hu - man - kind, with songs a - rise! Twelve the gates in - to the cit - y, Each one a pearl of shin - ing beau -

ing: Let voice to voice an - nounce his name! We
er— At last his might - y voice is heard. The
ty; The streets of gold ring out with praise. All

feel his foot - step near, The Bride - groom at the door—
Son of God has come To make with us his home:
crea - tures round the throne A - dore the ho - ly One

Al - le - lu - ia! The lamps will shine With light di - vine
Sing Ho - san - na! The fight is won, The feast be - gun;
With re - joic - ing: A - men be sung By ev - 'ry tongue

As Christ the Sav - ior comes to reign.
We fix our eyes on Christ a - lone.
To crown their wel - come to the King.

125 Comfort, Comfort, O My People

GENEVA 42 8.7.8.7.7.7.8.8

Isaiah 40:1-8; Johann Olearius (1671)
Trans. by Catherine Winkworth (1863), alt.

Genevan Psalter (1551)
Harm. adapt. from Claude Goudimel (1565)

1. Com - fort, com - fort, O my peo - ple, Speak of peace, now says our God; Com - fort those who sit in dark - ness, Mourn - ing 'neath their sor - row's load. Speak un - to Je - ru - sa - lem Of the peace that waits for them; Tell of all the sins I cov - er, And that war - fare now is o - ver.

2. Hark, the voice of one who's cry - ing In the des - ert far and near, Bid - ding all to full re - pent - ance Since the king - dom now is here. O that warn - ing cry o - bey! Now pre - pare for God a way; Let the val - leys rise to meet him And the hills bow down to greet him.

3. O make straight what long was crook - ed, Make the rough - er plac - es plain; Let your hearts be true and hum - ble, As be - fits his ho - ly reign. For the glo - ry of the Lord Now o'er earth is shed a - broad; And all flesh shall see the to - ken That his word is nev - er bro - ken.

Infant Holy, Infant Lowly

126

W ZLOBIE LEZY 4.4.7.4.4.7.4.4.4.4.7

Luke 2:6-20; Polish carol
Trans. by Edith M. G. Reed (1925)

Polish carol
Harm. by A. E. Rusbridge

1. In - fant ho - ly, In - fant low - ly, For his bed a
2. Flocks were sleep - ing: Shep-herds keep - ing Vig - il till the

cat - tle stall; Ox - en low - ing, Lit - tle know - ing
morn-ing new. Saw the glo - ry, Heard the sto - ry,

Christ the babe is Lord of all. Swift are wing - ing An - gels sing-ing,
Tid - ings of a gos-pel true. Thus re - joic-ing, Free from sor-row,

No - els ring-ing, Tid - ings bring-ing: Christ the babe is Lord of all.
Prais-es voic-ing Greet the mor-row: Christ the babe was born for you.

127   Let All Mortal Flesh Keep Silence

PICARDY 8.7.8.7.8.7

Liturgy of St. James (4th C.)
Trans. by Gerard Moultrie (1864)

French carol (17th C.)

1. Let all mor - tal flesh keep si - lence,
2. King of kings, yet born of Mar - y,
3. Rank on rank the host of heav - en
4. At his feet the six - winged ser - aph,

And with fear and trem - bling stand;
As of old on earth he stood,
Spreads its van - guard on the way,
Cher - u - bim with sleep - less eye,

Pon - der noth - ing earth - ly - mind - ed,
Lord of lords in hu - man ves - ture,
As the Light of Light de - scend - eth
Veil their fac - es to the Pres - ence,

For with bless - ing in his hand
In the Bod - y and the Blood
From the realms of end - less day,
As with cease - less voice they cry,

Christ our God to earth de - scend -
He will give to all the faith -
That the pow'rs of hell may van -
"Al - le - lu - ia, al - le - lu -

eth, Our full hom - age to de - mand.
ful His own self for heav'n - ly food.
ish As the dark - ness clears a - way.
ia! Al - le - lu - ia, Lord, Most High!"

128 The First Nowell

THE FIRST NOWELL Irregular with refrain

English carol (17th C.)

English carol
Harm. from *Christmas Carols New and Old* (1871)

1. The   first   Now - ell,   the   an - gel did   say,   Was   to
2. They   look - ed   up   and   saw   a   star   Shin - ing
3. And   by   the   light   of   that   same   star   Three
4. This   star   drew   nigh   to   the   north - west,   O'er
5. Then   en - tered   in   those   wise   men three,   Full
6. Then   let   us   all   with   one   ac - cord   Sing

cer - tain poor shep - herds   in   fields as   they   lay;   In
in   the   east,   be - yond   them   far,   And
wise   men   came   from   coun - try   far;   To
Beth - le - hem   it   took   its   rest;   And
rev - 'rent - ly   up - on   their   knee,   And
prais - es   to   our   heav - 'nly   Lord;   Who

fields   where   they   lay   keep - ing their   sheep,   On a
to   the   earth   it   gave   great   light,   And
seek   for a   king   was   their   in - tent,   And to
there   it   did   both   stop   and   stay,   Right
of - fered   there,   in   his   pres - ence,   Their
with   the   Fa - ther   we   a - dore   And

cold win - ter's night that was so deep.
so it con - tin - ued both day and night.
fol - low the star where - ev - er it went.
o - ver the place where Je - sus lay.
gold and myrrh and frank - in - cense.
Spir - it blest for ev - er - more.

Now - ell, Now - ell, Now - ell, Now - ell,

Born is the King of Is - ra - el.

129   The Snow Lay on the Ground

VENITE ADOREMUS 10.10.10.10 with refrain

English melody
Adapt. by Charles Winfred Douglas
Harm. by Leo Sowerby (1941)

Anglo-Irish carol (19th C.)

1. The snow lay on the ground, the stars shone bright, When Christ our Lord was born on Christ-mas night. Ve-ni-te a-do-re-mus Do-mi-

2. 'Twas Mar-y, daugh-ter pure of ho-ly Anne, That brought in-to this world the God made man. She laid him in a stall at Beth-le-

3. Saint Jo-seph, too, was by to tend the child; To guard him, and pro-tect his moth-er mild; The an-gels hov-ered round, and sang this

4. And thus that man-ger poor be-came a throne; For he whom Mar-y bore was God the Son. O come, then, let us join the heav'n-ly

num.   Ve - ni - te a - do - re - mus   Do - mi - num.
hem;   The ass and ox - en shared the   roof with   them.
song,   Ve - ni - te a - do - re - mus   Do - mi - num.
host;   To praise the Fa - ther, Son, and   Ho - ly   Ghost.

Ve - ni - te a - do - re - mus   Do - mi - num.   Ve -

ni - te a - do - re - mus   Do - mi - num.

130 ## Away in a Manger

CRADLE SONG 11.11.11.11

St. 1-2, anonymous
St. 3, John T. McFarland (1885)

William J. Kirkpatrick (1895)

1. A - way in a man - ger, no crib for a bed, The lit - tle Lord Je - sus laid down his sweet head; The stars in the bright sky looked down where he lay; The lit - tle Lord Je - sus a - sleep on the hay.

2. The cat - tle are low - ing, the ba - by a - wakes, But lit - tle Lord Je - sus, no cry - ing he makes. I love you, Lord Je - sus: look down from on high And stay by my side un - til morn - ing is nigh.

3. Be near me, Lord Je - sus; I ask you to stay Close by me for ev - er and love me, I pray. Bless all the dear chil - dren in your ten - der care; Pre - pare us for heav - en to live with you there.

Away in a Manger

131

MUELLER 11.11.11.11

St. 1-2, anonymous
St. 3, John T. McFarland (1885)

James R. Murray (1887)

1. A - way in a man - ger, no crib for a bed, The
2. The cat - tle are low - ing, the ba - by a - wakes, But
3. Be near me, Lord Je - sus; I ask you to stay Close

lit - tle Lord Je - sus laid down his sweet head; The
lit - tle Lord Je - sus, no cry - ing he makes. I
by me for ev - er and love me, I pray. Bless

stars in the bright sky looked down where he lay; The
love you, Lord Je - sus: look down from on high And
all the dear chil - dren in your ten - der care; Pre -

lit - tle Lord Je - sus a - sleep on the hay.
stay by my side un - til morn - ing is nigh.
pare us for heav - en to live with you there.

132   O Little Town of Bethlehem

ST. LOUIS 8.6.8.6.7.6.8.6

Phillips Brooks (1868)

Lewis Henry Redner (1868)

1. O lit - tle town of Beth - le - hem, How
2. For Christ is born of Mar - y, And
3. How si - lent - ly, how si - lent - ly, The
4. O ho - ly Child of Beth - le - hem! De -

still we see thee lie! A - bove thy deep and
gath - ered all a - bove, While mor - tals sleep, the
won - drous gift is giv'n! So God im - parts to
scend to us we pray; Cast out our sin and

dream - less sleep The si - lent stars go by;
an - gels keep Their watch of won - d'ring love.
hu - man hearts The bless - ings of his heav'n.
en - ter in, Be born in us to - day.

Yet in the dark streets shin - eth The
O morn - ing stars, to - geth - er Pro -
No ear may hear his com - ing, But
We hear the Christ - mas an - gels The

ev - er - last - ing Light; The hopes and fears of
claim the ho - ly birth! And prais - es sing to
in this world of sin, Where meek souls will re -
great glad tid - ings tell; O come to us, a -

all the years Are met in thee to - night.
God the King, And peace to all on earth.
ceive him, still The dear Christ en - ters in.
bide with us, Our Lord Em - man - u - el!

133   O Come, All Ye Faithful

ADESTE FIDELES Irregular with refrain

John F. Wade (c. 1743)
Trans. by Frederick Oakeley (1841)

John F. Wade (c. 1743)

O come, let us a - dore him, Christ, the Lord!

134   Angels, from the Realms of Glory

REGENT SQUARE 8.7.8.7.8.7

St. 1-3, James Montgomery (1816)
St. 4, *Christmas Box* (1825)

Henry Thomas Smart (1867)

1. An - gels, from the realms of glo - ry,
2. Shep - herds, in the fields a - bid - ing,
3. Sag - es, leave your con - tem - pla - tions,
4. Though an in - fant now we view him,

Wing your flight o'er all the earth; You who sang cre -
Watch-ing o'er your flocks by night, God on earth is
Bright - er vi - sions beam a - far; Seek the great De -
He shall fill his heav'n-ly throne, Gath - er all the

a - tion's sto - ry, Now pro-claim Mes - si - ah's birth:
now re - sid-ing, Yon - der shines the in - fant light:
sire of na-tions, You have seen his morn-ing star:
na - tions to him; Ev - 'ry knee shall then bow down:

Come and wor - ship, come and wor - ship,

Wor - ship   Christ,   the   new - born   King.

135   Once in Royal David's City

IRBY 8.7.8.7.7.7

Cecil Frances Alexander (1848)

Henry John Gauntlett (1849)
Harm. by Arthur Henry Mann (1919)

1. Once in roy - al Da - vid's cit - y Stood a low - ly cat - tle shed, Where a moth - er laid her ba - by In a man - ger for his bed. Mar - y
2. He came down to earth from heav - en Who is God and Lord of all, And his shel - ter was a sta - ble, And his cra - dle was a stall. With the
3. And through all his won - drous child - hood He would hon - or and o - bey, Love and watch the low - ly maid - en In whose gen - tle arms he lay. Chris - tian
4. For he is our child - hood's pat - tern, Day by day like us he grew; He was lit - tle, weak, and help - less, Tears and smiles like us he knew: And he
5. And our eyes at last shall see him, Through his own re - deem - ing love; For that child so dear and gen - tle Is our Lord in heav'n a - bove: And he

was   that moth - er   mild,   Je - sus
poor   and   mean   and   low - ly   Lived   on
chil - dren all   should be   Kind, o -
feels   for   all   our   sad - ness, And   he
leads   his   chil - dren   on   To   the

Christ   her   lit - tle   Child.
earth   our   Sav - ior   ho - ly.
be   -   dient, good   as   he.
shares   in   all   our   glad - ness.
place   where he   has   gone.

136

What Child Is This

GREENSLEEVES 8.7.8.7 with refrain

English melody (16th C.)
Harm. by John Stainer

William Chatterton Dix (1865)

1. What child is this, who, laid to rest, On
2. Why lies he in such low es - tate Where
3. So bring him in - cense, gold and myrrh, Come

Mar - y's lap is sleep - ing? Whom an - gels greet with
ox and ass are feed - ing? Good Chris - tian, fear; for
peas - ant, king to own him; The King of kings sal -

an - thems sweet, While shep - herds watch are keep - ing?
sin - ners here The si - lent Word is plead - ing.
va - tion brings, Let lov - ing hearts en - throne him.

This, this is Christ the King, Whom shep - herds guard and an - gels sing;

Haste, haste to bring him laud, The Babe, the Son of Mar - y.

While Shepherds Watched Their Flocks   137

WINCHESTER OLD CM

Thomas Est (1592)

Nahum Tate (1700)

Harm. from *Hymns Ancient and Modern* (1922)

1. While shep - herds watched their flocks by night, All
2. "Fear not," said he, for might - y dread Had
3. "To you, in Da - vid's town, this day Is
4. "The heav'n - ly babe you there shall find To
5. Thus spake the ser - aph, and forth - with Ap -
6. "All glo - ry be to God on high And

seat - ed on the ground, The an - gel of the
seized their troub - led mind; "Glad tid - ings of great
born of Da - vid's line The Sav - ior, who is
hu - man view dis - played, All mean - ly wrapped in
peared a shin - ing throng Of an - gels prais - ing
on the earth be peace; Good will hence - forth from

Lord came down, And glo - ry shone a - round.
joy I bring To you and all man - kind."
Christ the Lord; And this shall be the sign:
swath - ing bands, And in a man - ger laid."
God, who thus Ad - dressed their joy - ful song:
heav'n to men Be - gin and nev - er cease."

138   # God Rest You Merry, Gentlemen

GOD REST YOU MERRY 8.6.8.6.8.6 with refrain

English carol (18th C.)

English carol (18th C.)
Harm. by John Stainer

1. God rest you mer - ry, gen - tle - men, Let
2. In Beth - le - hem in Ju - dah This
3. From God our great Cre - a - tor A
4. The shep - herds at those tid - ings Re -
5. Now to the Lord sing prais - es, All

noth - ing you dis - may, For Je - sus Christ our
bless - ed babe was born, And laid with - in a
bless - ed an - gel came, And un - to cer - tain
joic - ed much in mind, And left their flocks a -
you with - in this place, And with true love and

Sav - ior Was born up - on this day,
man - ger Up - on this bless - ed morn:
shep - herds Brought tid - ings of the same,
feed - ing In tem - pest, storm, and wind,
char - i - ty Each oth - er now em - brace;

To   save   us   all   from   Sa - tan's pow'r When
For   which his   moth - er Mar   -   y   Did
How   that   in   Beth - le - hem   was   born   The
And   went   to   Beth - le - hem   straight - way, The
This   ho - ly tide of   Christ   -   mas   All

we   were   gone   a   -   stray.
noth - ing   take   in   scorn.
Son   of   God   by   name.
bless - ed   babe   to   find.
oth - ers   shall re   -   place.

O   tid - ings of   com - fort and   joy, com - fort and

joy;   O   tid - ings of   com - fort and   joy!

139   Angels We Have Heard on High

GLORIA 7.7.7.7 with refrain

French (c. 18th C.)
Trans. from *Crown of Jesus Music,* London (1862)

French traditional

1. An - gels   we   have   heard   on   high
2. Shep - herds,   why   this   ju - bi - lee?
3. Come   to   Beth - le - hem   and   see
4. See   him   in   a   man - ger   laid,

Sweet - ly   sing - ing   o'er   the   plains,
Why   your   joy - ous   strains   pro - long?
Him   whose   birth   the   an - gels   sing;
Whom   the   choirs   of   an - gels   praise;

And   the   moun - tains   in   re - ply
Say   what   may   the   tid - ings   be,
Come   a - dore,   on   bend - ed   knee,
Mar - y,   Jo - seph,   lend   your   aid,

Ech - o back their joy - ous strains.
Which in - spire your heav'n - ly song.
Christ, the Lord, the new - born King.
While our hearts in love we raise.

Glo - - - ri - a

in ex - cel - sis De - o, Glo - -

- - ri - a in ex - cel-sis De - o.

140

Go Tell It on the Mountain

GO TELL IT ON THE MOUNTAIN 7.6.7.6 with refrain

African-American spiritual
Adapt. by John W. Work, Jr. (1907)

African-American spiritual
Harm. by Paul Sjolund

Go tell it on the moun - tain, O - ver the hills and ev - 'ry - where; Go tell it on the moun - tain That Je - sus Christ is born!

D.C.

1. While shep - herds kept their watch - ing O'er
2. The shep - herds feared and trem - bled When
3. Down in a low - ly man - ger The

si - lent flocks by night, Be - hold through- out the
lo! a - bove the earth Rang out the an - gel
hum - ble Christ was born, And God sent us sal -

heav - ens There shone a ho - ly light.
cho - rus That hailed our Sav - ior's birth.
va - tion That bless - ed Christ - mas morn.

141   It Came upon the Midnight Clear

CAROL CMD

Luke 2:8-14
Edmund H. Sears (1849)

Richard Storrs Willis (1850)

1. It came up - on the mid - night clear, That
2. Still through the clo - ven skies they come, With
3. Yet with the woes of sin and strife, The
4. For, lo, the days are has - t'ning on, By

glo - rious song of old, From
peace - ful wings un - furled, And
world has suf - fered long; Be -
proph - ets seen of old, When

an - gels bend - ing near the earth To
still their heav'n - ly mu - sic floats O'er
neath the heav'n - ly hymn have rolled Two
with the ev - er - cir - cling years Shall

touch their harps of gold: "Peace
all the wea - ry world: A -
thou - sand years of wrong; And
come the time fore - told, When

142 Good Christian Friends, Rejoice

IN DULCI JUBILO 6.6.7.7.7.7.5.5

Latin and German (14th C.)
Trans. by John Mason Neale (1853)

Klug's *Geistliche Lieder* (1535)
Harm. by Robert L. Pearsall

1. Good Chris-tian friends, re-joice With heart and soul and voice; O give heed to what we say: Je-sus Christ is born to-day! Ox and ass be-fore him bow, And he is in the man-ger now.

2. Good Chris-tian friends, re-joice With heart and soul and voice; Now you hear of end-less bliss: Je-sus Christ was born for this! He has o-pened heav-en's door, And we are blest for ev-er-more.

3. Good Chris-tian friends, re-joice With heart and soul and voice; Now you need not fear the grave: Je-sus Christ was born to save! Calls you one and all To gain his ev-er-last-ing hall.

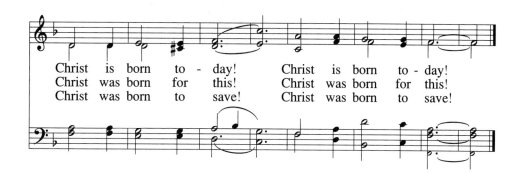

Christ is born to - day! Christ is born to - day!
Christ was born for this! Christ was born for this!
Christ was born to save! Christ was born to save!

143 Hark! The Herald Angels Sing

MENDELSSOHN 7.7.7.7 D with refrain

Charles Wesley (1739), alt.

Felix Mendelssohn (1840)

1. Hark! the her - ald an - gels sing, "Glo - ry to the
2. Christ, by high - est heav'n a - dored, Christ the ev - er-
3. Hail the heav'n - born Prince of Peace! Hail the Sun of

new - born King; Peace on earth, and mer - cy mild
last - ing Lord: Late in time be - hold him come,
Right - eous - ness! Light and life to all he brings,

God and sin - ners rec - on - ciled!" Joy - ful, all you
Off - spring of the Vir - gin's womb. Veiled in flesh the
Ris'n with heal - ing in his wings. Mild he lays his

na - tions, rise, Join the tri - umph of the skies;
God - head see: Hail the in - car - nate De - i - ty,
glo - ry by, Born that we no more may die,

144   From Heaven Above
VOM HIMMEL HOCH LM

Schumann's *Geistliche Lieder* (1539)

Vom Himmel hoch da komm ich her; Martin Luther

Harm. by Hans Leo Hassler

1. From heav'n a - bove to earth I come To bring good news
2. To you this night is born a child Of Mar - y, cho -
3. This is the Christ, God's Son most high, Who hears your sad
4. The bless - ing which the Fa - ther planned The Son holds in

to ev - 'ry - one! Glad tid - ings of great joy I bring
sen vir - gin mild; This new - born child of low - ly birth
and bit - ter cry; He will him - self your Sav - ior be
his in - fant hand, That in his king - dom bright and fair,

To all the world, and glad - ly sing:
Shall be the joy of all the earth.
And from all sin will set you free.
You may with us his glo - ry share.

5. These are the signs which you will see
   To let you know that it is he:
   In manger-bed, in swaddling clothes
   The child who all the earth upholds.

6. How glad we'll be to find it so!
   Then with the shepherds let us go
   To see what God for us had done
   In sending us his own dear Son.

7. Look, look, dear friends, look over there!
   What lies within that manger bare?
   Who is that lovely little one?
   The baby Jesus, God's dear Son.

8. Welcome to earth, O noble Guest,
   Through whom this sinful world is blest!
   You turned not from our needs away!
   How can our thanks such love repay?

9. O Lord, you have created all!
   How did you come to be so small,
   To sweetly sleep in manger-bed
   Where lowing cattle lately fed?

10. Were earth a thousand times as fair
    And set with gold and jewels rare,
    Still such a cradle would not do
    To rock a prince so great as you.

11. For velvets soft and silken stuff
    You have but hay and straw so rough
    On which as king so rich and great
    To be enthroned in humble state.

12. O dearest Jesus, holy child,
    Prepare a bed, soft, undefiled,
    A holy shrine, within my heart,
    That you and I need never part.

13. My heart for very joy now leaps;
    My voice no longer silence keeps;
    I too must join the angel-throng
    To sing with joy his cradle-song:

14. "Glory to God in highest heav'n,
    Who unto us his Son has giv'n."
    With angels sing in pious mirth:
    A glad new year to all the earth!

The extraordinary length of this hymn requires a special note of explanation. The Luthers sang hymns in their home in Wittenberg. For the Christmas Eve celebration, c. 1534, Luther wrote this fourteen stanza hymn, based upon a popular carol of the day, as the libretto for a family Christmas pageant.

The first five stanzas were sung by a neighbor dressed as an angel, heralding the birth of Christ. The next stanza was sung by the entire gathering, with stazas 7 through 13 sung by the children as they made their way to the crèche. The pageant was concluded with all singing the final stanza.

Stanzas 6 through 13 may be omitted.

145

Joy to the World

ANTIOCH CM with repeat

Psalm 98:4-9
Isaac Watts (1719)

George Frederick Handel (1742)
Arr. by Lowell Mason (1836)

1. Joy to the world! the Lord is come: Let earth re-
2. Joy to the world! the Sav-ior reigns: Let us, our
3. No more let sin and sor-rows grow, Nor thorns in-
4. He rules the world with truth and grace, And makes the

ceive her King; Let ev - 'ry heart pre-
songs em - ploy; While fields and floods, rocks,
fest the ground; He comes to make his
na - tions prove The glo - ries of his

pare him room, And heav'n and na - ture
hills, and plains Re - peat the sound - ing
bless - ings flow Far as the curse is
right - eous - ness, And won - ders of his

And
Re -
Far
And

146 Silent Night, Holy Night

STILLE NACHT 6.6.8.9.6.6

Joseph Mohr (1818)
Trans. by John F. Young (1863)

Franz X. Gruber (1818)

1. Si - lent night, ho - ly night, All is calm, all is bright Round yon Vir - gin Moth-er and Child, Ho - ly In - fant so ten - der and mild, Sleep in heav - en - ly peace, Sleep in heav - en - ly peace.

2. Si - lent night, ho - ly night, Shep - herds quake at the sight; Glo - ries stream from heav - en a - far, Heav'n-ly hosts sing al - le - lu - ia; Christ, the Sav - ior, is born! Christ, the Sav - ior, is born!

3. Si - lent night, ho - ly night, Son of God, love's pure light Ra - diant beams from thy ho - ly face, With the dawn of re - deem - ing grace, Je - sus, Lord, at thy birth, Je - sus, Lord, at thy birth.

As with Gladness Men of Old

147

DIX 7.7.7.7.7.7

Conrad Kocher (1838)

William Chatterton Dix (1860)

Arr. by William Henry Monk (1861)

1. As with glad-ness men of old Did the guid-ing star be-hold; As with joy they hailed its light, Lead-ing on-ward, beam-ing bright; So, most gra-cious Lord, may we Ev - er - more your splen-dor see.

2. As with joy-ful steps they sped To that low-ly man-ger-bed, There to bend the knee be-fore Christ whom heav'n and earth a - dore; So may we with hur - ried pace Run to seek your throne of grace.

3. As they of - fered gifts most rare At that man-ger crude and bare; So may we this ho - ly day, Drawn to you with - out de - lay, All our cost - liest treas - ures bring, Christ, to you, our heav'n-ly King.

4. Christ Re - deem - er, with us stay, Help us live your ho - ly way; And when earth - ly things are past, Bring our ran - somed souls at last Where they need no star to guide, Where no clouds your glo - ry hide.

5. In the heav'n-ly cit - y bright None shall need cre - at - ed light; You, its light, its joy, its crown, You, its sun which goes not down; There for ev - er may we sing Al - le - lu - ias to our King.

148 We Three Kings of Orient Are

KINGS OF ORIENT 8.8.4.4.6 with refrain

Matthew 2:1-11
John Henry Hopkins, Jr. (1857)

John Henry Hopkins, Jr. (1857)

1. We three kings of O - ri - ent are,
2. Born a babe on Beth - le - hem's plain,
3. Frank - in - cense to of - fer have I;
4. Myrrh is mine: its bit - ter per - fume
5. Glo - rious now be - hold him rise,

Bear - ing gifts we trav - erse a - far
Gold we bring to crown him a - gain;
In - cense owns a De - i - ty nigh,
Breathes a life of gath - 'ring gloom;
King and God and sac - ri - fice:

Field and foun - tain, Moor and
King for ev - er, Ceas - ing
Prayer and prais - ing Glad - ly
Sor - rowing, sigh - ing, Bleed - ing,
Heav'n sings, "Hal - le - lu - jah!"

moun - tain, Fol - low - ing yon - der star.
nev - er, O - ver us all to reign.
rais - ing, Wor - ship - ing God on high.
dy - ing, Sealed in the stone cold tomb.
"Hal - le - lu - jah!" earth re - plies.

O star of won - der, star of night, Star with

roy - al beau - ty bright, West - ward lead - ing,

still pro - ceed - ing, Guide us to the per - fect Light.

149 How Brightly Beams the Morning Star

WIE SCHÖN LEUCHTET 8.8.7.8.8.7.4.4.4.4.8

Philipp Nicolai (1599)
Trans. from *Lutheran Book of Worship* (1978), alt.

Philipp Nicolai (1599)
Harm. by Johann Sebastian Bach

1. How bright-ly beams the morn-ing star! What
2. Come, heav'n-ly bride-groom, light di-vine, And
3. O let the harps break forth in sound! Our

sud-den ra-diance from a-far A-glow with grace and
deep with-in our hearts now shine; There light a flame un-
joy be all with mu-sic crowned, Our voic-es rich-ly

mer - cy! Of Ja-cob's race, King Da-vid's Son, Our
dy - ing! In your one bod-y let us be As
blend - ing! For Christ goes with us all the way— To-

Lord and mas-ter, you have won Our hearts to serve you
liv-ing branch-es of a tree, Your life our lives sup-
day, to-mor-row, ev-'ry day! His love is nev-er

on - ly! Low - ly, ho - ly! Great and glo - rious,
ply - ing. Now, though dai - ly Earth's deep sad - ness
end - ing! Sing out! Ring out! Ju - bi - la - tion!

All vic - to - rious, Rich in bless - ing!
May per - plex us And dis - tress us,
Ex - ul - ta - tion! Tell the sto - ry!

Rule and might o'er all pos - sess - ing!
Yet with heav'n - ly joy you bless us.
Great is he, the King of glo - ry!

150   **Your Hands, O Lord, in Days of Old**
MOZART CMD

Matthew 14:35-36
Edward H. Plumptre, alt.

Adapt. from Wolfgang Amadeus Mozart

1. Your hands, O Lord, in days of old Were
2. And then your touch brought life and health, Gave
3. O be our might - y heal - er still, O

strong to heal and save; They tri - umphed o - ver
speech, and strength, and sight; And youth re - newed and
Lord of life and death; Re - store and strength-en,

pain and death, Fought dark - ness and the grave. To
health re - stored, Claimed you, the Lord of light: And
soothe and bless, With your al - might - y breath: On

you they went, the blind, the mute, The
so, O Lord, be near to bless, Al -
hands that work and eyes that see, Your

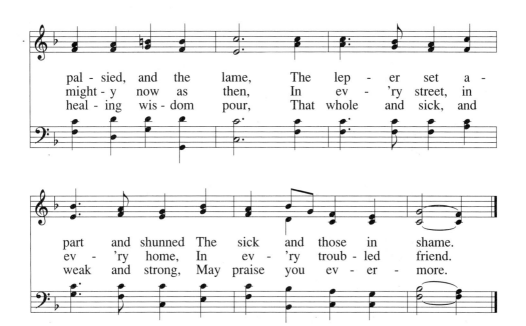

pal - sied, and the lame, The lep - er set a -
might - y now as then, In ev - 'ry street, in
heal - ing wis - dom pour, That whole and sick, and

part and shunned The sick and those in shame.
ev - 'ry home, In ev - 'ry troub - led friend.
weak and strong, May praise you ev - er - more.

151 Swiftly Pass the Clouds of Glory

GENEVA 8.7.8.7 D

Thomas H. Troeger (1985)

George Henry Day (1940)

1. Swift - ly pass the clouds of glo - ry,
2. Glimpsed and gone the rev - e - la - tion,
3. Lord, trans - fig - ure our per - cep - tion

Heav - en's voice, the daz - zling light; Mo - ses and E -
They shall gain and keep its truth, Not by build - ing
With the pur - est light that shines, And re - cast our

li - jah van - ish; Christ a - lone com - mands the height!
on the moun - tain An - y shrine or sa - cred booth,
life's in - ten - tions To the shape of your de - signs,

Pe - ter, James, and John fall si - lent,
But by fol - low - ing the Sav - ior
Till we seek no oth - er glo - ry

Turn - ing from the sum - mit's rise Down - ward toward the
Through the val - ley to the cross And by test - ing
Than what lies past Cal - v'ry's hill And our liv - ing

shad - owed val - ley Where their Lord has fixed his eyes.
faith's re - sil - ience Through be - tray - al, pain, and loss.
and our dy - ing And our ris - ing by your will.

152   Out of the Depths I Cry to You

AUS TIEFER NOT 8.7.8.7.8.8.7

Psalm 120:1-2, 130
Martin Luther (1524)
Trans. by Gracia Grindal (1978)

Attr. to Martin Luther (1524)
Harm. by Austin C. Lovelace (1963)

1. Out of the depths I cry to you; O Lord, now
2. All things you send are full of grace; You crown our
3. It is in God that we shall hope, And not in
4. My soul is wait - ing for the Lord As one who

hear me call - ing. In - cline your ear to my dis -
lives with fa - vor. All our good works are done in
our own mer - it; We rest our fears in God's good
longs for morn - ing; No watch - er waits with great - er

tress In spite of my re - bel - ling. Do
vain With - out our Lord and Sav - ior. We
Word And trust the Ho - ly Spir - it, Whose
hope Than I for Christ's re - turn - ing. I

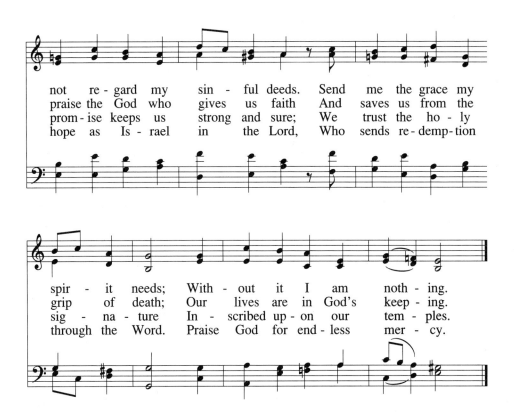

not re - gard my sin - ful deeds. Send me the grace my
praise the God who gives us faith And saves us from the
prom - ise keeps us strong and sure; We trust the ho - ly
hope as Is - rael in the Lord, Who sends re - demp - tion

spir - it needs; With - out it I am noth - ing.
grip of death; Our lives are in God's keep - ing.
sig - na - ture In - scribed up - on our tem - ples.
through the Word. Praise God for end - less mer - cy.

153

Wilt Thou Forgive

SO GIEBST DU NUN 10.10.10.10.8.4

Geist und Lehr-reiches Kirchen und Haus Buch (1694)

John Donne (1573-1631)

Harm. by Johann Sebastian Bach

1. Wilt thou for-give that sin, where I be - gun,
2. Wilt thou for-give that sin, by which I won
3. I have a sin of fear that when I've spun

Which is my sin, though it were done be - fore?
Oth - ers to sin, and made my sin their door?
My last thread, I shall per - ish on the shore;

Wilt thou for-give those sins through which I run,
Wilt thou for-give that sin which I did shun
Swear by thy - self, that at my death thy Son

And do run still, though still I do de - plore?
A year or two, but wal - lowed in a score?
Shall shine as he shines now, and here - to - fore.

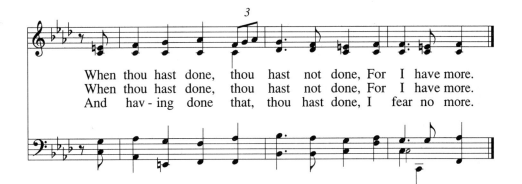

When thou hast done, thou hast not done, For I have more.
When thou hast done, thou hast not done, For I have more.
And hav-ing done that, thou hast done, I fear no more.

154　My Faith Looks Up to Thee

OLIVET 6.6.4.6.6.6.4

Ray Palmer (1875)　　　　　　　　　　　　　　　　　　Lowell Mason (1831)

1. My faith looks up to thee, Thou Lamb of
2. May thy rich grace im - part Strength to my
3. While life's dark maze I tread, And griefs a -

Cal - va - ry, Sav - ior di - vine! Now hear me
faint - ing heart, My zeal in - spire; As thou hast
round me spread, Be thou my guide; Bid dark - ness

while I pray, Take all my guilt a - way;
died for me, O may my love to thee
turn to day; Wipe sor - row's tears a - way,

O let me from this day Be whol - ly thine.
Pure, warm, and change - less be, A liv - ing fire.
Nor let me ev - er stray From thee a - side.

O Saving Victim

155

DUGUET LM

Attr. to Thomas Aquinas (13th C.)
Trans. by Edward Caswall, alt.

Dieu donne Duguet

1. O Sav - ing Vic - tim, o - p'ning wide The
2. To your great name be end - less praise, Im -

gate of heav'n to us be - low! Our foes press on from
mor - tal God - head, One - in - Three; O grant us end - less

ev - 'ry side: Your aid sup - ply, your strength be - stow.
length of days When our true na - tive land we see.

156   Lord, Who throughout These Forty Days

ST. FLAVIAN CM

Claudia Frances Hernaman (1873)

Day's *Psalter* (1562)
Adapt. and harm. by Richard Redhead

1. Lord, who through-out these for-ty days For
   us didst fast and pray, Teach us with thee to
   mourn our sins, And close by thee to stay.

2. As thou with Sa-tan didst con-tend And
   didst the vic-t'ry win, O give us strength in
   thee to fight, In thee to con-quer sin.

3. As thou didst hun-ger bear and thirst, So
   teach us, gra-cious Lord, To die to self, and
   chief-ly live By thy most ho-ly word.

4. And through these days of pen-i-tence, And
   through thy Pas-sion-tide, Yea, ev-er-more, in
   life and death, Je-sus! with us a-bide.

5. A-bide with us, that so, this life Of
   suf-f'ring o-ver-past, An Eas-ter of un-
   end-ing joy We may at-tain at last!

Jesus, Keep Me Near the Cross   157

NEAR THE CROSS 7.6.7.6 with refrain

Fanny J. Crosby (1869)   William H. Doane (1869)

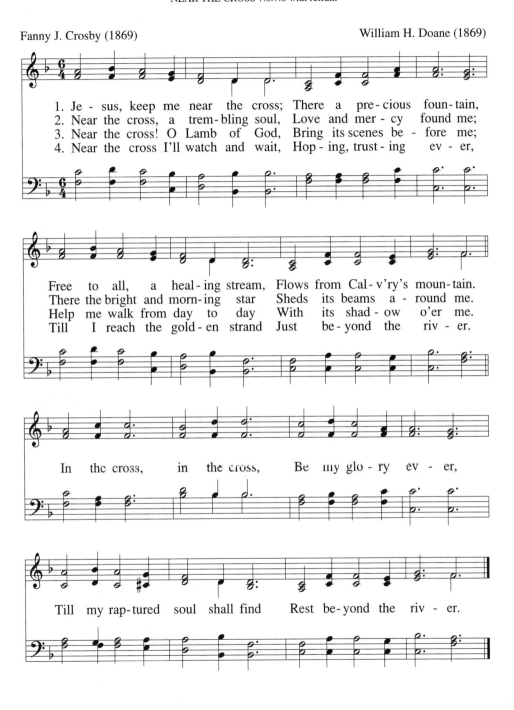

1. Je - sus, keep me near the cross; There a pre-cious foun-tain,
2. Near the cross, a trem-bling soul, Love and mer - cy found me;
3. Near the cross! O Lamb of God, Bring its scenes be - fore me;
4. Near the cross I'll watch and wait, Hop - ing, trust - ing ev - er,

Free to all, a heal-ing stream, Flows from Cal-v'ry's moun-tain.
There the bright and morn-ing star Sheds its beams a - round me.
Help me walk from day to day With its shad - ow o'er me.
Till I reach the gold-en strand Just be-yond the riv - er.

In the cross, in the cross, Be my glo - ry ev - er,

Till my rap-tured soul shall find Rest be-yond the riv - er.

158 By the Babylonian Rivers

KAS DZIEDAJA 8.7.8.7

Latvian folk melody
Acc. by Robert J. Batastini (1995)

Psalm 137

1. By the Bab - y - lo - nian riv - ers We sat
2. There our cap - tors in de - ri - sion Did re -
3. How shall we sing the Lord's song In a
4. Let the Cross be ben - e - dic - tion For those

down in grief and wept; Hung our harps up - on the
quire of us a song; So we sat with star - ing
strange and bit - ter land; Can our voic - es veil the
bound in tyr - an - ny; By the power of res - ur -

wil - low, Mourned for Zi - on when we slept.
vi - sion, And the days were hard and long.
sor - row? Lord God, hold your ho - ly band.
rec - tion Loose them from cap - tiv - i - ty.

Forty Days and Forty Nights

159

HEINLEIN 7.7.7.7

George H. Smyttan (1856), alt.

Attr. to Martin Herbst (1676), alt.
Harm. by William Henry Monk

1. For - ty days and for - ty nights Thou wast
2. Should not we thy sor - row share And from
3. Then if Sa - tan on us press, Je - sus,
4. So shall we have peace di - vine: Ho - lier
5. Keep, O keep us, Sav - ior dear, Ev - er

fast - ing in the wild; For - ty days and
world - ly joys ab - stain, Fast - ing with un -
Sav - ior, hear our call! Vic - tor in the
glad - ness ours shall be; Round us, too, shall
con - stant by thy side; That with thee we

for - ty nights Tempt - ed, and yet un - de - filed.
ceas - ing prayer, Strong with thee to suf - fer pain?
wil - der - ness, Grant we may not faint nor fall!
an - gels shine, Such as min - is - tered to thee.
may ap - pear At the e - ter - nal Eas - ter - tide.

160 Beneath the Cross of Jesus
ST. CHRISTOPHER 7.6.8.6.8.6.8.6

Elizabeth C. Clephane (1872)

Frederick C. Maker (1881)

1. Be - neath the cross of Je - sus I fain would take my
2. Up - on that cross of Je - sus Mine eye at times can
3. I take, O cross, thy shad - ow For my a - bid - ing

stand, The shad - ow of a might - y rock With -
see The ver - y dy - ing form of One Who
place; I ask no oth - er sun - shine than The

in a wea - ry land; A home with - in the
suf - fered there for me; And from my strick - en
sun - shine of his face; Con - tent to let the

wil - der - ness, A rest up - on the way, From the
heart with tears Two won - ders I con - fess: The
world go by, To know no gain nor loss, My

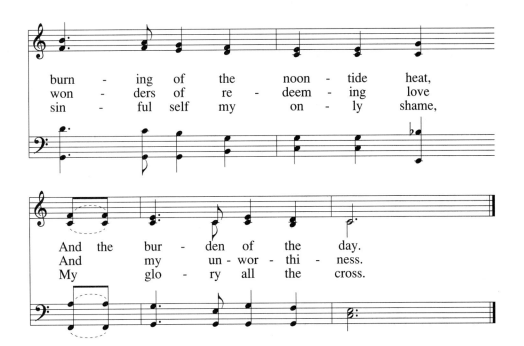

burn - ing of the noon - tide heat,
won - ders of re - deem - ing love
sin - ful self my on - ly shame,

And the bur - den of the day.
And my un - wor - thi - ness.
My glo - ry all the cross.

161 Lord Jesus, Think on Me

SOUTHWELL SM

Synesius of Cyrene (c. 370-414)
Trans. by Allen W. Chatfield (1876)

Daman's *Psalmes* (1579), alt.

1. Lord Je - sus, think on me, And
2. Lord Je - sus, think on me, A -
3. Lord Je - sus, think on me, Nor
4. Lord Je - sus, think on me, That,

purge a - way my sin; From earth - born pas - sions
mid the bat - tle's strife; In all my pain and
let me go a - stray; Through dark - ness and per -
when this life is past, I may the e - ter - nal

set me free, And make me pure with - in.
mis - er - y Be thou my health and life.
plex - i - ty Point thou the heav'n - ly way.
bright-ness see, And share thy joy at last.

Go to Dark Gethsemane

162

REDHEAD 76 7.7.7.7.7.7

James Montgomery (1825)   Richard Redhead (1853)

1. Go to dark Geth - sem - a - ne, Ye that feel the
2. Fol - low to the judg - ment hall; View the Lord of
3. Cal - v'ry's mourn - ful moun - tain climb; There, a - dor - ing

tempt - er's pow'r; Your Re - deem - er's con - flict see,
life ar - raigned; O the worm - wood and the gall!
at his feet, Mark the mir - a - cle of time,

Watch with him one bit - ter hour; Turn not from his
O the pangs his soul sus - tained! Shun not suf - f'ring,
God's own sac - ri - fice com - plete; "It is fin - ished!"

griefs a - way, Learn of Je - sus Christ to pray.
shame, or loss; Learn of him to bear the cross.
hear him cry; Learn of Je - sus Christ to die.

163 What Wondrous Love Is This

WONDROUS LOVE 12.9.12.12.9

Southern Harmony (1835)

Alexander Means (1823)

Harm. from *Cantate Domino* (1980)

1. What won-drous love is this, O my soul, O my soul?
2. To God and to the Lamb I will sing, I will sing;
3. And when from death I'm free, I'll sing on, I'll sing on;

What won-drous love is this, O my soul?
To God and to the Lamb, I will sing;
And when from death I'm free, I'll sing on;

What won-drous love is this that caused the Lord of bliss
To God and to the Lamb who is the great I AM,
And when from death I'm free, I'll sing and joy-ful be,

To   bear the dread - ful curse   for my   soul,   for my   soul;
While   mil - lions join the   theme,   I will   sing,   I will   sing;
And   through e - ter - ni - ty   I'll sing   on,   I'll sing   on!

To   bear   the   dread - ful   curse   for   my   soul?
While   mil - lions join   the   theme,   I   will   sing.
And   through e - ter - ni - ty   I'll   sing   on.

164   All Glory, Laud, and Honor

ST. THEODULPH 7.6.7.6 D

Theodulph of Orleans (c. 820)
Trans. by John Mason Neale (1851), alt.

Melchior Teschner (1615)

All glo-ry, laud, and hon - or To you, Re-deem-er, King!

To whom the lips of chil - dren Made sweet ho-san-nas ring.

1. You are the King of Is - ra - el, And
2. The com - pa - ny of an - gels Are
3. The peo - ple of the He - brews With
4. To you be - fore your pas - sion They
5. Their prais - es you ac - cept - ed, Ac -

Da - vid's roy - al Son, Now in the Lord's Name
prais - ing you on high; And mor - tals, joined with
palms be - fore you went: Our praise and prayers and
sang their hymns of praise: To you, now high ex -
cept the prayers we bring, Great source of love and

D.C.

com - ing, Our King and Bless - ed One.
all things Cre - at - ed, make re - ply.
an - thems Be - fore you we pre - sent.
alt - ed, Our mel - o - dy we raise.
good - ness, Our Sav - ior and our King.

D.C.

165
Ah, Holy Jesus
HERZLIEBSTER JESU 11.11.11.5

Johann Heermann (1630)
Trans. by Robert Seymour Bridges (1899)

Johann Crüger (1640), alt.

1. Ah, ho - ly Je - sus, how hast thou of -
2. Who was the guilt - y? Who brought this up -
3. Lo, the Good Shep - herd for the sheep is
4. For me, kind Je - sus, was thy in - car -
5. There - fore, kind Je - sus, since I can - not

fend - ed, That man to judge thee
on thee? A - las, my trea - son,
of - fered; The slave hath sin - ned,
na - tion, Thy mor - tal sor - row,
pay thee, I do a - dore thee,

hath in hate pre - tend - ed? By foes de -
Je - sus, hath un - done thee. 'Twas I, Lord
and the Son hath suf - fered; For our a -
and thy life's ob - la - tion; Thy death of
and will ev - er pray thee, Think on thy

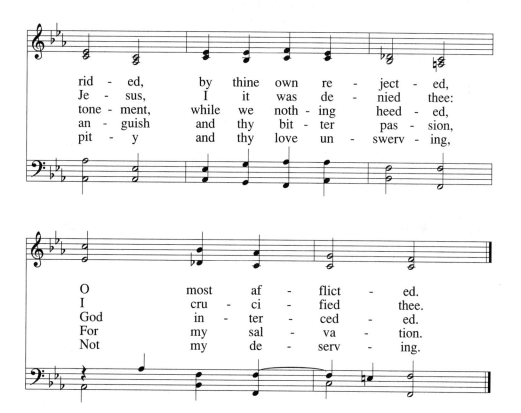

rid - ed, by thine own re - ject - ed,
Je - sus, I it was de - nied thee:
tone - ment, while we noth - ing heed - ed,
an - guish and thy bit - ter pas - sion,
pit - y and thy love un - swerv - ing,

O most af - flict - ed.
I cru - ci - fied thee.
God in - ter - ced - ed.
For my sal - va - tion.
Not my de - serv - ing.

166 There Is a Green Hill Far Away

HORSLEY CM

Cecil Frances Alexander, alt.   William Horsley

1. There is a green hill far a - way, Out -
side a cit - y wall, Where our dear Lord was
cru - ci - fied Who died to save us all.

2. We may not know, we can - not tell, What
pains he had to bear, But we be - lieve it
was for us He hung and suf - fered there.

3. He died that we might be for - giv'n, He
died to make us good, That we might go at
last to heav'n, Saved by his pre - cious blood.

4. There was no oth - er good e - nough To
pay the price of sin, He on - ly could un -
lock the gate Of heav'n and let us in.

5. O dear - ly, dear - ly has he loved! And
we must love him too, And trust in his re -
deem - ing blood, And try his works to do.

Alas! and Did My Savior Bleed

167

MARTYRDOM CM

Isaac Watts (1707)

Attr. to Hugh Wilson (1827)

1. A - las! And did my Sav - ior bleed, And did my Sov - 'reign die! Would he de - vote that sa - cred head For sin - ners such as I!
2. Was it for sins that I have done He suf - fered on the tree? A - maz - ing pit - y! Grace un - known! And love be - yond de - gree!
3. Well might the sun in dark - ness hide, And shut its glo - ries in, When Christ, the great Re - deem - er, died For hu - man crea - tures' sin.
4. But drops of grief can ne'er re - pay The debt of love I owe; Here, Lord, I give my - self a - way; 'Tis all that I can do.

168   O Sacred Head, Now Wounded

PASSION CHORALE 7.6.7.6 D

Matthew 27:27-31; Mark 15:16-20; John 19:1-5
Anonymous Latin
Trans. by Paul Gerhardt (1656) and
    James W. Alexander (1830)

Hans Leo Hassler (1601)
Harm. by Johann Sebastian Bach (1729), alt.

1. O   sa - cred Head,   now   wound - ed,   With
2. What   thou,   my   Lord,   hast   suf   - fered Was
3. What   lan - guage shall   I   bor   - row   To

grief   and   shame weighed   down,   Now   scorn - ful - ly   sur -
all   for   sin - ners'   gain;   Mine,   mine was   the   trans -
thank   thee,   dear - est   friend,   For   this   thy   dy - ing

round - ed With   thorns, thine   on - ly   crown: How
gres - sion, But   thine   the   dead - ly   pain.   Lo,
sor - row, Thy   pit - y   with - out   end?   O

pale thou art with an - guish, With
here I fall, my Sav - ior! 'Tis
make me thine for ev - er; And

sore a - buse and scorn! How does that vis - age
I de - serve thy place; Look on me with thy
should I faint - ing be, Lord, let me nev - er,

lan - guish Which once was bright as morn!
fa - vor, Vouch - safe to me thy grace.
nev - er Out - live my love to thee.

169   Were You There

WERE YOU THERE 10.10 with refrain

African-American spiritual
Harm. by Charles Winfred Douglas (1940)

African-American spiritual

1. Were you there when they cru - ci - fied my Lord? Were you
2. Were you there when they nailed him to the tree? Were you
3. Were you there when they pierced him in the side? Were you
4. Were you there when the sun re - fused to shine? Were you

there when they cru - ci - fied my Lord? Oh!
there when they nailed him to the tree? Oh!
there when they pierced him in the side? Oh!
there when the sun re - fused to shine? Oh!

Some-times it caus - es me to trem - ble, trem - ble, trem - ble,
Some-times it caus - es me to trem - ble, trem - ble, trem - ble,
Some-times it caus - es me to trem - ble, trem - ble, trem - ble,
Some-times it caus - es me to trem - ble, trem - ble, trem - ble,

Were you there when they cru - ci - fied my Lord?
Were you there when they nailed him to the tree?
Were you there when they pierced him in the side?
Were you there when the sun re - fused to shine?

Tune: Harm. copyright © 1940, 1943, 1961, The Church Pension Fund

5. Were you there when they laid him in the tomb?
   Were you there when they laid him in the tomb?
   Oh! Sometimes it causes me to tremble, tremble, tremble,
   Were you there when they laid him in the tomb?

6. Were you there when they rolled the stone away?
   Were you there when they rolled the stone away?
   Oh! Sometimes it causes me to tremble, tremble, tremble,
   Were you there when they rolled the stone away?

170   When I Survey the Wondrous Cross

ROCKINGHAM LM

Galatians 6:14
Isaac Watts (1707)

Second Supplement to Psalmody in Miniature (1783)
Adapt. by Edward Miller (1790)

1. When   I   sur - vey   the   won - drous
2. For - bid   it,   Lord,   that   I   should
3. See,   from   his   head,   his   hands,   his
4. Were   the   whole   realm   of   na - ture

cross   On   which   the   Prince   of   glo - ry
boast,   Save   in   the   death   of   Christ,   my
feet,   Sor - row   and   love   flow   min - gled
mine,   That   were   an   of - f'ring   far   too

died,   My   rich - est   gain   I   count   but
God;   All   the   vain   things   that   charm   me
down.   Did   e'er   such   love   and   sor - row
small;   Love   so   a - maz - ing,   so   di -

loss,   And   pour   con - tempt   on   all   my   pride.
most,   I   sac - ri - fice   them   to   his   blood.
meet,   Or   thorns   com - pose   so   rich   a   crown?
vine,   De - mands   my   soul,   my   life,   my   all.

When I Survey the Wondrous Cross   171

HAMBURG LM

Galatians 6:14
Isaac Watts (1707)

Lowell Mason (1824)

1. When I sur-vey the won-drous cross
2. For-bid it, Lord, that I should boast,
3. See, from his head, his hands, his feet,
4. Were the whole realm of na-ture mine,

On which the Prince of glo-ry died,
Save in the death of Christ, my God;
Sor-row and love flow min-gled down.
That were an of-f'ring far too small;

My rich-est gain I count but loss,
All the vain things that charm me most,
Did e'er such love and sor-row meet,
Love so a-maz-ing, so di-vine,

And pour con-tempt on all my pride.
I sac-ri-fice them to his blood.
Or thorns com-pose so rich a crown?
De-mands my soul, my life, my all.

172 Ride On! Ride On in Majesty!
ST. DROSTANE LM

Henry Hart Milman (1827)

John Bacchus Dykes (1862)

1. Ride on! Ride on in maj - es - ty! Hark!
2. Ride on! Ride on in maj - es - ty! In
3. Ride on! Ride on in maj - es - ty! The
4. Ride on! Ride on in maj - es - ty! In

all the tribes ho - san - na cry; O
low - ly pomp ride on to die: O
wing - ed squad - rons of the sky Look
low - ly pomp ride on to die; Bow

Sav - ior meek, pur - sue thy road With
Christ, thy tri - umphs now be - gin O'er
down with sad and won - d'ring eyes To
thy meek head to mor - tal pain, Then

palms and scat - tered gar - ments strowed.
cap - tive death and con - quered sin.
see the ap - proach - ing sac - ri - fice.
take, O God, thy pow'r, and reign.

That Easter Day with Joy Was Bright   173

PUER NOBIS LM

Claro paschali gaudio, Latin (5th C.)   Trier ms. (15th C.)
Trans. by John Mason Neale (1851), alt.   Adapt. by Michael Praetorius (1609)

1. That Eas - ter day with joy was bright, The sun shone
2. His ris - en flesh with ra - diance glowed; His wound - ed
3. O Je - sus, King of gen - tle - ness, Who with your
4. O Lord of all, with us a - bide In this our
5. All praise, to you, O ris - en Lord, Now both by

out with fair - er light, When to their long - ing
hands and feet he showed; Those scars their sol - emn
grace our hearts pos - sess That we may give you
joy - ful East - er - tide; From ev - 'ry weap - on
heav'n and earth a - dored; To God the Fa - ther

eyes re - stored, The a - pos - tles saw their ris - en Lord.
wit - ness gave That Christ was ris - en from the grave.
all our days The will - ing trib - ute of our praise.
death can wield Your own re - deemed for ev - er shield.
e - qual praise, And Spir - it blest, our songs we raise.

174 Good Christians All, Rejoice and Sing

GELOBT SEI GOTT 8.8.8 with alleluias

Cyril A. Alington (1925), alt.

Melchior Vulpius (1609)

1. Good Christians all, rejoice and sing!
   Now is the triumph of our King!
   To all the world glad news we bring:
   Alleluia, alleluia, alleluia!

2. The Lord of life is ris'n today.
   Sing songs of praise along his way.
   Let all the world rejoice and say:
   Alleluia, alleluia, alleluia!

3. Praise we in songs of victory
   That love, that life which cannot die,
   And sing with hearts uplifted high:
   Alleluia, alleluia, alleluia!

4. Your name we bless, O risen Lord,
   And sing today with one accord
   The life laid down, the life restored:
   Alleluia, alleluia, alleluia!

The Strife Is O'er

175

VICTORY 8.8.8 with alleluias

Anonymous Latin (12th C.)
Trans. by Francis Pott (1861), alt.

Giovanni da Palestrina (1591)
Adapt. by William Henry Monk (1861)

Al- le - lu - ia! Al- le - lu - ia! Al- le - lu - ia!

1. The strife is o'er, the bat - tle done; Now is the
2. Death's might - iest pow'rs have done their worst, And Je - sus
3. He closed the yawn - ing gates of hell; The bars from
4. On the third morn he rose a - gain, Glo - rious in

Vic - tor's tri - umph won; Now be the song of
has his foes dis - persed; Let shouts of praise and
heav'n's high por - tals fell; Let hymns of praise his
maj - es - ty to reign; O let us swell the

praise be - gun: Al - le - lu - ia!
joy out - burst: Al - le - lu - ia!
tri - umph tell: Al - le - lu - ia!
joy - ful strain: Al - le - lu - ia!

D.C.

176   Hail Thee, Festival Day

SALVE FESTA DIES Irregular with refrain

Venantius Honorius Fortunatus (c. 530-609)   Ralph Vaughan Williams (1906)

Refrain

Hail thee, fes - ti - val day! Blest day that art hal - lowed for

ev - er; Day when our Lord was raised, break - ing the

First time only | *All other times*

king - dom of death.   death.

Verse 1, 3, 5

1. All   the fair beau - ty of earth   from the
3. God   the Al - might - y, the Lord,   the
5. Spir - it of life   and of pow'r,   now

death of the win-ter a - ris - ing! Ev - 'ry good
rul - er of earth and the heav - ens, Guard us from
flow in us, fount of our be - ing, Light that en -

D.C.

gift of the year now with its mas - ter re-turns.
harm with - out; cleanse us from e - vil with-in.
light-ens us all, life that in all may a - bide.

Verses 2, 4, 6

2. Rise from the grave now, O Lord, the au - thor of
4. Je - sus, the health of the world, en - light - en our
6. Praise to the giv - er of good! O Lov - er and

life and cre - a - tion. Tread-ing the path-way of
minds great Re-deem - er. Son of the Fa - ther su -
Au - thor of con - cord, Pour out your balm on our

D.C.

death, new life you give to us all.
preme, on - ly be - got - ten of God.
days; or - der our ways in your peace.

Christh Is Alive

177

TRURO LM

Romans 6:5-11
Brian Wren (1975)

Williams' *Psalmodia Evangelica* (1789)

1. Christ is a - live! Let Chris - tians sing.
2. Christ is a - live! No long - er bound
3. In ev - 'ry in - sult, rift, and war,
4. Wom - en and men, in age and youth,
5. Christ is a - live, and comes to bring

The cross stands emp - ty to the sky.
To dis - tant years in Pal - es - tine,
Where col - or, scorn or wealth di - vide,
Can feel the Spir - it, hear the call,
Good news to this and ev - 'ry age,

Let streets and homes with prais - es ring.
But sav - ing, heal - ing, here and now,
Christ suf - fers still, yet loves the more,
And find the way, the life, the truth,
Till earth and sky and o - cean ring

Love, drowned in death, shall nev - er die.
And touch - ing ev - 'ry place and time.
And lives, where ev - en hope has died.
Re - vealed in Je - sus, freed for all.
With joy, with jus - tice, love and praise.

178   The Day of Resurrection

ELLACOMBE 7.6.7.6 D

John of Damascus (8th C.)
Trans. by John Mason Neale (1862)

Gesangbuch der Herzogl, Wirtemberg (1784)
Harm. by William Henry Monk (1868)

1. The day of res - ur - rec - tion! Earth, tell it out a -
2. Our hearts be pure from e - vil, That we may see a -
3. Now let the heav'ns be joy - ful, Let earth her song be -

broad; The Pass - o - ver of glad - ness, The
right The Lord in rays e - ter - nal Of
gin, The round world keep high tri - umph, And

Pass - o - ver of God. From death to life e -
res - ur - rec - tion light; And, lis - t'ning to his
all that is there - in; Let all things seen and

ter - nal, From earth un - to the sky, Our
ac - cents, May hear so calm and plain His
un - seen Their notes to - geth - er blend, For

Christ hath brought us o - ver With hymns of vic - to - ry.
own "All hail!" and, hear - ing, May raise the vic - tor strain.
Christ the Lord is ris - en, Our joy that hath no end.

179   At the Lamb's High Feast We Sing
SALZBURG 7.7.7.7 D

Ad regias agni dapes; Latin (4th C.)   Jakob Hintze (1678)
Trans. by Robert Campbell (1850), alt.   Harm. by Johann Sebastian Bach

1. At   the   Lamb's   high   feast   we   sing
2. Where the   Pas - chal   blood   is poured,
3. Might - y   vic - tim   from   the   sky,
4. East - er   tri - umph,   East -   er   joy,

Praise   to   our   vic - to - rious King.
Death's   dark   an - gel   sheathes his sword;
Hell's   fierce pow'rs be - neath you lie;
This   a - lone   can   sin de - stroy;

Who   has   washed   us   in   the   tide
Is - rael's   hosts   tri - umph - ant   go
You   have   con - quered in   the   fight,
From   sin's   pow'r, Lord,   set   us   free

Flow - ing   from   his   pierc - ed   side;
Through the   wave   that   drowns the   foe.
You   have   brought us   life   and   light:
New - born   souls   in   you   to   be.

Praise we him, whose love di - vine
Praise we Christ, whose blood was shed,
Now no more can death ap - pall,
Fa - ther, who the crown shall give,

Gives his sa - cred Blood for wine,
Pas - chal vic - tim, Pas - chal bread;
Now no more the grave en - thrall;
Sav - ior, by whose death we live,

Gives his Bod - y for the feast,
With sin - cer - i - ty and love
You have o - pened par - a - dise,
Spir - it, guide through all our days,

Christ the vic - tim, Christ the priest.
Eat we man - na from a - bove.
And in you your saints shall rise.
Three in One, your name we praise.

180   O Sons and Daughters, Let Us Sing!

O FILII ET FILIAE 8.8.8 with alleluias

Attr. to Jean Tisserand   French tune (15th C.)
Trans. by John Mason Neale (1852)   *Airs sur les hymnes sacrez, odes et nöels* (1623)

Al - le - lu - ia! Al - le - lu - ia!

Al - le - lu - ia! Al - le - lu - ia!

1. O   sons   and   daugh - ters,   let   us   sing!   The
2. That   Eas - ter   morn,   at   break   of   day,   The
3. An   an - gel   clad   in   white   they see,   Who
4. That   night   the a - pos - tles   met   in   fear;   A -
5. On   this   most   ho - ly   day   of   days,   To

King   of heav'n,   the   glo - rious King,   O'er
faith - ful   wom - en   went   their   way   To
sat   and   spoke   un - to   the   three,   "Your
mong   them   came   their   Lord   most   dear,   And
God   your   hearts   and   voic - es   raise,   In

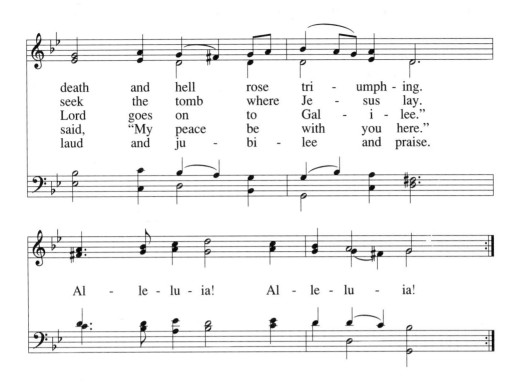

death   and   hell   rose   tri - umph - ing.
seek   the   tomb   where   Je   -   sus   lay.
Lord   goes   on   to   Gal - i - lee."
said,   "My   peace   be   with   you   here."
laud   and   ju -   bi -   lee   and   praise.

Al - le - lu - ia! Al - le - lu - ia!

181 Hail, Thou Once Despised Jesus

IN BABILONE 8.7.8.7 D

Revelation 4:2-11
Attr. to John Bakewell (1757)
and Martin Madan (1760), alt.

Traditional Dutch melody
Arr. by Julius Röntgen (1906)

1. Hail, thou once de - spis - ed Je - sus! Hail, thou Gal - i -
2. Pas - chal Lamb, by God ap - point - ed, All our sins on
3. Je - sus, hail! en - throned in glo - ry, There for ev - er
4. Wor - ship, hon - or, pow'r, and bless - ing Christ is wor - thy

le - an King! Thou didst suf - fer to re - lease us;
thee were laid; By al - might - y love a - noint - ed,
to a - bide; All the heav'n - ly hosts a - dore thee,
to re - ceive; Loud - est prais - es, with - out ceas - ing,

Thou didst free sal - va - tion bring. Hail, thou u - ni -
Thou hast full a - tone - ment made. Ev - 'ry sin may
Seat - ed at thy Fa - ther's side. There for sin - ners
Right it is for us to give. Help, ye bright an -

ver - sal Sav - ior, Who hast borne our sin and shame!
be for - giv - en Through the vir - tue of thy blood;
thou art plead-ing; There thou dost our place pre - pare;
gel - ic spir - its, Bring your sweet - est, no - blest lays;

By thy mer - its we find fa - vor;
O - pened is the gate of heav - en,
Thou for saints art in - ter - ced - ing
Help to sing of Je - sus' mer - its,

Life is giv - en through thy name.
Rec - on - ciled are we with God.
Till in glo - ry they ap - pear.
Help to chant Em - man - uel's praise!

182 Welcome, Happy Morning

FORTUNATUS 11.11.11.11.11

Venantius Honorius Fortunatus (7th C.)
Trans. by John Ellerton, alt.

Arthur Seymour Sullivan (1871)

1. "Wel-come, hap-py morn-ing!" age to age shall say:
2. Earth her joy con-fess-es, cloth-ing her for spring,
3. Months in due suc-ces-sion, days of length-'ning light,
4. Mak-er and Re-deem-er, life and health of all,
5. Thou, of life the au-thor, death didst un-der-go,
6. Loose the souls long pris-oned, bound with Sa-tan's chain;

Hell to-day is van-quished, heav'n is won to-day!
All fresh gifts re-turned with her re-turn-ing King:
Hours and pass-ing mo-ments praise thee in their flight.
Thou from heav'n be-hold-ing hu-man na-ture's fall,
Tread the path of dark-ness, sav-ing strength to show;
All that now is fal-len raise to life a-gain;

Lo! the dead is liv-ing, God for ev-er-more!
Bloom in ev-'ry mead-ow, leaves on ev-'ry bough,
Bright-ness of the morn-ing, sky and fields and sea,
Of the Fa-ther's God-head true and on-ly Son,
Come then, true and faith-ful, now ful-fill thy word,
Show thy face in bright-ness, bid the na-tions see;

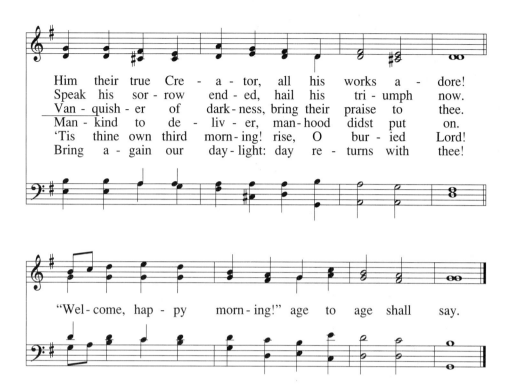

Him their true Cre - a - tor, all his works a - dore!
Speak his sor - row end - ed, hail his tri - umph now.
Van - quish - er of dark - ness, bring their praise to thee.
Man - kind to de - liv - er, man - hood didst put on.
'Tis thine own third morn - ing! rise, O bur - ied Lord!
Bring a - gain our day - light: day re - turns with thee!

"Wel - come, hap - py morn - ing!" age to age shall say.

183   Christ Jesus Lay in Death's Strong Bands

CHRIST LAG IN TODESBANDEN 8.7.8.7.7.8.7.4

Martin Luther (1524)   *Geystliche gesangk Buchleyn* (1524)
Trans. by Richard Massie (1854), alt.   Adapt. and harm. by Johann Sebastian Bach (c.1707)

1. Christ Je - sus lay in death's strong bands For
2. It was a strange and dread - ful strife When
3. So let us keep the fes - ti - val To
4. Then let us feast this ho - ly day On

our of - fens - es giv - en; But
life and death con - tend - ed; The
which the Lord in - vites us; Christ
the true bread of heav - en; The

now at God's right hand he stands And
vic - to - ry re - mained with life, The
is him - self the joy of all, The
word of grace hath purged a - way The

brings us life from heav - en; There - fore let us
reign of death was end - ed; Stripped of pow'r, no
sun that warms and lights us; By his grace he
old and wick - ed leav - en; Christ a - lone our

joy - ful be, And sing to God right
more he reigns, An emp - ty form a -
doth im - part E - ter - nal sun - shine
souls will feed, He is our meat and

thank - ful - ly Loud songs of al - le -
lone re - mains; His sting is lost for
to the heart; The night of sin is
drink in - deed; Faith lives up - on no

lu - ia! Al - le - lu - ia!
ev - cr! Al - le - lu - ia!
end - ed! Al - le - lu - ia!
oth - er! Al - le - lu - ia!

184   Come, Ye Faithful, Raise the Strain

ST. KEVIN 7.6.7.6 D

John of Damascus (c. 675-749)
Trans. by John Mason Neale (1859), alt.

Arthur Seymour Sullivan (1872)

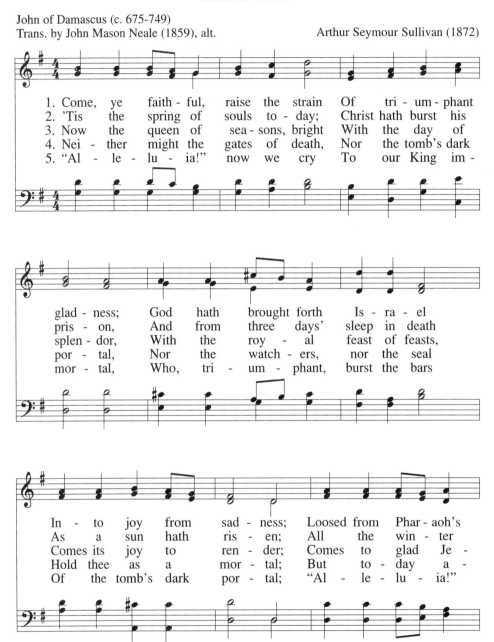

1. Come, ye faith - ful, raise the strain Of tri - um - phant glad - ness; God hath brought forth Is - ra - el In - to joy from sad - ness; Loosed from Phar - aoh's
2. 'Tis the spring of souls to - day; Christ hath burst his pris - on, And from three days' sleep in death As a sun hath ris - en; All the win - ter
3. Now the queen of sea - sons, bright With the day of splen - dor, With the roy - al feast of feasts, Comes its joy to ren - der; Comes to glad Je -
4. Nei - ther might the gates of death, Nor the tomb's dark por - tal, Nor the watch - ers, nor the seal Hold thee as a mor - tal; But to - day a -
5. "Al - le - lu - ia!" now we cry To our King im - mor - tal, Who, tri - um - phant, burst the bars Of the tomb's dark por - tal; "Al - le - lu - ia!"

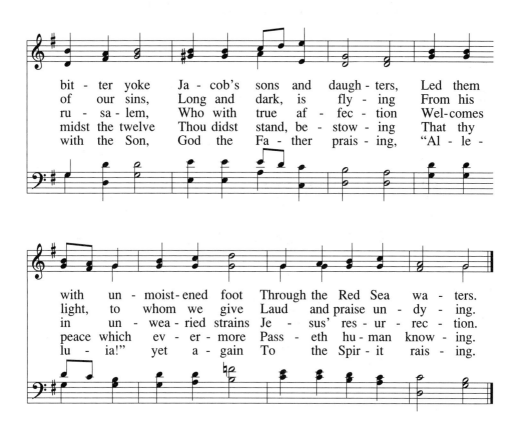

bit - ter yoke   Ja - cob's   sons   and   daugh - ters,   Led them
of   our   sins,   Long and   dark,   is   fly - ing   From his
ru - sa - lem,   Who with   true   af - fec - tion   Wel - comes
midst the twelve   Thou didst   stand, be - stow - ing   That thy
with   the Son,   God the   Fa - ther   prais - ing,   "Al - le -

with   un - moist-ened   foot   Through the Red Sea   wa - ters.
light,   to   whom we   give   Laud   and praise un - dy - ing.
in   un - wea - ried strains   Je - sus' res - ur - rec - tion.
peace which   ev - er - more   Pass - eth hu - man know - ing.
lu - ia!"   yet   a - gain   To   the Spir - it   rais - ing.

185   Christ the Lord Is Risen Today

EASTER HYMN 7.7.7.7 with alleluias

Charles Wesley (1739)   *Lyra Davidica* (1708)

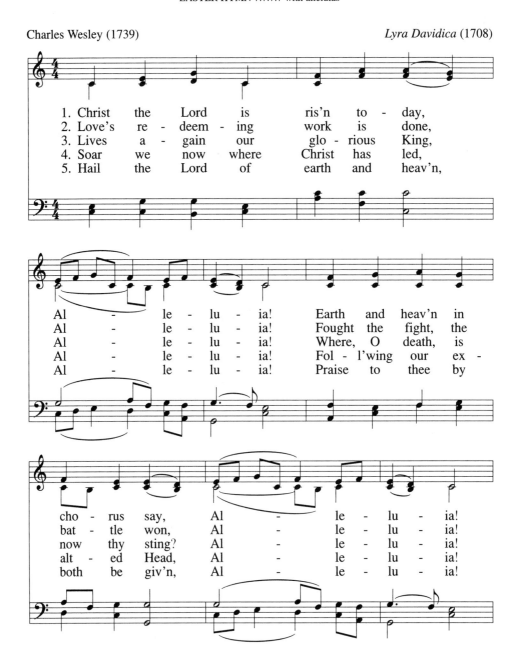

1. Christ the Lord is ris'n to - day,
2. Love's re - deem - ing work is done,
3. Lives a - gain our glo - rious King,
4. Soar we now where Christ has led,
5. Hail the Lord of earth and heav'n,

Al - le - lu - ia! Earth and heav'n in
Al - le - lu - ia! Fought the fight, the
Al - le - lu - ia! Where, O death, is
Al - le - lu - ia! Fol - l'wing our ex -
Al - le - lu - ia! Praise to thee by

cho - rus say, Al - le - lu - ia!
bat - tle won, Al - le - lu - ia!
now thy sting? Al - le - lu - ia!
alt - ed Head, Al - le - lu - ia!
both be giv'n, Al - le - lu - ia!

Raise your joys and tri - umphs high,
Death in vain for - bids him rise,
Once he died our souls to save,
Made like him, like him we rise,
Thee we greet tri - um - phant now,

Al - le - lu - ia! Sing, ye heav'ns, and
Al - le - lu - ia! Christ has o - pened
Al - le - lu - ia! Where's thy vic - t'ry,
Al - le - lu - ia! Ours the cross, the
Al - le - lu - ia! Hail the Res - ur -

earth re - ply, Al - le - lu - ia!
par - a - dise, Al - le - lu - ia!
boast - ing grave? Al - le - lu - ia!
grave, the skies, Al - le - lu - ia!
rec - tion, thou, Al - le - lu - ia!

186 Alleluia! Sing to Jesus

HYFRYDOL 8.7.8.7 D

Revelation 5:9
William Chatterton Dix (1866)

Rowland H. Prichard (1831)

1. Al - le - lu - ia! sing to Je - sus!
2. Al - le - lu - ia! not as or - phans
3. Al - le - lu - ia! Bread of An - gels,
4. Al - le - lu - ia! King e - ter - nal,

His the scep - ter, his the throne;
Are we left in sor - row now;
Here on earth our food, our stay!
You the Lord of lords we own;

Al - le - lu - ia! his the tri - umph,
Al - le - lu - ia! he is near us,
Al - le - lu - ia! here the sin - ful
Al - le - lu - ia! born of Mar - y,

His the vic - to - ry a - lone;
Faith be - lieves, nor ques - tions how:
Flee to you from day to day:
Earth your foot - stool, heav'n your throne:

Hark! the songs of peace - ful Zi - on
Though the cloud from sight re - ceived him,
In - ter - ces - sor, friend of sin - ners,
You, with - in the veil, have en - tered,

Thun - der like a might - y flood;
When the for - ty days were o'er,
Earth's re - deem - er, plead for me,
Robed in flesh, our great high priest;

Je - sus out of ev - 'ry na - tion
Shall our hearts for - get his prom - ise,
Where the songs of all the sin - less
Here on earth both priest and vic - tim

Has re - deemed us by his blood.
"I am with you ev - er - more?"
Sweep a - cross the crys - tal sea.
In the eu - cha - ris - tic feast.

187   Crown Him with Many Crowns

DIADEMATA SMD

Revelation 19:12
St. 1, 3, 4, Matthew Bridges (1851)
St. 2, Godfrey Thring (1874)

George J. Elvey (1868)

1. Crown him with man - y crowns, The Lamb up - on his
2. Crown him the Lord of life, Who tri - umphed o'er the
3. Crown him the Lord of love, Be - hold his hands and
4. Crown him the Lord of peace, Whose power a scep - ter

throne; Hark! how the heav'n - ly an - them drowns All
grave, And rose vic - to - rious in the strife For
side, Rich wounds yet vis - i - ble a - bove In
sways From pole to pole, that wars may cease, Ab -

mu - sic but its own. A - wake, my soul, and sing Of
those he came to save. His glo - ries now we sing, Who
beau - ty glo - ri - fied. No an - gel in the sky Can
sorbed in prayer and praise. His reign shall know no end, And

him who set us free, And hail him as your
died and rose on high, Who died, e - ter - nal
ful - ly bear that sight, But down - ward bends his
round his pierc - ed feet Fair flow'rs of Par - a -

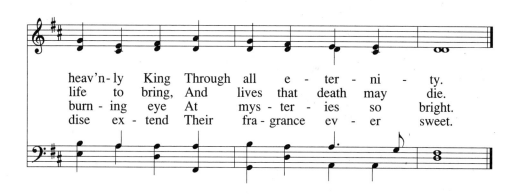

heav'n- ly King Through all e - ter - ni - ty.
life to bring, And lives that death may die.
burn - ing eye At mys - ter - ies so bright.
dise ex - tend Their fra - grance ev - er sweet.

188   ## Rejoice, the Lord Is King
DARWALL'S 148TH 6.6.6.6.8.8

John Darwall (1770)
Harm. from *The Hymnal 1940*

Charles Wesley (1744)

1. Re - joice, the Lord is King! Your Lord and King a - dore!
2. The Lord, our Sav - ior, reigns, The God of truth and love;
3. His king-dom can - not fail, He rules o'er earth and heav'n;
4. Re - joice in glo - rious hope! Our Lord the judge shall come

Re - joice, give thanks, and sing, And tri - umph ev - er - more:
When he had purged our sins, He took his seat a - bove:
The keys of death and hell Are to our Je - sus giv'n:
And take his ser - vants up To their e - ter - nal home:

Lift up your heart, lift up your voice!

Re - joice, a - gain I say, re - joice!

Spirit of God, Who Dwells within My Heart 189

MORECAMBE 10.10.10.10

George Croly (1867), alt.   Frederick C. Atkinson (1870)

1. Spir - it of God, who dwells with - in my heart,
2. I ask no dream, no proph - et ec - sta - sies,
3. Did you not bid us love you, God and King,
4. Teach me to feel that you are al - ways nigh;
5. Teach me to love you as your an - gels love,

Wean it from sin, through all its puls - es move.
No sud - den rend - ing of the veil of clay,
Love you with all our heart and strength and mind?
Teach me the strug - gles of the soul to bear,
One ho - ly pas - sion fill - ing all my frame:

Stoop to my weak - ness, might - y as you are,
No an - gel vi - si - tant, no o - pening skies;
I see the cross— there teach my heart to cling.
To check the ris - ing doubt, the reb - el sigh;
The full - ness of the heav'n - de - scen - ded Dove;

And make me love you as I ought to love.
But take the dim - ness of my soul a - way.
O let me seek you and O let me find!
Teach me the pa - tience of un - ceas - ing prayer.
My heart an al - tar, and your love the flame.

190 Holy Ghost, Dispel Our Sadness

GENEVA 8.7.8.7 D

Paul Gerhardt (1648)
Trans. by John Christian Jacobi (c. 1725), alt.

George Henry Day (1940)

1. Ho - ly Ghost, dis - pel our sad - ness; Pierce the
2. Au - thor of the new cre - a - tion, Come, a -

clouds of na - ture's night; Come, O source of
noint us with your pow'r. Make our hearts your

joy and glad - ness, Breathe your life, and spread your light.
hab - i - ta - tion; With your grace our spir - its show'r.

From the height which knows no meas - ure, As a gra - cious
Hear, O hear our sup - pli - ca - tion, Bless - ed Spir - it,

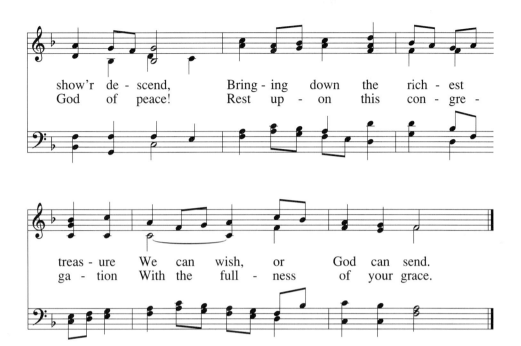

show'r de - scend, Bring - ing down the rich - est
God of peace! Rest up - on this con - gre -

treas - ure We can wish, or God can send.
ga - tion With the full - ness of your grace.

191 **For Your Gift of God the Spirit**

BLAENWERN 8.7.8.7 D

Margaret Clarkson (1959)   William P. Rowlands (1905)

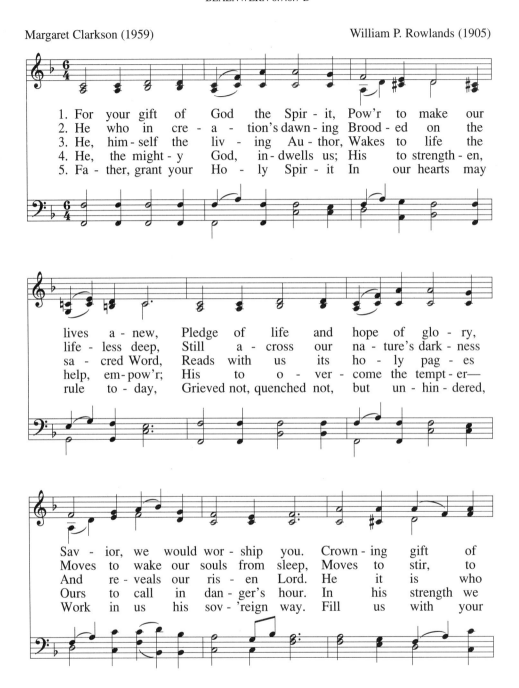

1. For your gift of God the Spir-it, Pow'r to make our
2. He who in cre-a-tion's dawn-ing Brood-ed on the
3. He, him-self the liv-ing Au-thor, Wakes to life the
4. He, the might-y God, in-dwells us; His to strength-en,
5. Fa-ther, grant your Ho-ly Spir-it In our hearts may

lives a-new, Pledge of life and hope of glo-ry,
life-less deep, Still a-cross our na-ture's dark-ness
sa-cred Word, Reads with us its ho-ly pag-es
help, em-pow'r; His to o-ver-come the tempt-er—
rule to-day, Grieved not, quenched not, but un-hin-dered,

Sav-ior, we would wor-ship you. Crown-ing gift of
Moves to wake our souls from sleep, Moves to stir, to
And re-veals our ris-en Lord. He it is who
Ours to call in dan-ger's hour. In his strength we
Work in us his sov-'reign way. Fill us with your

res - ur - rec - tion Sent from your as - cend - ed throne,
draw, to quick - en, Thrusts us through with sense of sin;
works with - in us, Teach - ing reb - el hearts to pray,
dare to bat - tle All the rag - ing hosts of sin,
ho - ly full - ness, God the Fa - ther, Spir - it, Son;

Full - ness of the ver - y God - head,
Brings to birth and seals and fills us—
He whose ho - ly in - ter - ces - sions
And by him a - lone we con - quer
In us, through us, then, for ev - er,

Come to make your life our own.
Sav - ing Ad - vo - cate with - in.
Rise for us both night and day.
Foes with - out and foes with - in.
Shall your per - fect will be done.

192   # Breathe on Me, Breath of God
TRENTHAM SM

Edwin Hatch (1878), alt.   Robert Jackson (1894)

1. Breathe on me, breath of God, Fill me with
2. Breathe on me, breath of God, Un - til my
3. Breathe on me, breath of God, So shall I

life a - new, That I may love the
heart is pure, Un - til my will is
nev - er die, But live with you the

way you love, And do what you would do.
one with yours, To do and to en - dure.
per - fect life For all e - ter - ni - ty.

I Greet Thee, Who My Sure Redeemer Art　193
TOULON 10.10.10.10

Adapt. from GENEVAN 124
French Psalter, Strassburg (1545)　　　　　　　　　*Genevan Psalter* (1551)

1. I greet thee, who my sure Re-deem-er art,
2. Thou art the King of mer - cy and of grace,
3. Thou art the life, by which a - lone we live,
4. Thou hast the true and per - fect gen - tle - ness,
5. Our hope is in no oth - er save in thee;

My on - ly trust and Sav - ior of my heart,
Reign - ing om - nip - o - tent in ev - 'ry place:
And all our sub - stance and our strength re - ceive;
No harsh-ness hast thou and no bit - ter - ness:
Our faith is built up - on thy prom - ise free;

Who pain didst un - der - go for my poor sake;
So come, O King, and our whole be - ing sway;
Sus - tain us by thy faith and by thy pow'r,
O grant to us the grace we find in thee,
Lord, give us peace, and make us calm and sure,

I pray thee from our hearts all cares to take.
Shine on us with the light of thy pure day.
And give us strength in ev - 'ry try - ing hour.
That we may dwell in per - fect u - ni - ty.
That in thy strength we ev - er - more en - dure.

194 Fairest Lord Jesus

ST. ELIZABETH 5.6.8.5.5.8

Münster Gesangbuch (1677)
Trans. by Joseph August Seiss (1873)

Schlesische Volkslieder (1842)
Arr. by Richard Storrs Willis (1850)

1. Fair - est Lord Je - sus, Rul - er of all na - ture,
2. Fair are the mead - ows, Fair - er still the wood-lands,
3. Fair is the sun - shine, Fair - er still the moon-light,
4. Beau - ti - ful Sav - ior! Lord of all the na - tions!

O thou of God and man the Son,
Robed in the bloom - ing garb of spring:
And all the twin - kling, star - ry host:
Son of God and Son of Man!

Thee will I cher - ish, Thee will I
Je - sus is fair - er, Je - sus is
Je - sus shines bright - er, Je - sus shines
Glo - ry and hon - or, Praise, ad - o -

hon - or, Thou, my soul's glo - ry, joy, and crown.
pur - er, Who makes the woe - ful heart to sing.
pur - er, Than all the an - gels heav'n can boast.
ra - tion, Now and for ev - er - more be thine.

Jesus Shall Reign

195

DUKE STREET LM

Based on Psalm 72
Isaac Watts (1719), alt.

John Hatton (1793)

1. Je - sus shall reign wher - e'er the sun
2. To him shall end - less prayer be made,
3. Peo - ple and realms of ev - 'ry tongue
4. Bless - ings a - bound wher - e'er he reigns;
5. Let ev - 'ry crea - ture rise and bring

Does his suc - ces - sive jour - neys run;
And prais - es throng to crown his head;
Dwell on his love with sweet - est song;
The pris - 'ner leaps to lose his chains;
Bless - ing and hon - or to our King;

His king - dom stretch from shore to shore,
His Name like sweet per - fume shall rise
And in - fant voic - es shall pro - claim
The wea - ry find e - ter - nal rest,
An - gels de - scend with songs a - gain,

Till moons shall wax and wane no more.
With ev - 'ry morn - ing sac - ri - fice.
Their ear - ly bless - ings on his Name.
And all who suf - fer want are blest.
And earth re - peat the loud A - men.

196   Christ Is the World's Light

CHRISTE SANCTORUM 10.11.11.6

Fred Pratt Green (1969)   *Paris Antiphoner* (1681)

1. Christ is the world's Light, he and none oth - er;
2. Christ is the world's Peace, he and none oth - er;
3. Christ is the world's Life, he and none oth - er;
4. Give God the glo - ry, God and none oth - er;

Born in our dark - ness, he be - came our
No one can serve him and de - spise an -
Sold once for sil - ver, mur - dered here, our
Give God the glo - ry, Spir - it, Son and

Broth - er. If we have seen him, we have seen the
oth - er. Who else u - nites us, one in God the
Broth - er— He, who re - deems us, reigns with God the
Fa - ther; Give God the glo - ry, God in Man my

Fa - ther: Glo - ry to God on high.
Fa - ther? Glo - ry to God on high.
Fa - ther: Glo - ry to God on high.
broth - er: Glo - ry to God on high.

There's a Spirit in the Air   197

LAUDS 7.7.7.7

Brian Wren (1979)   John W. Wilson (1967)

1. There's a spir-it in the air, Tell-ing Chris-tians
2. Lose your shy-ness, find your tongue; Tell the world what
3. When be-liev-ers break the bread, When a hun-gry
4. Still the Spir-it gives us light, See-ing wrong and
5. When a stran-ger's not a-lone, Where the home-less

ev-'ry-where, "Praise the love that Christ re-vealed,
God has done: God in Christ has come to stay,
child is fed: Praise the love that Christ re-vealed,
set-ting right: God in Christ has come to stay,
find a home, Praise the love that Christ re-vealed,

Liv-ing, work-ing in our world."
Live to-mor-row's life to-day.
Liv-ing, work-ing in our world.
Live to-mor-row's life to-day.
Liv-ing, work-ing in our world.

6. May the Spirit fill our praise,
   Guide our thoughts and change our ways.
   God in Christ has come to stay,
   Live tomorrow's life today.

7. There's a Spirit in the air,
   Calling people ev'rywhere;
   Praise the love that Christ revealed;
   Living, working in our world

198   Ask Ye What Great Thing I Know

HENDON 7.7.7.7.7

Johann C. Schwedler (1741)
Trans. by Benjamin H. Kennedy (1863)

H. A. César Malan (1827)
Harm. by Lowell Mason (1841)

1. Ask ye what great thing I know, That de-lights and
2. Who de-feats my fierc-est foes? Who con-soles my
3. Who is life in life to me? Who the death of
4. This is that great thing I know; This de-lights and

stirs me so? What the high re-ward I win?
sad-dest woes? Who re-vives my faint-ing heart,
death will be? Who will place me on his right,
stirs me so: Faith in him who died to save,

Whose the name I glo-ry in?
Heal-ing all its hid-den smart?
With the count-less hosts of light?
Him who tri-umphed o'er the grave:

Je - sus Christ, the cru-ci-fied.

To Jesus Christ, Our Sovereign King   199

ICH GLAUB AN GOTT 8.7.8.7 with refrain

Martin B. Hellrigel, alt.

Mainz Gesangbuch (1870)
Harm. by Richard Proulx (1986)

1. To Jesus Christ, our sov-'reign King, Who is the world's sal-va-tion, All praise and hom-age do we bring And thanks and ad-o-ra-tion.
2. Your reign ex-tend, O King be-nign, To ev-'ry land and na-tion; For in your King-dom, Lord di-vine, A-lone we find sal-va-tion.
3. To you, and to your church, great King, We pledge our heart's ob-la-tion; Un-til be-fore your throne we sing In end-less ju-bi-la-tion.

Christ Je-sus, Vic-tor! Christ Je-sus, Rul-er! Christ Je-sus, Lord and Re-deem-er!

200 I Love to Tell the Story

HANKEY 7.6.7.6 D with refrain

Katherine Hankey (c. 1868)

William G. Fischer (1869)

1. I love to tell the sto - ry Of un - seen things a -
2. I love to tell the sto - ry; More won - der - ful it
3. I love to tell the sto - ry; 'Tis pleas - ant to re -
4. I love to tell the sto - ry, For those who know it

bove, Of Je - sus and his glo - ry, Of
seems Than all the gold - en fan - cies Of
peat What seems, each time I tell it, More
best Seem hun - ger - ing and thirst - ing To

Je - sus and his love. I love to tell the sto-ry,
all our gold - en dreams. I love to tell the sto-ry,
won - der - ful - ly sweet. I love to tell the sto-ry,
hear it like the rest. And when, in scenes of glo-ry,

Be - cause I know 'tis true; It sat - is - fies my
It did so much for me; And that is just the
For some have nev - er heard The mes - sage of sal -
I sing the new, new song, 'Twill be the old, old

long-ings   As   noth - ing else   can   do.
rea - son   I   tell   it   now   to   thee.
va - tion   From God's own ho - ly Word.
sto - ry   That   I   have loved   so   long.

I   love   to   tell   the   sto - ry,   'Twill

be   my theme in   glo-ry, To   tell   the old, old

sto - ry   Of   Je - sus and   his   love.

201 All Hail the Power of Jesus' Name

CORONATION CM with repeat

Edward Perronet (1780)
Alt. by John Rippon (1787)

Oliver Holden (1793)

1. All hail the pow'r of Je - sus' name! Let
2. Crown him, ye mar - tyrs of our God, Who
3. Ye cho - sen seed of Is - rael's race, A
4. O that, with yon - der sa - cred throng, We

an - gels pros - trate fall; Bring forth the roy - al
from his al - tar call; Ex - tol the stem of
rem - nant weak and small, Hail him who saved you
at his feet may fall, Join in the ev - er -

di - a - dem And crown him Lord of all; Bring
Jes - se's rod, And crown him Lord of all; Ex -
by his grace, And crown him Lord of all; Hail
last - ing song, And crown him Lord of all; Join

forth the roy - al di - a - dem And crown him Lord of all.
tol the stem of Jes - se's rod, And crown him Lord of all.
him who saved you by his grace, And crown him Lord of all.
in the ev - er - last - ing song, And crown him Lord of all.

At the Name of Jesus

202

KING'S WESTON 6.5.6.5 D

Philippians 2:5-7
Caroline M. Noel (1870), alt.

Ralph Vaughan Williams (1925), alt.

1. At the name of Je - sus Ev - 'ry knee shall bow,
2. Hum-bled for a sea - son To re - ceive a name
3. Bore it up tri - um - phant With its hu - man light,
4. In your hearts en - throne him; There let him sub - due

Ev - 'ry tongue con - fess him King of glo - ry now;
From the lips of sin - ners Un - to whom he came,
Through all ranks of crea - tures, To the cen - tral height,
All that is not ho - ly, All that is not true:

'Tis the Fa - ther's pleas - ure We should call him Lord,
Faith - ful - ly he bore it, Spot-less to the last,
To the throne of God - head, To the Fa - ther's breast;
Crown him as your Cap - tain In temp - ta - tion's hour;

Who from the be - gin - ning Was the might - y Word.
Brought it back vic - to - rious When through death he passed.
Filled it with the glo - ry Of that per - fect rest.
Let his will en - fold you In its light and pow'r.

203 Jesus, the Very Thought of Thee

ST. AGNES CM

Attr. to Bernard of Clairvaux (12th C.)
Trans. by Edward Caswall (1849)

John Bacchus Dykes (1866)

1. Je - sus, the ver - y thought of thee
2. O hope of ev - 'ry con - trite heart,
3. But what to those who find? Ah, this
4. Je - sus, our on - ly joy be thou,

With sweet - ness fills the breast; But sweet - er far thy
O joy of all the meek, To those who fall, how
Nor tongue nor pen can show; The love of Je - sus,
As thou our prize wilt be; Je - sus, be thou our

face to see, And in thy pres - ence rest.
kind thou art! How good to those who seek!
what it is, None but his loved ones know.
glo - ry now, And through e - ter - ni - ty.

O Christ, the Healer
ERHALT UNS HERR LM

Klug's *Geistliche Lieder* (1543)
Harm. by Johann Sebastian Bach

Fred Pratt Green (1969)

1. O Christ, the heal - er, we have come To
2. From ev - 'ry ail - ment flesh en - dures Our
3. How strong, O Lord, are our de - sires, How
4. In con - flicts that de - stroy our health We
5. Grant that we all, made one in faith, In

pray for health, to plead for friends. How can we fail to
bod - ies clam - or to be freed; Yet in our hearts we
weak our knowl-edge of our-selves! Re - lease in us those
rec - og - nize the world's dis - ease; Our com - mon life de -
your com-mun - i - ty may find The whole - ness that, en -

be re - stored, When reached by love that nev - er ends?
would con - fess That whole-ness is our deep - est need.
heal - ing truths Un - con-scious pride re - sists or shelves.
clares our ills: Is there no cure, O Christ, for these?
rich - ing us, Shall reach the whole of hu - man - kind.

205 O Love, How Deep

DEO GRACIAS LM

Attr. to Thomas à Kempis (15th C.)
Trans. by Benjamin Webb (1854), alt.

English melody
Harm. from *Hymns Ancient and Modern,*
Revised (1950)

1. O love, how deep, how broad, how high,
2. For us bap - tized, for us he bore
3. For us he prayed; for us he taught;
4. For us to e - vil pow'r be - trayed,
5. For us he rose from death a - gain;
6. All glo - ry to our Lord and God

It fills the heart with ec - sta - sy,
His ho - ly fast and hun - gered sore,
For us his dai - ly works he wrought;
Scourged, mocked, in pur - ple robe ar - rayed,
For us he went on high to reign;
For love so deep, so high, so broad:

That God, the Son of God, should take
For us temp - ta - tion sharp he knew;
By words and signs and ac - tions thus
He bore the shame - ful cross and death,
For us he sent his Spir - it here,
The Trin - i - ty whom we a - dore,

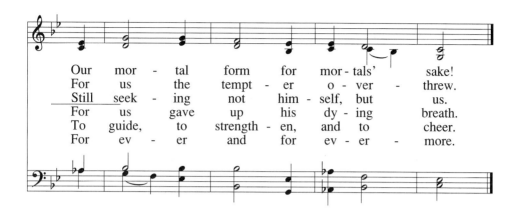

Our mor - tal form for mor - tals' sake!
For us the tempt - er o - ver - threw.
Still seek - ing not him - self, but us.
For us gave up his dy - ing breath.
To guide, to strength - en, and to cheer.
For ev - er and for ev - er - more.

206 Of the Father's Love Begotten

DIVINUM MYSTERIUM 8.7.8.7.8.7.7

Aurelius Clemens Prudentius (4th C.)
Trans. by John Mason Neale (1854),
and Henry Williams Baker (1859)

Plainsong, Mode V
Harm. by Charles Winfred Douglas (1940)

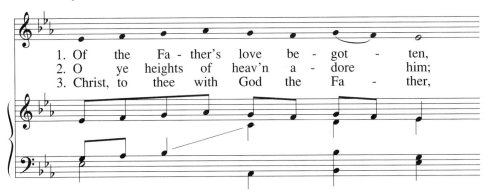

1. Of the Fa - ther's love be - got - ten,
2. O ye heights of heav'n a - dore him;
3. Christ, to thee with God the Fa - ther,

Ere the worlds be - gan to be,
An - gel hosts, his prais - es sing;
And, O Ho - ly Ghost, to thee,

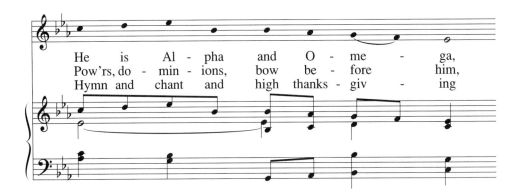

He is Al - pha and O - me - ga,
Pow'rs, do - min - ions, bow be - fore him,
Hymn and chant and high thanks - giv - ing

207   # I Am the Bread of Life

BREAD OF LIFE Irregular with refrain

John 6
Suzanne Toolan, SM (1966)   Suzanne Toolan, SM (1966)

1. ___ I am the Bread of life. You who
2. The bread that ___ I will give is my
3. Un - less ___ you ___ eat of the
4. ___ I am the Res - ur - rec - tion, ___
5. Yes, Lord, ___ I be - lieve that ___

come to me shall not hun - ger; and who be -
flesh for the life of the world, ___ and if you
flesh of the Son of Man ___ and ___
I ___ am the life. ___ If you be -
you ___ are the Christ, ___ the ___

lieve in me shall not thirst. ___ No one can come to
eat ___ of this bread, ___ you shall ___ live for
drink ___ of his blood, and drink ___ of his
lieve ___ in ___ me, ___ e - ven ___ though you
Son ___ of ___ God, ___ Who ___ has ___

me   un - less   the___   Fa - ther   beck-ons.
ev - er,___   you   shall___   live   for   ev - er.
blood,   you   shall   not have   life   with - in   you.
die,___   you   shall___   live   for   ev - er.
come   in - to___   the___   world.___

And   I   will   raise   you   up,   and   I   will

raise   you   up,   and   I   will   raise   you

up   on   the   last   day.

208

Lift High the Cross

CRUCIFER 10.10 with refrain

1 Corinthians 1:18
George W. Kitchin and Michael R. Newbolt (1916), alt.   Sidney Hugo Nicholson (1916)

Unison

Lift high the cross, the love of Christ pro - claim Till

all the world a - dore his sa - cred name.

Harmony

1. Come, Chris-tians, fol - low where the Mas - ter trod, Our
2. Led on their way by this tri - um - phant sign, The
3. Each new - born fol - l'wer of the Cru - ci - fied Bears
4. O Lord, once lift - ed on the glo - rious tree, Your
5. So shall our song of tri - umph ev - er be: Praise

D.C.

King vic - to - rious, Christ, the Son of God.
hosts of God in con - quering ranks com - bine.
on the brow the seal of him who died.
death has bought us life e - ter - nal - ly.
to the Cru - ci - fied for vic - to - ry!

Jesus Loves Me

209

JESUS LOVES ME 7.7.7.7 with refrain

St. 1, Anna B. Warner (1860)
Sts. 2-3, David Rutherford McGuire

William B. Bradbury (1862)

1. Je - sus loves me! This I know, For the Bi - ble tells me so.
2. Je - sus loves me! This I know, As he loved so long a - go,
3. Je - sus loves me still to - day, Walk - ing with me on my way,

Lit - tle ones to him be - long; They are weak, but he is strong.
Tak - ing chil - dren on his knee, Say - ing, "Let them come to me."
Want - ing as a friend to give Light and love to all who live.

Yes, Je - sus loves me! Yes, Je - sus loves me!

Yes, Je - sus loves me! The Bi - ble tells me so.

210

The King of Glory

KING OF GLORY 12.12 with refrain

Israeli folk song
Harm. by Richard Proulx (1986)

Willard F. Jabusch (1966)

The King of glo-ry comes, the na-tion re-joic-es.

O-pen the gates be-fore him, lift up your voic-es. lift up your voic-es.

1.-5. *To verses* *6.*

1. Who is the king of glo-ry; how shall we call him?
2. In all of Gal-i-lee, in cit-y or vil-lage,
3. Sing then of Da-vid's Son, our Sav-ior and broth-er;
4. He gave his life for us, the pledge of sal-va-tion,
5. He con-quered sin and death; he tru-ly has ris-en.

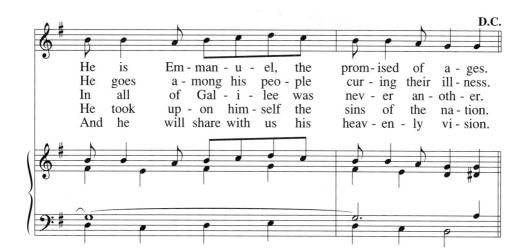

D.C.

He   is   Em - man - u - el,   the   prom - ised   of   a - ges.
He   goes   a - mong his   peo - ple   cur - ing their   ill - ness.
In   all   of   Gal - i - lee   was   nev - er   an - oth - er.
He   took   up - on   him - self   the   sins   of   the   na - tion.
And   he   will share with   us   his   heav - en - ly   vi - sion.

211   # We Come, O Christ, to You
DARWALL'S 148TH 6.6.6.6.4.4.8

Margaret Clarkson (1946)   John Darwall (1770)

1. We come, O Christ, to you, True Son of God and man;
2. You are the way to God, Your blood our ran - som paid;
3. You are the liv - ing truth, All wis - dom dwells in you,
4. You on - ly are true life, To know you is to live
5. We wor - ship you, Lord Christ, Our Sav - ior and our King;

By whom all things con - sist, In whom all life be - gan:
In you we face our judge And mak - er un - a - fraid;
The source of ev - 'ry skill, The one e - ter - nal true!
The more a - bun - dant life That earth can nev - er give.
To you our youth and strength A - dor - ing - ly we bring:

In you a - lone We live and move,
Be - fore the throne Ab - solved we stand:
O great I AM! In you we rest,
O ris - en Lord! We live in you:
So fill our hearts That all may view

And have our be - ing in your love.
Your love has met your law's de - mand.
Sure an - swer to our ev - 'ry quest.
In us each day your life re - new!
Your life in us, and turn to you!

Text: Copyright © 1957, 1985, Hope Publishing Co.

How Sweet the Name of Jesus

ST. PETER CM

212

John Newton

Alexander Robert Reinagle (c. 1836)

1. How sweet the Name of Je - sus sounds In a be - liev - er's ear! It soothes our sor - rows, heals our wounds, And drives a - way our fear.

2. It makes the wound - ed spir - it whole, And calms the troub - led breast; 'Tis man - na to the hun - gry soul, And to the wea - ry, rest.

3. Dear Name, the rock on which I build, My shield and hid - ing - place, My nev - er - fail - ing treas - 'ry, filled With bound - less stores of grace!

4. O Je - sus! Shep - herd, Guard - ian, Friend, O Proph - et, Priest, and King, My Lord, my Life, my Way, my End, Ac - cept the praise I bring.

5. Weak is the ef - fort of my heart, And cold my warm - est thought; But when I see thee as thou art, I'll praise thee as I ought.

213 All Praise to Thee, for Thou, O King Divine
SINE NOMINE 10.10.10 with alleluias

Philippians 2:5-11
F. Bland Tucker (1938)

Ralph Vaughan Williams (1906)

1. All praise to thee, for thou, O King di - vine, Didst
2. Thou cam'st to us, in low - li - ness of thought; By
3. Let this mind be in us which was in thee,
4. Where-fore, by God's e - ter - nal pur-pose, thou
5. Let ev - 'ry tongue con - fess with one ac - cord In

yield the glo - ry that of right was thine,
thee the out - cast and the poor were sought,
Who wast a ser - vant, that we might be free,
Art high ex - alt - ed o'er all crea - tures now,
heav'n and earth that Je - sus Christ is Lord;

That in our dark - ened hearts thy grace might shine:
And by thy death was God's sal - va - tion wrought:
Hum - bling thy - self to death on Cal - va - ry:
And giv'n the name to which all knees shall bow:
And God the Fa - ther be by all a - dored:

Al – le - lu – ia! Al – le - lu – ia!

Alternate tune: ENGELBERG

214 Sing, My Soul, His Wondrous Love

ST. BEES 7.7.7.7

Anonymous (1800), alt.

John Bacchus Dykes

1. Sing, my soul, his won - drous love,
2. Heav'n and earth by him were made;
3. God, the mer - ci - ful and good,
4. Sing, my soul, a - dore his name!

Who, from yon bright throne a - bove, Ev - er watch - ful
All is by his scep - ter swayed; What are we that
Bought us with the Sav - ior's blood, And, to make sal -
Let his glo - ry be thy theme: Praise him till he

o'er our race, Still to us ex - tends his grace.
he should show So much love to us be - low?
va - tion sure, Guides us by his Spir - it pure.
calls thee home; Trust his love for all to come.

Like the Murmur of the Dove's Song   215

BRIDEGROOM 8.7.8.7.6

Carl P. Daw, Jr. (1981)   Peter Cutts (1968)

1. Like the mur - mur of the dove's song, Like the chal - lenge of her flight, Like the vig - or of the wind's rush, Like the new flame's ea - ger might: Come, Ho - ly Spir - it, come.

2. To the mem - bers of Christ's bod - y, To the branch - es of the vine, To the church in faith as - sem - bled, To her midst as gift and sign: Come, Ho - ly Spir - it, come.

3. With the heal - ing of di - vi - sion, With the cease - less voice of prayer, With the pow'r to love and wit - ness, With the peace be - yond com - pare: Come, Ho - ly Spir - it, come.

216 Every Time I Feel the Spirit

FEEL THE SPIRIT Irregular

Romans 8:15-17
African-American spiritual

African-American spiritual
Adapt. and arr. by William Farley Smith (1986)

Ev-'ry time I feel the Spir-it Mov-ing in my heart, I will pray.

Yes, ev-'ry time I feel the Spir-it Mov-ing in my heart, I will pray.

1. Up - on the moun - tain, my Lord spoke, Out his
2. ⁊ Jor - dan riv - er runs right cold, Chills the

mouth came fire and smoke. All a-round me looks so
bod - y, not the soul. Ain't but one train on this

D.C.

shine, Ask my Lord if all was mine.
track, Runs to heav - en and right back.

Tune: Adapt. and arr. copyright © 1989, The United Methodist Publishing House

Come, Gracious Spirit, Heavenly Dove 217

MENDON LM

Methodist Harmonist (1821)
Adapt. and harm. by Lowell Mason

Simon Browne (1720), alt.

1. Come, gra - cious Spir - it, heav'n - ly Dove,
2. The light of truth to us dis - play,
3. Lead us to Christ, the liv - ing way,
4. Lead us to heav'n, that we may share

With light and com - fort from a - bove;
And make us know and choose thy way;
Nor let us from his pre - cepts stray;
Full - ness of joy for ev - er there;

Be thou our guard - ian, thou our guide
Plant ho - ly fear in ev - 'ry heart,
Lead us to ho - li - ness, the road
Lead us to God, our fi - nal rest,

O'er ev - 'ry thought and step pre - side.
That we from thee may ne'er de - part.
That we must take to dwell with God.
To be with him for ev - er blest.

218 **Of All the Spirit's Gifts to Me**

MEYER 8.8.8.4

Fred Pratt Green (1979)

Meyer's *Seelenfreud* (1692)

1. Of all the Spir - it's gifts to me, I
2. The Spir - it shows me love's the root Of
3. The Spir - it shows if I pos - sess A
4. Though what's a - head is mys - ter - y, And
5. We go in peace, but made a - ware That,

pray that I may nev - er cease To take and treas - ure
ev - 'ry gift sent from a - bove, Of ev - 'ry flow'r, of
love no e - vil can de - stroy; How - ev - er great is
life it - self is ours on lease, Each day the Spir - it
in a need - y world like this, Our clear - est pur - pose

most these three: Love, joy, and peace.
ev - 'ry fruit, That God is love.
my dis - tress, Then this is joy.
says to me, "Go forth in peace!"
is to share Love, joy, and peace.

Come, Holy Ghost, Our Hearts Inspire   219

WINCHESTER OLD CM

Est's *Whole Booke of Psalmes* (1592)
Harm. from *Hymns Ancient and Modern* (1861)

Charles Wesley (1740)

1. Come, Ho - ly Ghost, our hearts in - spire, Let us thine in - fluence prove; Source of the old pro - phet - ic fire, Foun - tain of life and love.
2. Come, Ho - ly Ghost (for moved by thee The proph - ets wrote and spoke), Un - lock the truth, thy - self the key, Un - seal the sa - cred book.
3. Ex - pand thy wings, ce - les - tial Dove, Brood o'er our na - ture's night; On our dis - or - dered spir - its move, And let there now be light.
4. God, through the Spir - it we shall know If thou with - in us shine, And sound, with all thy saints be - low, The depths of love di - vine.

220   O Spirit of the Living God

FOREST GREEN CMD

Acts 2
Henry H. Tweedy (1935)

Traditional English melody
Adapt. and harm. by Ralph Vaughan Williams (1906)

1. O Spir - it of the liv - ing God, Thou
2. Blow, wind of God! With wis - dom blow Un -
3. Teach us to ut - ter liv - ing words Of
4. So shall we know the pow'r of Christ Who

light and fire di - vine, De - scend up - on thy
til our minds are free From mists of er - ror,
truth which all may hear, The lan - guage all may
came this world to save; So shall we rise with

church once more, And make it tru - ly thine.
clouds of doubt, Which blind our eyes to thee.
un - der - stand When love speaks loud and clear;
him to life Which soars be - yond the grave;

Tune: Arr. copyright © 1906, *The English Hymnal*, Oxford University Press

Fill it with love and joy and pow'r, With
Burn, wing - ed fire! In - spire our lips With
Till ev - 'ry age and race and clime Shall
And earth shall win true ho - li - ness, Which

right - eous - ness and peace; Till Christ shall dwell in
flam - ing love and zeal, To preach to all thy
blend their creeds in one, And earth shall form one
makes thy chil - dren whole; Till, per - fect - ed by

hu - man hearts, And sin and sor - row cease.
great good news, God's glo - rious com - mon - weal.
fam - i - ly By whom thy will is done.
thee, we reach Cre - a - tion's glo - rious goal!

221 Onward, Christian Soldiers

ST. GERTRUDE 6.5.6.5 with refrain

Sabine Baring-Gould (1864)   Arthur Seymour Sullivan (1871)

1. On - ward, Chris - tian sol - diers, March-ing as to war,
2. Like a might - y ar - my Moves the church of God;
3. Crowns and thrones may per - ish, King-doms rise and wane,
4. On - ward, then, ye peo - ple, Join our hap - py throng:

With the cross of Je - sus Go - ing on be - fore.
Chris-tians, we are tread - ing Where the saints have trod,
But the church of Je - sus Con - stant will re - main,
Blend with ours your voic - es In the tri - umph song,

Christ, the roy - al Mas - ter, Leads a - gainst the foe;
We are not di - vid - ed; All one bod - y we—
Gates of hell can nev - er 'Gainst that church pre - vail.
Glo - ry, laud, and hon - or Un - to Christ the King,

For - ward in - to bat - tle See his ban-ners go!
One in hope and doc - trine, One in char - i - ty.
We have Christ's own prom - ise, And that can-not fail.
We through count-less a - ges With the an - gels sing.

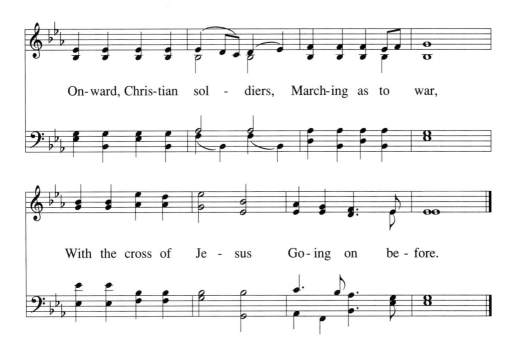

On- ward, Chris-tian sol - diers, March-ing as to war,

With the cross of Je - sus Go- ing on be - fore.

222 God of Grace and God of Glory

CWM RHONDDA 8.7.8.7.8.7.7

Harry Emerson Fosdick (1930), alt.

John Hughes (1905)

1. God of grace and God of glo - ry,
2. Lo! the hosts of e - vil round us
3. Cure thy chil - dren's war - ring mad - ness,
4. Save us from weak res - ig - na - tion

On thy peo - ple pour thy pow'r;
Scorn thy Christ, as - sail his ways!
Bend our pride to thy con - trol;
To the e - vils we de - plore;

Crown thine an - cient Chur - ch's sto - ry;
From the fears that long have bound us
Shame our wan - ton, self - ish glad - ness,
Let the gift of thy sal - va - tion

Bring her bud to glo - rious flow'r.
Free our hearts to faith and praise:
Rich in things and poor in soul.
Be our glo - ry ev - er - more.

Grant us wis - dom, grant us cour - age,
Grant us wis - dom, grant us cour - age,
Grant us wis - dom, grant us cour - age,
Grant us wis - dom, grant us cour - age,

For the fac - ing of this hour,
For the liv - ing of these days,
Lest we miss thy king - dom's goal,
Serv - ing thee whom we a - dore,

For the fac - ing of this hour.
For the liv - ing of these days.
Lest we miss thy king - dom's goal.
Serv - ing thee whom we a - dore.

223   Christ Is Made the Sure Foundation

WESTMINSTER ABBEY 8.7.8.7.8.7

Angularis fundamentum (11th C.)
Trans. by John Mason Neale (1851), alt.

Adapt. from an anthem of Henry Purcell

1. Christ is made the sure foun-da-tion, Christ the head and
2. To this tem-ple where we call you, Come, O Lord of
3. Grant, we pray, to all your peo-ple, All the grace they

cor-ner-stone; Cho-sen of the Lord, and pre-cious,
hosts, to-day; With your wont-ed lov-ing kind-ness
ask to gain; What they gain from you for ev-er

Bind-ing all the Church in one; Ho-ly Zi-on's
Hear your ser-vants as they pray, And your full-est
With the bless-ed to re-tain, And here-af-ter

help for ev-er, And her con-fi-dence a-lone.
ben-e-dic-tion Shed in all its bright ar-ray.
in your glo-ry Ev-er-more with you to reign.

In Christ There Is No East or West   224

MC KEE CM

African-American spiritual
Jubilee Songs (1884)
Adapt. by Harry T. Burleigh (1940)

Galatians 3:23
John Oxenham (1908)

1. In Christ there is no east or west, In
2. In him shall true hearts ev - 'ry - where Their
3. Join hands, dis - ci - ples in the faith, What -
4. In Christ now meet both east and west, In

him no south or north, But one great fam - 'ly
high com - mun - ion find; His serv - ice is the
e'er your race may be! Who serve each oth - er
him meet south and north, All Christ - ly souls are

bound by love Through - out the whole wide earth.
gold - en cord Close - bind - ing hu - man - kind.
in Christ's love Are sure - ly kin to me.
one in him, Through - out the whole wide earth.

225 Blest Be the Tie That Binds

DENNIS SM

John Fawcett (1782)

Johann Georg Nägeli
Arr. by Lowell Mason (1845)

1. Blest be the tie that binds Our hearts in
2. Be - fore our Fa - ther's throne We pour our
3. We share each oth - er's woes, Each oth - er's
4. From sor - row, toil, and pain, And sin we

Chris - tian love; The fel - low - ship of
ar - dent prayers; Our fears, our hopes, our
bur - dens bear; And of - ten for each
shall be free; And per - fect love and

kin - dred minds Is like to that a - bove.
aims are one, Our com - forts and our cares.
oth - er flows The sym - pa - thiz - ing tear.
joy shall reign Through all e - ter - ni - ty.

I Love Thy Kingdom, Lord

226

ST. THOMAS SM

Aaron Williams (1770)
Harm. by Lowell Mason

Timothy Dwight (1880)

1. I love thy king - dom, Lord, The house of thine a - bode, The Church our blest Re - deem - er saved With his own pre - cious blood.
2. For her my tears shall fall; For her my prayers as - cend; To her my cares and toils be giv'n, Till toils and cares shall end.
3. Be - yond my high - est joy I prize her heav'n - ly ways, Her sweet com - mun - ion, sol - emn vows, Her hymns of love and praise.
4. Je - sus, thou friend di - vine, Our Sav - ior and our King, Thy hand from ev - 'ry snare and foe Shall great de - liv - 'rance bring.
5. Sure as thy truth shall last, To Zi - on shall be giv'n The bright - est glo - ries earth can yield, And bright - er bliss of heav'n.

227 The Church's One Foundation

AURELIA 7.6.7.6 D

Samuel J. Stone (1866)

Samuel Sebastian Wesley (1864)

1. The chur-ch's one foun - da - tion Is Je - sus Christ her
2. E - lect from ev - 'ry na - tion, Yet one o'er all the
3. Though with a scorn - ful won - der We see her sore op -
4. Mid toil and trib - u - la - tion, And tu - mult of her
5. Yet she on earth hath un - ion With God the Three - in -

Lord; She is his new cre - a - tion By wa - ter and the
earth; Her char - ter of sal - va - tion, One Lord, one faith, one
pressed, By schis-ms rent a - sun - der, By her - e - sies dis -
war, She waits the con - sum - ma - tion Of peace for ev - er -
One, And mys - tic sweet com - mu - nion With those whose rest is

Word. From heav'n he came and sought her To
birth; One ho - ly name she bless - es, Par -
tressed, Yet saints their watch are keep - ing; Their
more; Till, with the vi - sion glo - rious, Her
won. O hap - py ones and ho - ly! Lord,

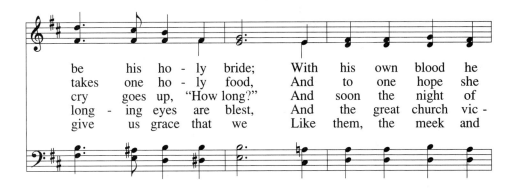

be	his	ho -	ly	bride;	With	his	own	blood	he
takes	one	ho -	ly	food,	And	to	one	hope	she
cry	goes	up,	"How	long?"	And	soon	the	night	of
long -	ing	eyes	are	blest,	And	the	great	church	vic -
give	us	grace	that	we	Like	them,	the	meek	and

bought	her,	And	for	her	life	he	died.
press -	es,	With	ev -	'ry	grace	en -	dued.
weep -	ing	Shall	be	the	morn	of	song.
to -	rious	Shall	be	the	church	at	rest.
low -	ly,	On	high	may	dwell	with	thee.

228   O Zion, Haste

TIDINGS 11.10.11.10 with refrain

Mary A. Thomson (1894)

James Walch (1875)

1. O Zi - on, haste, thy mis - sion high ful - fill - ing,
2. Be - hold how man - y thou-sands still are ly - ing
3. Pro - claim to ev - 'ry peo - ple, tongue, and na - tion
4. Give of thine own to bear the mes - sage glo-rious;

To tell to all the world that God is light,
Bound in the dark - some pris - on - house of sin,
That God, in whom they live and move, is love;
Give of thy wealth to speed them on their way;

That he who made all na - tions is not will - ing
With none to tell them of the Sav - ior's dy - ing,
Tell how he stooped to save his lost cre - a - tion,
Pour out thy soul for them in prayer vic - to - rious;

One soul should per - ish, lost in shades of night.
Or of the life he died for them to win.
And died on earth that we might live a - bove.
O Zi - on, haste to bring the bright - er day.

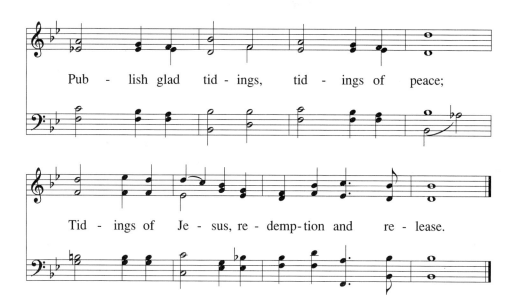

Pub - lish glad tid - ings, tid - ings of peace;

Tid - ings of Je - sus, re - demp-tion and re - lease.

229

Come, Labor On

ORA LABORA 4.10.10.10.4

Jane Laurie Borthwick (1859, 1863)　　　　　Thomas Tertius Noble (1918)

1. Come, la-bor on. Who dares stand i - dle on the har - vest plain While all a - round us waves the gold - en grain? And to each ser - vant
2. Come, la-bor on. The en - e - my is watch-ing night and day, To sow the tares, to snatch the seed a - way; While we in sleep our
3. Come, la-bor on. A - way with gloom - y doubts and faith - less fear! No arm so weak but may do serv - ice here: By fee - blest a - gents
4. Come, la-bor on. Claim the high call - ing an - gels can - not share: To young and old the gos - pel glad - ness bear. Re - deem the time— its
5. Come, la-bor on. No time for rest, till glows the west - ern sky, Till the long shad - ows o'er our path-way lie And a glad sound comes

does the Mas - ter say, "Go work to - day."
du - ty have for - got, He slum - bers not.
may our God ful - fill His right - eous will.
hours so swift - ly fly— The night draws nigh.
with the set - ting sun: "Ser - vants, well done."

230 Wonderful Words of Life

WORDS OF LIFE 8.6.8.6.6.6 with refrain

Philip P. Bliss (1874)   Philip P. Bliss (1874)

1. Sing them o - ver a - gain to me, Won-der-ful words of
2. Christ, the bless-ed one, gives to all Won-der-ful words of
3. Sweet - ly ech - o the gos - pel call, Won-der-ful words of

life; Let me more of their beau - ty see,
life; Sin - ner, list to the lov - ing call,
life; Of - fer par - don and peace to all,

Won-der - ful words of life; Words of life and
Won-der - ful words of life; All so free - ly
Won-der - ful words of life; Je - sus, on - ly

beau - ty Teach me faith and du - ty.
giv - en, Woo - ing us to heav - en.
Sav - ior, Sanc - ti - fy for ev - er.

Beau - ti - ful words, won - der - ful words,

won - der - ful words of life. life.

231 O Word of God Incarnate

MUNICH 7.6.7.6 D

Neuvermehrtes Meiningisches Gesangbuch (1693)
Harm. by Felix Mendelssohn (1847)

William W. How (1867)

1. O Word of God in - car - nate, O Wis - dom from on high, O Truth un - changed, un - chang - ing, O Light of our dark sky: We praise you for the ra - diance That

2. The church from you, our Sav - ior, Re - ceived the gift di - vine, And still that light is lift - ed O'er all the earth to shine. It is the sa - cred ves - sel Where

3. The Scrip - ture is a ban - ner Be - fore God's host un - furled; It is a shin - ing bea - con A - bove the dark - ling world. It is the chart and com - pass That

4. O make your church, dear Sav - ior, A lamp of pur - est gold, To bear be - fore the na - tions Your true light as of old. O teach your wan - d'ring pil - grims By

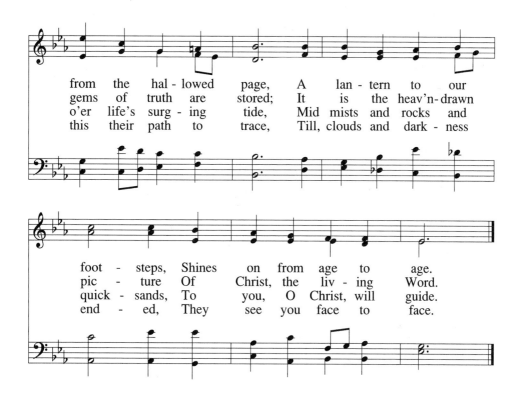

from the hal - lowed page, A lan - tern to our
gems of truth are stored; It is the heav'n-drawn
o'er life's surg - ing tide, Mid mists and rocks and
this their path to trace, Till, clouds and dark - ness

foot - steps, Shines on from age to age.
pic - ture Of Christ, the liv - ing Word.
quick - sands, To you, O Christ, will guide.
end - ed, They see you face to face.

232 Break Thou the Bread of Life
BREAD OF LIFE 6.4.6.4 D

Mary Ann Lathbury (1877), alt.　　　　　　　　　　William Fisk Sherwin (1877), alt.

1. Break thou the bread of life, Dear Lord, to me,
2. Bless thou the truth, dear Lord, Now un - to me,

As thou didst break the loaves Be - side the sea;
As thou didst bless the bread By Gal - i - lee;

Be - yond the sa - cred page I seek thee, Lord;
Then shall all bond - age cease, All fet - ters fall;

My spir - it pants for thee, O liv - ing Word!
And I shall find my peace, My all in all.

Thanks to God Whose Word Was Spoken 233

WYLDE GREEN 8.7.8.7.4.7

R. T. Brooks (1954)

Peter Cutts (1966)

1. Thanks to God whose Word was spo - ken In the deed that made the earth. His the voice that called a na - tion; His the fires that tried its worth. God has spo - ken; Praise him for his o - pen Word.

2. Thanks to God whose Word In - car - nate, Our new life in him be - gan. Deeds and words and death and ris - ing, Tell the grace in heav - en's plan. God has spo - ken; Praise him for his o - pen Word.

3. Thanks to God whose Word is an-swered By the Spir - it's voice with - in. Here we drink of joy un - meas-ured, Life re - deemed from death and sin. God is speak - ing; Praise him for his o - pen Word.

234   One Bread, One Body

1 Corinthians 10:16, 17, 12:4; Galatians 3:28; The *Didache* 9
John B. Foley, SJ (1978)   John B. Foley, SJ (1978)

One bread, one bod-y, one Lord of all, one cup of bless - ing which we bless. And we, though man-y, through - out the earth, we are one

Last time to coda ✛

bod - y in this one Lord.

Verses

1. Gen - tile or Jew, ser - vant or free,
2. Man - y the gifts, man - y the works,
3. Grain for the fields, scat-tered and grown,

wom-an or man no more.
one in the Lord of all.
gath-ered to one for all.

D.C. ✛ Coda

Lord.

Bread of the World, in Mercy Broken   235

EUCHARISTIC HYMN 9.8.9.8

Reginald Heber (1827)   John S. B. Hodges (1868)

1. Bread of the world, in mer - cy bro - ken,
2. Look on the heart by sor - row bro - ken,

Wine of the soul, in mer - cy shed,
Look on the tears by sin - ners shed,

By whom the words of life were spo - ken,
And be thy feast to us the to - ken

And in whose death our sins are dead:
That by thy grace our souls are fed.

I Come with Joy

236

LAND OF REST CM

American folk melody
Brian Wren (1969, rev. 1995)
Harm. by Annabel M. Buchanan (1938)

1. I come with joy, a child of God, For-
2. I come with Chris-tians far and near To
3. As Christ breaks bread, and bids us share, Each
4. The Spir-it of the ris-en Christ, Un-
5. To-geth-er met, to-geth-er bound, By

giv-en, loved, and free, The life of Je-sus
find, as all are fed, The new com-mu-ni-
proud di-vi-sion ends. The love that made us,
seen, but al-ways near, Is in such friend-ship
all that God has done, We'll go with joy, to

to re-call, In love laid down for me.
ty of love In Christ's com-mu-nion bread.
makes us one, And stran-gers now are friends.
bet-ter known, A-live a-mong us here.
give the world The love that makes us one.

Living Word of God Eternal   237

KOMM, O KOMM, DU GEIST DES LEBENS 8.7.8.7.8.7

Jeffery Rowthorn (1983)   *Neuvermehrtes Meiningisches Gesangbuch* (1693)

1. Liv-ing word of God e-ter-nal, Lay-ing claim to ev-'ry age, Je-sus, speak through all our speak-ing, Bring to life the Bi-ble's page; Let your gos-pel, heard and heed-ed, Set our course of pil-grim-age.

2. Lov-ing Sav-ior, whose em-brac-es Our true selves a-lone un-mask, In this fel-low-ship's small com-pass Train us for our com-mon task: By our love to grow more like you And to dare what you will ask.

3. Liv-ing bread come down from heav-en, Bro-ken, shared, dis-trib-ut-ed, Feed us, gath-ered at this ta-ble, With your grace un-lim-it-ed, And as ser-vants then em-ploy us Till this hun-gry world is fed.

4. Lov-ing Spir-it, pray-ing in us, Giv-ing voice to all our sighs, Show the wide-ness of your mer-cy To deaf ears and blind-ed eyes; Free our tongues to come be-fore you With our neigh-bors' joys and cries.

5. May your word a-mong us spo-ken, May the lov-ing which we dare, May your bread a-mong us bro-ken, May the prayers in which we share Dai-ly make us faith-ful peo-ple, Liv-ing signs, Lord, of your care.

Text: Copyright © 1983, Hope Publishing Co.

238 Let Us Break Bread Together

LET US BREAK BREAD 10.10.6.8.7

American folk hymn
Harm. by David Hurd (1968)

American folk hymn

1. Let us break bread to - geth - er on our knees;
2. Let us drink wine to - geth - er on our knees;
3. Let us praise God to - geth - er on our knees;

Let us break bread to - geth - er on our knees;
Let us drink wine to - geth - er on our knees;
Let us praise God to - geth - er on our knees;

When I fall on my knees, With my
face to the ris - ing sun, O Lord, have
mer - cy on me.

Jesus, Thou Joy of Loving Hearts   239
QUEBEC LM

Attr. to Bernard of Clairvaux (12th C.)
Trans. by Ray Palmer (1858)   Henry Baker (1854)

1. Je - sus, thou joy of lov - ing hearts,
2. Thy truth un - changed hath ev - er stood;
3. We taste thee, O thou liv - ing bread,
4. Our rest - less spir - its yearn for thee,
5. O Je - sus, ev - er with us stay,

Thou fount of life, thou light of all,
Thou sav - est those that on thee call;
And long to feast up - on thee still;
Wher - e'er our change - ful lot is cast,
Make all our mo - ments calm and bright;

From the best bliss that earth im - parts
To them that seek thee thou art good,
We drink of thee, the foun - tain - head,
Glad when thy gra - cious smile we see,
O chase the night of sin a - way,

We turn, un - filled, to heed thy call.
To them that find thee, all in all.
And thirst our souls from thee to fill.
Blest when our faith can hold thee fast.
Shed o'er the world thy ho - ly light.

240

Gather Us In

GATHER US IN Irregular

Marty Haugen (1982)   Marty Haugen (1982)

1. Here in this place new light is stream-ing,
2. We are the young— our lives are a mys-t'ry,
3. Here we will take the wine and the wa-ter,
4. Not in the dark of build-ings con-fin-ing,

Now is the dark-ness van-ished a-way,
We are the old— who yearn for your face,
Here we will take the bread of new birth,
Not in some heav-en, light-years a-way,

See in this space our fears and our dream-ings, Brought here to
We have been sung through-out all of his-t'ry, Called to be
Here you shall call your sons and your daugh-ters, Call us a-
here in this place the new light is shin-ing, Now is the

you in the light of this day!
light to the whole hu-man race.
new to be salt for the earth.
King-dom, now is the day.

Gath-er us in—the lost and for-sak-en, Gath-er us in—the
Gath-er us in—the rich and the haugh-ty, Gath-er us in—the
Give us to drink the wine of com-pas-sion, Give us to eat the
Gath-er us in and hold us for ev-er, Gath-er us in and

blind and the lame; Call to us now, and
proud and the strong; Give us a heart so
bread that is you; Nour-ish us well, and
make us your own; Gath-er us in— all

we shall a-wak-en, We shall a-rise at the
meek and so low-ly, Give us the cour-age to
teach us to fash-ion Lives that are ho-ly and
peo-ples to-geth-er, Fire of love in our

sound of our name.
en - ter the song.
hearts that are true.
flesh and our bone.

241   Deck Thyself, My Soul, with Gladness

SCHMUCKE DICH LMD

John 6:35-58, Johann Franck (1649)
Trans. by Catherine Winkworth (1863), alt.

Johann Crüger (1653)

1. Deck thy - self, my soul, with glad - ness,
2. Sun, who all my life dost bright - en;
3. Je - sus, bread of life, I pray thee,

Leave the gloom - y haunts of sad - ness.
Light, who dost my soul en - light - en;
Let me glad - ly here o - bey thee;

Come in - to the day - light's splen - dor;
Joy, the best that an - y know - eth;
Nev - er to my hurt in - vit - ed,

There with joy thy prais - es ren - der
Fount, whence all my be - ing flow - eth;
Be thy love with love re - quit - ed.

Un - to Christ, whose grace un - bound - ed
At thy feet I cry, my Mak - er,
From this ban - quet let me meas - ure,

Hath this won - drous ban - quet found - ed.
Let me be a fit par - tak - er
Lord, how vast and deep its treas - ure;

High o'er all the heav'ns he reign - eth,
Of this bless - ed food from heav - en,
Through the gifts thou here dost give me,

Yet to dwell with thee he deign - eth.
For our good, thy glo - ry, giv - en.
As thy guest in heav'n re - ceive me.

242

Gift of Finest Wheat

BICENTENNIAL CM with refrain

John 6:34, 10:1-5; 1 Corinthians 10:16-17
Omer Westendorf (1977)   Robert E. Kreutz (1977)

You sat-is-fy the hun-gry heart With gift of fin-est wheat.

Come, give to us, O sav-ing Lord, The bread of life to eat.

1. As when the shep - herd calls his sheep, They
2. With joy - ful lips we sing to you Our
3. Is not the cup we bless and share The
4. The mys - t'ry of your pres - ence, Lord, No
5. You give your - self to us, O Lord; Then

know and heed his voice, So when you call your
praise and grat - i - tude, That you should count us
blood of Christ out-poured? Do not one cup, one
mor - tal tongue can tell; Whom all the world can -
self - less let us be, To serve each oth - er

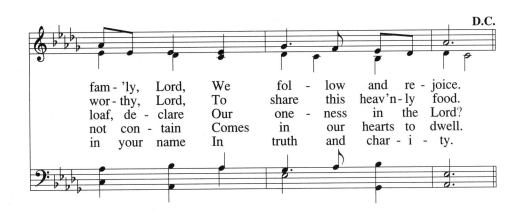

D.C.

fam - 'ly, Lord, We fol - low and re - joice.
wor - thy, Lord, To share this heav'n - ly food.
loaf, de - clare Our one - ness in the Lord?
not con - tain Comes in our hearts to dwell.
in your name In truth and char - i - ty.

243
Here, O My Lord
ADORO TE DEVOTE 10.10.10.10

Thomas Aquinas (c. 1225-1274)
Trans. James Russell Woodford (1850)

Benedictine plainsong, Mode V (13th C.)
Harm. from *Hymnal for Colleges and Schools* (1956)

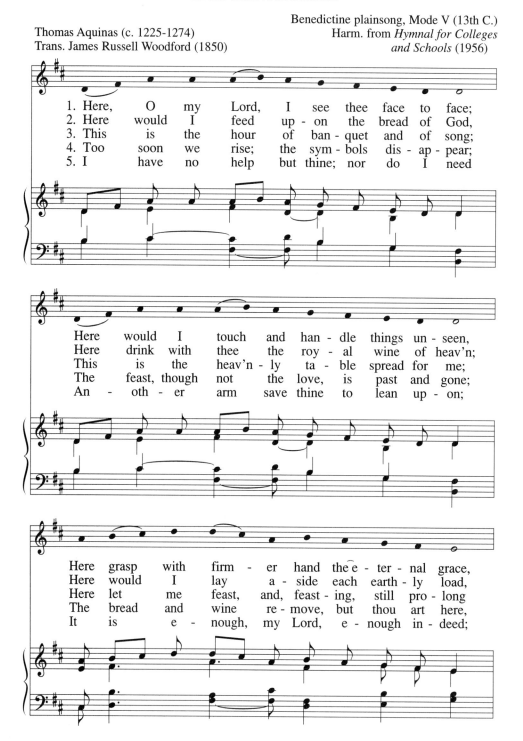

1. Here, O my Lord, I see thee face to face;
2. Here would I feed up-on the bread of God,
3. This is the hour of ban-quet and of song;
4. Too soon we rise; the sym-bols dis-ap-pear;
5. I have no help but thine; nor do I need

Here would I touch and han-dle things un-seen,
Here drink with thee the roy-al wine of heav'n;
This is the heav'n-ly ta-ble spread for me;
The feast, though not the love, is past and gone;
An-oth-er arm save thine to lean up-on;

Here grasp with firm-er hand the e-ter-nal grace,
Here would I lay a-side each earth-ly load,
Here let me feast, and, feast-ing, still pro-long
The bread and wine re-move, but thou art here,
It is e-nough, my Lord, e-nough in-deed;

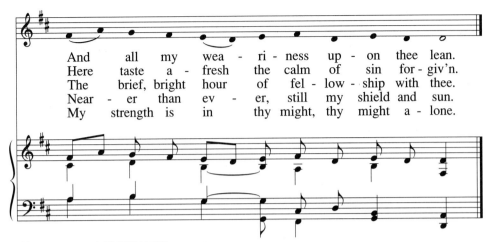

And all my wea - ri - ness up - on thee lean.
Here taste a - fresh the calm of sin for - giv'n.
The brief, bright hour of fel - low - ship with thee.
Near - er than ev - er, still my shield and sun.
My strength is in thy might, thy might a - lone.

Alternate tune: MORECAMBE

244 Eat This Bread

John 6
Adapt. by Robert J. Batastini and the Taizé Community (1984)   Jacques Berthier (1984)

Refrain

Eat this bread, drink this cup, come to me and nev-er be hun-gry.

Eat this bread, drink this cup, trust in me and you will not thirst.

Verses

1. I am the bread of life, the
2. Your an-ces-tors ate man-na in the des-ert, but
3. Eat my flesh and drink my blood, and
4. An-y-one who eats this bread, will
5. If you be-lieve and eat this bread,

true bread sent from the Fa - ther. **D.C.**

this is the bread come down from heav - en. **D.C.**

I will raise you up on the last day. **D.C.**

live for ev - er. **D.C.**

you will have e - ter - nal life. **D.C.**

Flute

245 We Know That Christ Is Raised

ENGELBERG 10.10.10 with alleluia

Romans 6:4, 9
John Brownlow Geyer (1969)

Charles Villiers Stanford (1904)

1. We know that Christ is raised and dies no more.
2. We share by wa - ter in his sav - ing death.
3. The Fa - ther's splen - dor clothes the Son with life.
4. A new cre - a - tion comes to life and grows

Em - braced by death, he broke its fear - ful hold,
Re - born, we share with him an East - er life
The Spir - it's fis - sion shakes the Church of God.
As Christ's new bod - y takes on flesh and blood.

And our de - spair he turned to blaz - ing joy.
As liv - ing mem - bers of our Sav - ior Christ.
Bap - tized, we live with God the Three - in - One.
The u - ni - verse re - stored and whole will sing:

Text: Copyright © 1972, John B. Geyer

Al – le - lu – ia!
Al – le - lu – ia!
Al – le - lu – ia!

Al – le - lu – ia!

246   May the Grace of Christ Our Savior
STAINER 8.7.8.7

John Newton (1779)

John Stainer (1898)

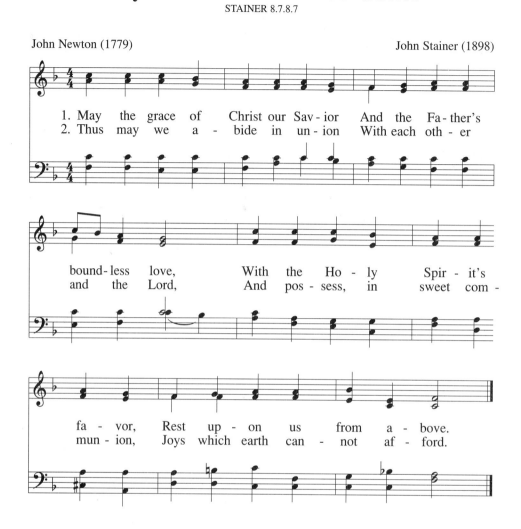

1. May the grace of Christ our Sav-ior And the Fa-ther's
2. Thus may we a - bide in un-ion With each oth - er

bound-less love, With the Ho - ly Spir - it's
and the Lord, And pos - sess, in sweet com -

fa - vor, Rest up - on us from a - bove.
mun - ion, Joys which earth can - not af - ford.

I Need Thee Every Hour

NEED 6.4.6.4 with refrain

247

John 15:5
Annie S. Hawks (1872)　　　　　　　　　　　　　　　Robert Lowry (1873)

1. I need thee ev-'ry hour, Most gra - cious Lord;
2. I need thee ev-'ry hour; Stay thou near - by;
3. I need thee ev-'ry hour, In joy or pain;
4. I need thee ev-'ry hour; Teach me thy will;
5. I need thee ev-'ry hour, Most Ho - ly One;

No ten - der voice like thine Can peace af - ford.
Temp - ta - tions lose their pow'r When thou art nigh.
Come quick - ly and a - bide, Or life is vain.
And thy rich prom - is - es In me ful - fill.
O make me thine in - deed, Thou bless - ed Son.

I need thee, O I need thee; Ev - 'ry hour I need thee;

O bless me now, my Sav - ior, I come to thee.

248   Just As I Am, without One Plea

WOODWORTH LM

Charlotte Elliott (1835)   William B. Bradbury (1849)

1. Just as I am, without one plea,
2. Just as I am, though tossed about
3. Just as I am, poor, wretch - ed, blind;
4. Just as I am, thou wilt re - ceive;
5. Just as I am, thy love un - known
6. Just as I am, of thy great love

But that thy blood was shed for me,
With man - y a con - flict, man - y a doubt;
Sight, rich - es, heal - ing of the mind,
Wilt wel - come, par - don, cleanse, re - lieve,
Has bro - ken ev - 'ry bar - rier down;
The breadth, length, depth, and height to prove,

And that thou bidd'st me come to thee,
Fight - ings and fears with - in, with - out,
Yea, all I need, in thee to find,
Be - cause thy prom - ise I be - lieve,
Now to be thine, yea, thine a - lone,
Here for a sea - son, then a - bove:

O Lamb of God, I come, I come.

I Sought the Lord

249

FAITH 10.10.10.6

Matthew 14:22-23
Anonymous (c. 1878)

Harold Moyer (1969)

1. I sought the Lord, and af-ter-ward I knew He
2. Thou didst reach forth thy hand and mine en-fold, I
3. I find, I walk, I love, but O the whole Of

moved my soul to seek him, seek-ing me;
walked and sank not on the storm-vexed sea;
love is but my an-swer, Lord, to thee!

It was not I that found, O Sav-ior
'Twas not so much that I on thee took
For thou wert long be - fore-hand with my

true, No, I was found of thee.
hold As thou, dear Lord, on me.
soul; Al - ways thou lov - edst me.

250 There Is a Balm in Gilead

BALM IN GILEAD Irregular with refrain

Jeremiah 8:22
African-American spiritual

African-American spiritual
Acc. by Robert J. Batastini (1987)

Refrain

There is a balm in Gil - e - ad To make the wound - ed whole, There is a balm in Gil - e - ad To heal the sin - sick soul.

Verses

1. Some - times I feel dis - cour - aged And
2. If you can - not preach like Pe - ter, If you
3. Don't ev - er feel dis - cour - aged, For

think my work's in vain, But then the Ho - ly
can - not pray like Paul, You can tell the love of
Je - sus is your friend; And if you lack for

D.C.

Spir - it Re - vives my soul a - gain.
Je - sus, And say, "He died for all!"
knowl - edge He'll ne'er re - fuse to lend.

251 Take My Life

HENDON 7.7.7.7.7

Frances Ridley Havergal (1874)

H. A. César Malan (1827)

1. Take my life, and let it be Con - se - crat - ed,
2. Take my hands, and let them move At the im - pulse
3. Take my voice, and let me sing, Al - ways, on - ly,
4. Take my sil - ver and my gold, Not a mite would
5. Take my will, and make it thine; It shall be no
6. Take my love; my Lord, I pour At thy feet its

Lord, to thee. Take my mo - ments and my days;
of thy love. Take my feet, and let them be
for my King. Take my lips, and let them be
I with - hold; Take my in - tel - lect, and use
long - er mine. Take my heart, it is thine own;
treas - ure store. Take my - self, and I will be

Let them flow in cease - less praise,
Swift and beau - ti - ful for thee,
Filled with mes - sa - ges from thee,
Ev - 'ry pow'r as thou shalt choose,
It shall be thy roy - al throne,
Ev - er, on - ly, all for thee,

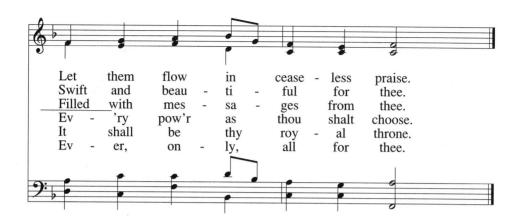

Let them flow in cease - less praise.
Swift and beau - ti - ful for thee.
Filled with mes - sa - ges from thee.
Ev - 'ry pow'r as thou shalt choose.
It shall be thy roy - al throne.
Ev - er, on - ly, all for thee.

252   It Is Well with My Soul

VILLE DU HAVRE 11.8.11.9 with refrain

Horatio G. Spafford (1873)   Philip P. Bliss (1876)

1. When peace, like a riv-er, at-tend-eth my way, When sor-rows like sea bil-lows roll; What-ev-er my lot, thou hast taught me to say, It is well, it is well with my soul.

2. Though Sa-tan should buf-fet, though tri-als should come, Let this blest as-sur-ance con-trol, That Christ has re-gard-ed my help-less es-tate, And hath shed his own blood for my soul.

3. My sin, oh, the bliss of this glo-ri-ous thought! My sin, not in part but the whole, Is nailed to the cross, and I bear it no more, Praise the Lord, praise the Lord, O my soul!

4. And, Lord, haste the day when my faith shall be sight, The clouds be rolled back as a scroll; The trump shall re-sound, and the Lord shall de-scend, E-ven so, it is well with my soul.

253 We Remember

Marty Haugen (1980)   Marty Haugen (1980)

We re-mem-ber how you loved us to your death,

and still we cel-e-brate, for you are with us here;

and we be-lieve that we will see you when you come

in your glo-ry, Lord. We re-mem-ber, we

Last time to coda

cel-e-brate, we be-lieve.

D.C.

Verses

1. Here, a mil - lion wound-ed souls are yearn-ing just to
2. Now we re - cre - ate your love, we bring the bread and
3. Christ, the Fa-ther's great "A-men" to all the hopes and
4. See the face of Christ re - vealed in ev - 'ry per-son

touch you and be healed. Gath-er all your
wine to share a meal. Sign of grace and
dreams of ev - 'ry heart, Peace be-yond all
stand - ing by your side, Gift to one an-

peo - ple, and hold them to your heart.
mer - cy, the pres - ence of the Lord.
tell - ing, and free - dom from all fear.
oth - er, and tem - ples of your love.

⊕ Coda

Take Time to Be Holy

HOLINESS 6.5.6.5 D

1 Peter 1:16
William D. Longstaff (c. 1882)

George C. Stebbins (1890)

254

1. Take time to be ho - ly, Speak oft with thy Lord;
2. Take time to be ho - ly, The world rush - es on;
3. Take time to be ho - ly, Let him be thy guide,
4. Take time to be ho - ly, Be calm in thy soul,

A - bide in him al - ways, And feed on his word.
Spend much time in se - cret With Je - sus a - lone.
And run not be - fore him, What - ev - er be - tide.
Each thought and each mo - tive Be - neath his con - trol.

Make friends of God's chil - dren, Help those who are weak,
By look - ing to Je - sus, Like him thou shalt be;
In joy or in sor - row, Still fol - low the Lord,
Thus led by his spir - it To foun - tains of love,

For - get - ting in noth - ing His bless - ing to seek.
Thy friends in thy con - duct His like - ness shall see.
And, look - ing to Je - sus, Still trust in his word.
Thou soon shalt be fit - ted For serv - ice a - bove.

255   Come to the Water

Isaiah 55:1, 2; Matthew 11:28-30
John B. Foley, SJ (1978)

John B. Foley, SJ (1978)

1. O   let   all   who   thirst,   let them come to the wa-ter. And let all who have noth-ing, let them come to the Lord:
2. And let all who seek, let them come to the wa-ter. And let all who have noth-ing, let them come to the Lord:
3. And let all who toil, let them come to the wa-ter. And let all who are wea-ry, let them come to the Lord:
4. And let all the poor, let them come to the wa-ter. Bring the ones who are lad-en, bring them all to the Lord:

With-out mon-ey,   with-out price.
With-out mon-ey,   with-out strife.
All   who la-bor,   with-out rest.
Bring the chil-dren   with-out might.

Why   should you   pay   the   price,   ex-cept for the
Why   should you   spend your   life,   ex-cept for the
How   can   your   soul   find   rest,   ex-cept for the
Eas - y   the   load   and   light: come to the

Lord?
Lord?
Lord?
Lord.

Keyboard only

1. 3.

4.

256   Savior, Like a Shepherd Lead Us

BRADBURY 8.7.8.7 D

John 10:1-29
Attr. to Dorothy A. Thrupp (1836)   William B. Bradbury (1859)

1. Sav - ior, like a shep-herd lead us,
2. We are thine, thou dost be - friend us,
3. Thou hast prom-ised to re - ceive us,
4. Ear - ly let us seek thy fa - vor,

Much we need thy ten - der care;
Be the guard - ian of our way;
Poor and sin - ful though we be;
Ear - ly let us do thy will;

In thy pleas - ant pas - tures feed us,
Keep thy flock, from sin de - fend us,
Thou hast mer - cy to re - lieve us,
Bless - ed Lord and on - ly Sav - ior,

For our use thy folds pre - pare.
Seek us when we go a - stray.
Grace to cleanse and pow'r to free.
With thy love our bos - oms fill.

Bless - ed Je - sus, bless - ed Je - sus! Thou hast
Bless - ed Je - sus, bless - ed Je - sus! Hear, O
Bless - ed Je - sus, bless - ed Je - sus! We will
Bless - ed Je - sus, bless - ed Je - sus! Thou hast

bought us, thine we are. Bless - ed Je - sus, bless - ed
hear us when we pray. Bless - ed Je - sus, bless - ed
ear - ly turn to thee. Bless - ed Je - sus, bless - ed
loved us, love us still. Bless - ed Je - sus, bless - ed

Je - sus! Thou hast bought us, thine we are.
Je - sus! Hear, O hear us when we pray.
Je - sus! We will ear - ly turn to thee.
Je - sus! Thou hast loved us, love us still.

257   I Am Thine, O Lord

I AM THINE 10.7.10.7 with refrain

Fanny J. Crosby (1875)

William H. Doane (1875)

1. I am thine, O Lord, I have heard thy voice, And it
2. Con - se - crate me now to thy serv - ice, Lord, By the
3. O, the pure de - light of a sin - gle hour That be -
4. There are depths of love that I can - not know Till I

told thy love to me; But I long to rise in the
pow'r of grace di - vine; Let my soul look up with a
fore thy throne I spend, When I kneel in prayer, and with
cross the nar - row sea; There are heights of joy that I

arms of faith, And be clos - er drawn to thee.
stead - fast hope, And my will be lost in thine.
thee, my God, I com - mune as friend with friend!
may not reach Till I rest in peace with thee.

Draw me near - er, near - er, bless - ed Lord, To the

cross where thou hast died; Draw me near - er, near - er,

near - er, bless - ed Lord, To thy pre - cious, bleed - ing side.

258 Blessed Assurance: Jesus Is Mine

ASSURANCE 9.10.9.9 with refrain

St. 1&3, Fanny J. Crosby (1873)
St. 2, Marie J. Post (1985)

Phoebe P. Knapp (1873)

1. Bless-ed as - sur - ance: Je-sus is mine! Oh, what a
2. Joy - ful con - fes - sion: I am his own! Fol - low-ing
3. Per - fect sub - mis - sion: all is at rest, I in my

fore - taste of glo - ry di - vine! Heir of sal -
Je - sus, I'm nev - er a - lone. Born of his
Sav - ior am hap - py and blest; Watch-ing and

va - tion, pur - chase of God, Born of his
Spir - it, I am re - stored, Chal - lenged to
wait - ing, look - ing a - bove, Filled with his

Spir - it, washed in his blood.
serve my Sav - ior and Lord.
good - ness, kept in his love.

This is my sto - ry, this is my song, Prais-ing my
Sav - ior all the day long; This is my sto - ry, this is my
song, Prais-ing my Sav - ior all the day long.

259   O Happy Day, That Fixed My Choice

HAPPY DAY LM with refrain

2 Chronicles 15:15
Philip Doddridge (1755)
Refrain from *Wesleyan Sacred Harp* (1854)

Anonymous
Refrain attr. to Edward F. Rimbault (1854)

1. O hap - py day, that fixed my choice On thee, my
2. O hap - py bond, that seals my vows To him who
3. It's done: the great trans - ac - tion's done! I am the
4. Now rest, my long - di - vid - ed heart, Fixed on this
5. High heav'n, that heard the sol - emn vow, That vow re -

Sav - ior and my God! Well may this glow - ing heart re -
mer - its all my love! Let cheer - ful an - thems fill his
Lord's and he is mine; He drew me and I fol - lowed
bliss - ful cen - ter, rest. Here have I found a no - bler
newed shall dai - ly hear, Till in life's lat - est hour I

joice, And tell its rap - tures all a - broad.
house, While to that sa - cred shrine I move.
on, Charmed to con - fess the voice di - vine.
part; Here heav'n - ly pleas - ures fill my breast.
bow And bless in death a bond so dear.

Hap - py day, hap - py day, When Je - sus washed my sins a -

way! He taught me how to watch and pray, And live re-

joic - ing ev - 'ry day. Hap - py day, hap - py

day, When Je - sus washed my sins a - way!

260   In the Cross of Christ I Glory
RATHBUN 8.7.8.7

John Bowring (1825)

Ithamar Conkey (1849)

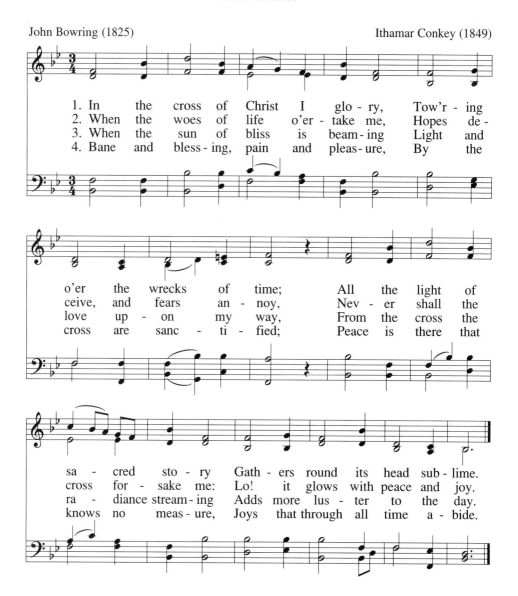

1. In the cross of Christ I glo - ry, Tow'r - ing
2. When the woes of life o'er - take me, Hopes de -
3. When the sun of bliss is beam - ing Light and
4. Bane and bless - ing, pain and pleas - ure, By the

o'er the wrecks of time; All the light of
ceive, and fears an - noy, Nev - er shall the
love up - on my way, From the cross the
cross are sanc - ti - fied; Peace is there that

sa - cred sto - ry Gath - ers round its head sub - lime.
cross for - sake me: Lo! it glows with peace and joy.
ra - diance stream - ing Adds more lus - ter to the day.
knows no meas - ure, Joys that through all time a - bide.

Amazing Grace

261

NEW BRITAIN CM

St. 1-4, John Newton (1779)
St. 5, ascr. to John Rees

Virginia Harmony (1831)
Harm. by John Barnard (1982)

1. A - maz - ing grace! how sweet the sound, That
2. 'Twas grace that taught my heart to fear, And
3. The Lord has prom - ised good to me, His
4. Through man - y dan - gers, toils, and snares, I
5. When we've been there ten thou - sand years, Bright

saved a wretch like me! I once was lost, but
grace my fears re - lieved; How pre - cious did that
word my hope se - cures; He will my shield and
have al - read - y come; 'Tis grace has brought me
shin - ing as the sun, We've no less days to

now am found, Was blind, but now I see.
grace ap - pear The hour I first be - lieved!
por - tion be As long as life en - dures.
safe thus far, And grace will lead me home.
sing God's praise Than when we'd first be - gun.

262 Be Thou My Vision

SLANE 10.10.9.10

Irish poem; trans. by Mary E. Byrne (1905)
Vrs. by Eleanor Hull (1912), alt.

Irish ballad
Harm. by David Evans (1927)

1. Be thou my vi - sion, O Lord of my heart;
2. Rich-es I heed not, nor vain, emp - ty praise,
3. Be thou my wis - dom, and thou my true word;

Nought be all else to me, save that thou art—
Thou mine in - her - i - tance, now and al - ways:
I ev - er with thee and thou with me, Lord;

Thou my best thought, by day or by night,
Thou and thou on - ly, first in my heart,
Heart of my own heart, what - ev - er be - fall,

Wak - ing or sleep - ing, thy pres - ence my light.
Great God of heav - en, my treas - ure thou art.
Still be my vi - sion, O Rul - er of all.

Tune: Harm. copyright © 1927, *Revised Church Hymnary,* Oxford University Press

Jesus Calls Us

GALILEE 8.7.8.7

263

Matthew 4:18-22
Cecil Frances Alexander (1852)

William H. Jude (1874)

1. Je - sus calls us o'er the tu - mult Of our
2. As of old the a - pos - tles heard it By the
3. Je - sus calls us from the wor - ship Of the
4. In our joys and in our sor - rows, Days of
5. Je - sus calls us! By thy mer - cies, Sav - ior,

life's wild, rest - less sea; Day by day his
Gal - i - le - an lake, Turned from home and
vain world's gold - en store, From each i - dol
toil and hours of ease, Still he calls, in
may we hear thy call, Give our hearts to

sweet voice sound - eth, Say - ing "Chris - tian, fol - low me!"
toil and kin - dred, Leav - ing all for Je - sus' sake.
that would keep us, Say - ing, "Chris - tian, love me more!"
cares and pleas - ures, "Chris - tian, love me more than these!"
thine o - be - dience, Serve and love thee best of all.

264   Nobody Knows the Trouble I See

DUBOIS Irregular with refrain

African-American spiritual

African-American spiritual
Adapt. and arr. by William Farley Smith (1986)

Refrain

No-bod - y knows the troub-le I see,

No-bod - y knows but Je - sus; Oh, no-bod - y knows the

troub-le I see, Glo - ry hal - le - lu - jah!

Verses

1. Some - times I'm up, some - times I'm down,
2. Al - though you see me going long so, Oh, yes,
3. What makes old Sa - tan hate me so?

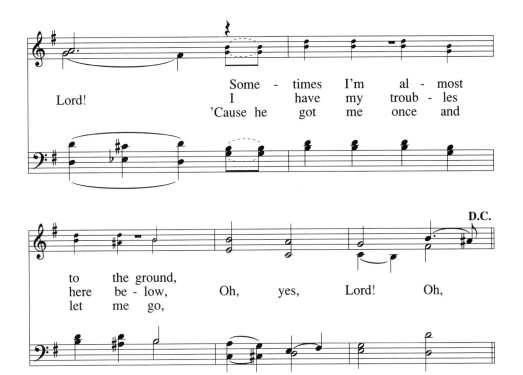

Lord!

Some - times I'm al - most
I have my troub - les
'Cause he got me once and

D.C.

to the ground,
here be - low, Oh, yes, Lord! Oh,
let me go,

Dear Lord and Father of Mankind　265

REST 8.6.8.8.6

John Greenleaf Whittier (1872)　　　　　　　　　Frederick C. Maker (1887)

1. Dear Lord and Fa - ther of man - kind, For -
2. In sim - ple trust like theirs who heard, Be -
3. O sab - bath rest by Gal - i - lee, O
4. Drop thy still dews of qui - et - ness, Till
5. Breathe through the heats of our de - sire Thy

give our fool - ish ways; Re - clothe us in our
side the Syr - ian sea, The gra - cious call - ing
calm of hills a - bove, Where Je - sus knelt to
all our striv - ings cease; Take from our souls the
cool - ness and thy balm; Let sense be dumb, let

right - ful mind, In pur - er lives thy
of the Lord, Let us, like them, with -
share with thee The si - lence of e -
strain and stress, And let our or - dered
flesh re - tire; Speak through the earth - quake,

serv - ice find, In deep - er rev - 'rence, praise.
out a word, Rise up and fol - low thee.
ter - ni - ty, In - ter - pret - ed by love!
lives con - fess The beau - ty of thy peace.
wind, and fire, O still, small voice of calm.

266   Be Not Afraid

Isaiah 43:2-3; Luke 6:20ff
Bob Dufford, SJ (1975)

Bob Dufford, SJ (1975)
Acc. by Sr. Theophane Hytrek, OSF

Verses 1, 2

1. You shall cross the bar-ren des-ert, but you

2. If you pass through rag-ing wa-ters in the

shall not die of thirst. You shall wan-der far in

sea, you shall not drown. If you walk a-mid the

safe - ty though you do not know the

burn-ing flames, you shall not be

way. You shall speak your words in for-eign lands and

harmed. If you stand be - fore the pow'r of hell and

all will un - der - stand. You shall see the

death is at your side, know that I am

face of God and live.

with you through it all.

Refrain
Melody:

Be not a - fraid. I go be -

fore you al - ways. Come, fol-low me, and

I will give you rest.

Last time

267 O God of Bethel, by Whose Hand

DUNDEE CM

Philip Doddridge (1736) and
John Logan (1781), alt.

Scottish Psalter (1615)

1. O God of Beth - el, by whose hand
2. Our vows, our prayers, we now pre - sent
3. Through each per - plex - ing path of life
4. O spread thy cov - 'ring wings a - round

Thy peo - ple still are fed;
Be - fore thy throne of grace;
Our wan - d'ring foot - steps guide;
Till all our wan - d'rings cease,

Who through this wea - ry pil - grim - age
God of our fa - thers, be the God
Give us each day our dai - ly bread,
And at our Fa - ther's loved a - bode

Hast all our fa - thers led.
Of their suc - ceed - ing race.
And rai - ment fit pro - vide.
Our souls ar - rive in peace.

Day By Day

SUMNER Irregular

268

Attr. to Richard of Chichester   Arthur Henry Biggs

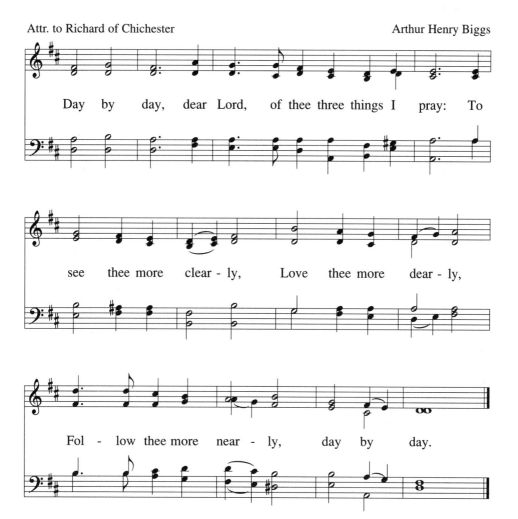

Day by day, dear Lord, of thee three things I pray: To see thee more clear - ly, Love thee more dear - ly, Fol - low thee more near - ly, day by day.

269   I Want to Walk as a Child of the Light

HOUSTON 10.7.10.8.9.9.10.7

Ephesians 5:8-10; Revelation 21:23;
  John 12:46; 1 John 1:5; Hebrews 12:1
Kathleen Thomerson (1970)   Kathleen Thomerson (1970)

1. I want to walk as a child of the light.
2. I want to see the bright-ness of God.
3. I'm look - ing for the com - ing of Christ.

I want to fol - low Je - sus.
I want to look at Je - sus.
I want to be with Je - sus.

God set the stars to give light to the world. The
Clear sun of right-eous-ness shine on my path, And
When we have run with pa - tience the race, We

star of my life is Je - sus.
show me the way to the Fa - ther.
shall know the joy of Je - sus.

270   Stand Up, Stand Up for Jesus

WEBB 7.6.7.6 D

Ephesians 6:10-17
George Duffield, Jr. (1858)

George J. Webb (1830)

1. Stand up, stand up for Je - sus, Ye sol - diers of the
2. Stand up, stand up for Je - sus, The trum - pet call o -
3. Stand up, stand up for Je - sus, Stand in his strength a -
4. Stand up, stand up for Je - sus, The strife will not be

cross; Lift high his roy - al ban - ner, It must not
bey; Forth to the might - y con - flict, In this his
lone; The arm of flesh will fail you, Ye dare not
long; This day the noise of bat - tle, The next the

suf - fer loss. From vic - t'ry un - to vic - t'ry His
glo - rious day. Ye that are brave now serve him A -
trust your own. Put on the gos - pel ar - mor, Each
vic - tor's song. To those who van - quish e - vil A

ar - my shall he lead, Till ev - 'ry foe is
gainst un - num - bered foes; Let cour - age rise with
piece put on with prayer; Where du - ty calls or
crown of life shall be; They with the King of

van - quished, And Christ is Lord in - deed.
dan - ger, And strength to strength op - pose.
dan - ger, Be nev - er want - ing there.
Glo - ry Shall reign e - ter - nal - ly.

271 Love Divine, All Loves Excelling

HYFRYDOL 8.7.8.7 D

Charles Wesley (1747), alt.

Rowland H. Prichard (c. 1830)

1. Love di - vine, all loves ex - cel - ling, Joy of
2. Come, al - might - y to de - liv - er, Let us
3. Fin - ish then your new cre - a - tion, Pure and

heav'n to earth come down! Fix in us your
all your life re - ceive; Sud - den - ly re -
spot - less, gra - cious Lord, Let us see your

hum - ble dwell - ing, All your faith - ful mer - cies crown.
turn and nev - er, Nev - er more your tem - ples leave.
great sal - va - tion Per - fect - ly in you re - stored.

Je - sus, source of all com - pas - sion, Love un -
Lord, we would be al - ways bless - ing, Serve you
Changed from glo - ry in - to glo - ry, Till in

bound - ed,　love　all　pure;　Vis - it　us　with
as　your　hosts　a - bove,　Pray,　and　praise　you
heav'n　we　take　our　place,　Till　we　sing　be -

your　sal - va - tion,　Let　your love　in　us　en - dure.
with - out　ceas - ing,　Glo - ry　in　your pre - cious love.
fore　the al - might - y　Lost　in　won - der,　love　and　praise.

272   Come, Thou Fount of Every Blessing

NETTLETON 8.7.8.7 D

Robert Robinson (1758)   Wyeth's *Repository of Sacred Music* (1813)

1. Come, thou Fount of ev-'ry bless-ing, Tune my heart to sing thy grace; Streams of mer-cy, nev-er ceas-ing, Call for songs of loud-est praise. Teach me some me-lo-dious son-net, Sung by
2. Here I raise mine Eb-e-ne-zer; Hith-er by thy help I'm come; And I hope, by thy good pleas-ure, Safe-ly to ar-rive at home. Je-sus sought me when a stran-ger, Wan-d'ring
3. O to grace how great a debt-or Dai-ly I'm con-strained to be! Let thy good-ness, like a fet-ter, Bind my wan-d'ring heart to thee. Prone to wan-der, Lord, I feel it, Prone to

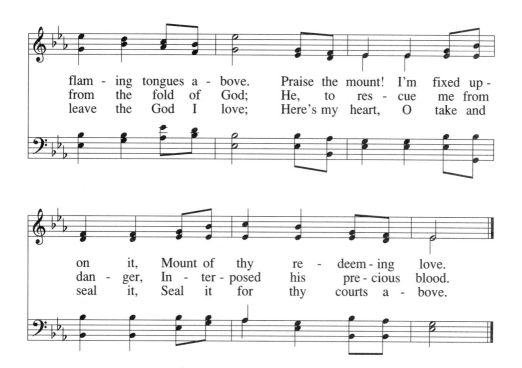

flam - ing tongues a - bove. Praise the mount! I'm fixed up -
from the fold of God; He, to res - cue me from
leave the God I love; Here's my heart, O take and

on it, Mount of thy re - deem - ing love.
dan - ger, In - ter - posed his pre - cious blood.
seal it, Seal it for thy courts a - bove.

273

'Tis the Gift to Be Simple

SIMPLE GIFTS Irregular with refrain

Shaker melody
Arr. by Margaret W. Mealy

Shaker song (18th C.)

'Tis the gift to be sim-ple, 'tis the gift to be free, 'tis the

gift to come down where we ought to be, and

when we find our-selves in the place just right, 'twill

be in the val - ley of love and de - light.

When true sim - plic - i - ty is gained to

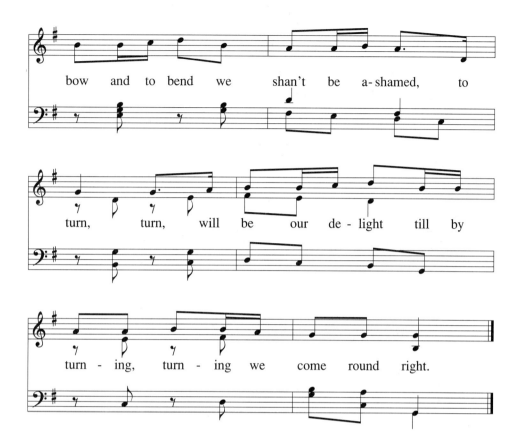

bow   and   to   bend   we   shan't   be   a- shamed,   to

turn,   turn,   will   be   our   de - light   till   by

turn - ing,   turn - ing   we   come   round   right.

274   # God Be in My Head
LYTLINGTON Irregular

Sarum Primer (1514)   Sydney Hugo Nicholson

God be in my head, and in my un-der-stand-ing;

God be in mine eyes, and in my look-ing;

God be in my mouth, and in my speak-ing;

God be in my heart, and in my think-ing;

God be at mine end, and at my de-part-ing.

Tune: Copyright © Royal School of Church Music

O Savior, in This Quiet Place

ST. STEPHEN CM

275

Fred Pratt Green (1974)

William Jones (1789)

1. O Sav - ior, in this qui - et place, Where
2. If pain of bod - y, stress of mind, De -
3. If self up - on its sick - ness feeds And
4. You nev - er said, "You ask too much," To
5. But if the thing I most de - sire Is
6. Of all my prayers, may this be chief: Till

an - y - one may kneel, I al - so come to
stroys my in - ward peace, In prayer for oth - ers
turns my life to gall, Let me not brood up -
an - y troub - led soul. I long to feel your
not your way for me, May faith, when test - ed
faith is ful - ly grown, Lord, dis - be - lieve my

ask for grace, Be - liev - ing you can heal.
may I find The se - cret of re - lease.
on my needs, But sim - ply tell you all.
heal - ing touch; Will you not make me whole?
in the fire, Prove its in - teg - ri - ty.
un - be - lief, And claim me as your own.

276   How Firm a Foundation

FOUNDATION 11.11.11.11

2 Timothy 2:19; Isaiah 41:10, 43:2, 46:4;   Funk's *Compilation of Genuine*
   Hebrews 13:5   *Church Music* (1832)
Rippon's *A Selection of Hymns* (1787)   Harm. by Richard Proulx (1975)

1. How   firm   a foun - da - tion, ye saints   of   the
2. "Fear   not,   I   am   with   thee, O   be   not dis -
3. "When through the deep wa - ters I call   thee   to
4. "When through fier - y   tri - als thy path - ways shall
5. "E'en   down   to old   age   all my peo - ple shall
6. "The   soul   that on   Je - sus still leans   for   re -

Lord,   Is   laid   for your faith   in   his   ex - cel - lent
mayed, For   I   am thy God   and will still give thee
go,   The   riv - ers of woe   shall not thee   o - ver -
lie,   My   grace, all suf - fi - cient, shall be   thy sup -
prove   My   sov - 'reign, e - ter - nal, un - change - a - ble
pose,   I   will not, I will   not de - sert   to   its

Tune: Harm. copyright © 1975, GIA Publications, Inc.

Word! What more can he say than to you he hath
aid; I'll strength - en and help thee, and cause thee to
flow; For I will be with thee, thy troub - les to
ply; The flame shall not hurt thee; I on - ly de -
love; And when hoar - y hairs shall their tem - ples a -
foes; That soul, though all hell should en - deav - or to

said, To you who for ref - uge to Je - sus have fled?
stand, Up - held by my right - eous, om - nip - o - tent hand."
bless, And sanc - ti - fy to thee thy deep - est dis - tress."
sign Thy dross to con - sume, and thy gold to re - fine."
dorn, Like lambs they shall still in my bos - om be borne."
shake, I'll nev - er, no, nev - er, no, nev - er for - sake."

277 Tell Me the Stories of Jesus

STORIES OF JESUS 8.4.8.4.5.4.5.4

Matthew 16:13-15, 21:8-9;
Mark 10:13-16, 11:8-10; John 12:13
William H. Parker (1885)

Frederick A. Challinor (1903)

1. Tell me the sto-ries of Je - sus I love to
2. First let me hear how the chil - dren Stood 'round his
3. In - to the cit - y I'd fol - low The chil - dren's

hear; Things I would ask him to tell me
knee, And I shall fan - cy his bless - ing
band, Wav - ing a branch of the palm tree

If he were here: Scenes by the
Rest - ing on me; Words full of
High in my hand; One of his

way - side, Tales of the sea,
kind - ness, Deeds full of grace,
her - alds, Yes, I would sing

Sto - ries of Je - sus, Tell them to me.
All in the love - light Of Je - sus' face.
Loud - est ho - san - nas, "Je - sus is King!"

278 Jesus, Lover of My Soul

ABERYSTWYTH 7.7.7.7 D

Charles Wesley (1740), alt.

Joseph Parry (1879)

1. Je - sus, Lov - er of my soul, Let me to thy
2. Oth - er ref - uge have I none, Hangs my help - less
3. Plen - teous grace with thee is found, Grace to cleanse from

bos - om fly, While the near - er wa - ters roll,
soul on thee; Leave, ah! leave me not a - lone,
ev - 'ry sin; Let the heal - ing streams a - bound,

While the tem - pest still is high: Hide me, O my
Still sup - port and com - fort me! All my trust on
Make and keep me pure with - in. Thou of life the

Sav - ior, hide, Till the storm of life be past;
thee is stayed; All my help from thee I bring;
foun - tain art, Free - ly let me take of thee:

Safe in - to the ha - ven guide,
Cov - er my de - fense - less head
Spring thou up with - in my heart,

O re - ceive my soul at last.
With the shad - ow of thy wing.
Rise to all e - ter - ni - ty.

279   Jesus, Priceless Treasure

JESU, MEINE FREUDE 6.6.5.6.6.5.7.8.6

Johann Franck (1653)   *Praxis Pietatis Melica* (1656)
Trans. by Catherine Winkworth (1863)   Harm. by Johann Sebastian Bach (1723)

1. Je - sus, price - less treas - ure, Source of pur - est
2. In thine arms I rest me; Foes who would mo -
3. Hence, all thoughts of sad - ness! For the Lord of

pleas - ure, Tru - est friend to me,
lest me Can - not reach me here.
glad - ness, Je - sus, en - ters in.

Long my heart hath pant - ed, Till it well - nigh
Though the earth be shak - ing, Ev - 'ry heart be
Those who love the Fa - ther, Though the storms may

faint - ed, Thirst - ing af - ter thee.
quak - ing, Je - sus calms our fear;
gath - er, Still have peace with - in;

Thine I am, O spot - less Lamb,	I will suf - fer
Sin and hell in con - flict fell	With their heav - iest
Yea, what-e'er we here must bear,	Still in thee lies

naught to hide thee,	Ask for naught be - side	thee.
storms as - sail us;	Je - sus will not fail	us.
pur - est pleas - ure,	Je - sus, price - less treas - ure!

280   God Will Take Care of You

MARTIN CM with refrain

Civilla D. Martin (1904)

W. Stillman Martin (1905)

God   will   take   care   of you,   Through ev - 'ry   day,

o'er   all   the   way;   He   will   take

care   of you,   God will take   care   of   you.

281 O Master, Let Me Walk with Thee

MARYTON LM

Washington Gladden (1879)   H. Percy Smith (1874)

1. O Mas - ter, let me walk with thee
2. Help me the slow of heart to move
3. Teach me thy pa - tience; still with thee
4. In hope that sends a shin - ing ray

In low - ly paths of serv - ice free;
By some clear, win - ning word of love;
In clos - er, dear - er com - pa - ny,
Far down the fu - ture's broad - 'ning way,

Tell me thy se - cret; help me bear
Teach me the way - ward feet to stay,
In work that keeps faith sweet and strong,
In peace that on - ly thou canst give,

The strain of toil, the fret of care.
And guide them in the home - ward way.
In trust that tri - umphs o - ver wrong;
With thee, O Mas - ter, let me live.

May the Mind of Christ, My Savior   282

ST. LEONARDS 8.7.8.5

Kate B. Wilkinson (1925)   A. Cyril Barham-Gould (1925)

1. May the mind of Christ, my Savior, Live in me from day to day, By his love and pow'r controlling All I do and say.

2. May the word of God dwell richly In my heart from hour to hour, So that all may see I triumph Only through his pow'r.

3. May the peace of God, my Father, Rule my life in ev'rything, That I may be calm to comfort Sick and sorrowing.

4. May the love of Jesus fill me As the waters fill the sea. Him exalting, self abasing: This is victory.

5. May we run the race before us, Strong and brave to face the foe, Looking only unto Jesus As we onward go.

Tune: Copyright © A. C. Barham-Gould estate

283 Seek the Lord

GENEVA 8.7.8.7 D

Isaiah 55:6-11
Fred Pratt Green (1986)

George Henry Day (1940)

1. Seek the Lord who now is pres - ent,
2. "Judge me not by hu - man stan - dards!
3. "So my word re - turns not fruit - less;

Pray to One who is at hand. Let the wick - ed
As the vault of heav - en soars High a - bove the
Does not from its la - bors cease Till it has a -

cease from sin - ning, E - vil - do - ers change their mind.
earth, so high - er Are my thoughts and ways than yours.
chieved my pur - pose In a world of joy and peace."

284 My Shepherd Will Supply My Need

RESIGNATION CMD

Psalm 23
Isaac Watts (1719), alt.

Funk's *Compilation of Genuine Church Music* (1832)
Harm. by Richard Proulx (1975)

1. My Shep-herd will sup - ply my need; The God of love su - preme; In pas - tures green you make me feed, Be - side the liv - ing stream. You

2. When I walk through the shades of death, Your pres - ence is my stay; One word of your sup - port - ing breath Drives all my fears a - way. Your

3. The sure pro - vi - sions of my God At - tend me all my days; O may your house be my a - bode, And all my work be praise! There

bring my wan - d'ring spir - it back, When I for -
hand, in sight of all my foes, Does still my
would I find a set - tled rest, While oth - ers

sake your ways; And lead me for your
ta - ble spread; My cup with bless - ings
go and come, No more a stran - ger

mer - cy's sake, In paths of truth and grace.
o - ver - flows, Your oil a - noints my head.
nor a guest; But like a child at home.

285   What a Friend We Have in Jesus

CONVERSE 8.7.8.7 D

Joseph M. Scriven (c. 1855)   Charles C. Converse (1868)

1. What a friend we have in Jesus,
2. Have we tri-als and temp-ta-tions?
3. Are we weak and heav-y-la-den,

All our sins and griefs to bear!
Is there troub-le an-y-where?
Cum-bered with a load of care?

What a priv-i-lege to car-ry
We should nev-er be dis-cour-aged—
Pre-cious Sav-ior, still our ref-uge—

Ev-'ry-thing to God in prayer!
Take it to the Lord in prayer.
Take it to the Lord in prayer.

O   what peace we of - ten   for   -   feit,
Can   we   find   a   friend   so   faith   -   ful
Do   thy friends de - spise,   for - sake   thee?

O   what need - less pain   we   bear,
Who   will   all   our   sor - rows   share?
Take   it   to   the   Lord   in   prayer;

All   be - cause we   do   not   car   -   ry
Je   -   sus knows our ev - 'ry   weak   -   ness—
In   his arms he'll take and   shield   thee—

Ev   -   'ry - thing to   God   in   prayer!
Take   it   to   the Lord   in   prayer.
Thou   wilt find   a   sol - ace   there.

286 Near to the Heart of God

McAFEE CM with refrain

Cleland B. McAfee (1903)   Cleland B. McAfee (1903)

1. There is a place of qui - et rest,
2. There is a place of com - fort sweet,
3. There is a place of full re - lease,

Near to the heart of God; A place where sin can -
Near to the heart of God; A place where we our
Near to the heart of God; A place where all is

not mo - lest, Near to the heart of God.
Sav - ior meet, Near to the heart of God.
joy and peace, Near to the heart of God.

O Je - sus, blest Re - deem - er, Sent from the heart of God,

Hold us who wait be - fore thee Near to the heart of God.

Lord of All Hopefulness

SLANE 10.11.11.12

Irish ballad
Adapt. from *The Church Hymnary* (1927)
Jan Struther (1931)   Harm. from *The Hymnal 1982*

287

1. Lord of all hope-ful-ness, Lord of all joy, Whose
2. Lord of all ea-ger-ness, Lord of all faith, Whose
3. Lord of all kind-li-ness, Lord of all grace, Your
4. Lord of all gen-tle-ness, Lord of all calm, Whose

trust, ev-er child-like, no cares could de-stroy, Be
strong hands were skilled at the plane and the lathe, Be
hands swift to wel-come, your arms to em-brace, Be
voice is con-tent-ment, whose pres-ence is balm, Be

there at our wak-ing, and give us, we pray, Your
there at our la-bors, and give us, we pray, Your
there at our hom-ing, and give us, we pray, Your
there at our sleep-ing, and give us, we pray, Your

bliss in our hearts, Lord, at the break of the day.
strength in our hearts, Lord, at the noon of the day.
love in our hearts, Lord, at the eve of the day.
peace in our hearts, Lord, at the end of the day.

288 Jesu, Jesu, Fill Us with Your Love

CHEREPONI Irregular with refrain

John 13:3-5
Tom Colvin (1963)

Ghanaian folk song
Adapt. by Tom Colvin (1963)
Arr. by Jane M. Marshall (1982)

Refrain

Je - su Je - su fill us with your love, show
us how to serve the neigh-bors we have from you.

Capo 5: (C)/F ... (G⁷)/C⁷ ... (C)/F ... (F)/B♭ (G⁷)/C⁷ (C)/F

Verses

1. Kneels at the feet of his friends,
2. Neigh - bors are rich and poor,
3. These are the ones we should serve,
4. Kneel at the feet of our friends,

(C)/F ... (Am)/Dm ... (Dm)/Gm

Si - lent - ly wash - es their feet,
Var - ied in col - or and race,
These are the ones we should love.
Si - lent - ly wash - ing their feet,

(G⁷)
C⁷

(C)
F

D.C.

Mas - ter who pours out him - self for them.
Neigh-bors are near and far a - way.
All are neigh-bors to us and you.
This is the way we should live with you.

(Am)
Dm

(F)
B♭

(G⁷)
C⁷

(C)
F

289 O Jesus Christ, May Grateful Hymns Be Rising

CHARTERHOUSE 11.10.11.10

Bradford G. Webster (1954)

David Evans (1927)

1. O Jesus Christ, may grateful hymns be rising
2. Grant us new courage, sacrificial, humble,
3. Show us your Spirit, brooding o'er each city

In ev'ry city for your love and care:
Strong in your strength to venture and to dare,
As you once wept above Jerusalem,

Inspire our worship, grant the glad surprising
To lift the fallen, guide the feet that stumble,
Seeking to gather all in love and pity,

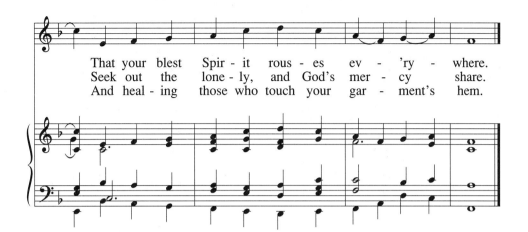

That your blest Spir - it rous - es ev - 'ry - where.
Seek out the lone - ly, and God's mer - cy share.
And heal - ing those who touch your gar - ment's hem.

290 Lord, You Give the Great Commission

ABBOT'S LEIGH 8.7.8.7 D

Jeffery Rowthorn (1978) Cyril V. Taylor (1942)

1. Lord, you give the great com - mis - sion:
2. Lord, you call us to your serv - ice:
3. Lord, you make the com - mon ho - ly:
4. Lord, you show us love's true meas - ure:
5. Lord, you bless with words as - sur - ing:

"Heal the sick and preach the word."
"In my name bap - tize and teach."
"This my bod - y, this my blood."
"Fa - ther, what they do, for - give."
"I am with you to the end."

Lest the Church ne - glect its mis - sion,
That the world may trust your prom - ise,
Let us all, for earth's true glo - ry,
Yet we hoard as pri - vate treas - ure,
Faith and hope and love re - stor - ing,

And the Gos - pel go un - heard,
Life a - bun - dant meant for each,
Dai - ly lift life heav - en - ward,
All that you so free - ly give.
May we serve as you in - tend,

Help us wit - ness to your pur - pose
Give us all new fer - vor, draw us
Ask - ing that the world a - round us
May your care and mer - cy lead us
And, a - mid the cares that claim us,

With re - newed in - teg - ri - ty;
Clos - er in com - mun - i - ty;
Share your chil - dren's lib - er - ty;
To a just so - ci - e - ty;
Hold in mind e - ter - ni - ty;

With the Spir - it's gifts em - pow'r us

For the work of min - is - try.

291   Not for Tongues of Heaven's Angels

BRIDEGROOM 8.7.8.7.6

1 Corinthians 13
Timothy Dudley-Smith (1985)

Peter Cutts (1969)

1. Not for tongues of heav-en's an - gels, Not for wis-dom to dis - cern, Not for faith that mas-ters moun - tains— For this bet - ter gift we yearn: May love be ours, O Lord.

2. Love is hum - ble, love is gen - tle, Love is ten - der, true and kind; Love is gra - cious, ev - er - pa - tient, Gen - er - ous of heart and mind— May love be ours, O Lord.

3. Nev - er jeal - ous, nev - er self - ish, Love will not re - joice in wrong; Nev - er boast - ful nor re - sent - ful, Love be - lieves and suf - fers long— May love be ours, O Lord.

4. In the day this world is fad - ing, Faith and hope will play their part; But when Christ is seen in glo - ry, Love shall reign in ev - 'ry heart: May love be ours, O Lord.

Christ for the World We Sing

292

MOSCOW 6.6.4.6.6.6.6.4

Felice de Giardini (1769)
Samuel Wolcott (1869)
Harm. from *The New Hymnal* (1916)

1. Christ for the world we sing! The world to Christ we bring With lov - ing zeal; The poor, and them that mourn, The faint and o - ver - borne, Sin - sick and sor - row - worn, Whom Christ doth heal.

2. Christ for the world we sing! The world to Christ we bring With fer - vent prayer; The way - ward and the lost, By rest - less pas - sions tossed, Re - deemed at count - less cost From dark de - spair.

3. Christ for the world we sing! The world to Christ we bring With one ac - cord; With us the work to share, With us re - proach to dare, With us the cross to bear, For Christ our Lord.

4. Christ for the world we sing! The world to Christ we bring With joy - ful song; The new - born souls, whose days, Re - claimed from er - ror's ways, In - spired with hope and praise, To Christ be - long.

293   Here I Am, Lord

Isaiah 6
Dan Schutte (1981)

Dan Schutte (1981)
Arr. by Michael Pope, SJ and John Weissrock

1. I, the Lord of sea and sky, I have heard my peo-ple cry.
2. I, the Lord of snow and rain, I have borne my peo-ple's pain.
3. I, the Lord of wind and flame, I will tend the poor and lame.

All who dwell in dark and sin My hand will save.
I have wept for love of them. They turn a-way.
I will set a feast for them. My hand will save.

I who made the stars of night, I will make their
I will break their hearts of stone, Give them hearts for
Fin-est bread I will pro-vide Till their hearts be

dark-ness bright. Who will bear my light to them? Whom shall I
love a-lone. I will speak my word to them. Whom shall I
sat-is-fied. I will give my life to them. Whom shall I

294   Fight the Good Fight

PENTECOST LM

John Samuel Bewley Monsell (1863), alt.   William Boyd (1864)

1. Fight the good fight with all thy might,
2. Run the straight race through God's good grace,
3. Cast care aside, lean on thy Guide;
4. Faint not nor fear, his arms are near;

Christ is thy strength and Christ thy right;
Lift up thine eyes and seek his face;
His boundless mercy will provide;
He changeth not, and thou art dear;

Lay hold on life, and it shall be
Life with its way before us lies,
Trust, and thy trusting soul shall prove
Only believe, and thou shalt see

Thy joy and crown eternally.
Christ is the path and Christ the prize.
Christ is its life and Christ its love.
That Christ is all in all to thee.

O Day of God, Draw Nigh   **295**

ST. MICHAEL SM

Robert B. Y. Scott (1937)

Genevan Psalter (1551)
Arr. by William Crotch (1836)

1. O day of God, draw nigh In beau - ty and in pow'r; Come with thy time - less judg - ment now To match our pres - ent hour.
2. Bring to our troub - led minds, Un - cer - tain and a - fraid, The qui - et of a stead - fast faith, Calm of a call o - beyed.
3. Bring jus - tice to our land, That all may dwell se - cure, And fine - ly build for days to come Foun - da - tions that en - dure.
4. Bring to our world of strife Thy sov - 'reign word of peace, That war may haunt the earth no more, And des - o - la - tion cease.
5. O day of God, draw nigh As at cre - a - tion's birth; Let there be light a - gain, and set Thy judg - ments on the earth.

296 Make Me a Channel of Your Peace

Prayer of St. Francis
Adapt. by Sebastian Temple (1967)

Sebastian Temple (1967)
Acc. by Robert J. Batastini (1996)

1. Make me a chan-nel of your peace. Where there is ha-tred, let me bring your love. Where there is in-ju-ry, your par-don, Lord, And where there's doubt, true faith in you.

2. Make me a chan-nel of your peace. Where there's de-spair in life, let me bring hope. Where there is dark-ness, on-ly light, And where there's sad-ness, ev - er joy.

4. Make me a chan-nel of your peace. It is in par-don-ing that we are par-doned, in giv-ing of our-selves that we re - ceive, and in dy - ing that we're born to e-ter-nal life.

297

O God of Every Nation

LLANGLOFFAN 7.6.7.6 D

Welsh hymn melody
Evans' *Hymnau a Thonau* (1865)

William Watkins Reid, Jr. (1958), alt.

1. O God of ev - 'ry na - tion, Of ev - 'ry race and
2. From search for wealth and pow - er And scorn of truth and
3. Lord, strength - en all who la - bor That we may find re -
4. Keep bright in us the vi - sion Of days when war shall

land, Re - deem the whole cre - a - tion With
right, From trust in bombs that show - er De -
lease From fear of rat - tling sa - ber, From
cease, When ha - tred and di - vi - sion Give

your al - might - y hand; Where hate and fear di -
struc - tion through the night, From pride of race and
dread of war's in - crease; When hope and cour - age
way to love and peace, Till dawns the morn - ing

vide us And bit - ter threats are hurled, In
na - tion And blind - ness to your way, De -
fal - ter, Your still small voice be heard; With
glo - rious When truth and jus - tice reign And

love and mer - cy   guide us   And   heal our strife - torn world.
liv - er ev - 'ry   na - tion, E - ter - nal God, we pray!
faith that none can   al - ter, Your   ser - vants un - der - gird.
Christ shall rule vic - to - rious O'er   all   the world's do - main.

298 # God the Omnipotent

RUSSIA 11.10.11.9

Sts. 1-2, Henry Fothergill Chorley, alt.
Sts. 3-4, John Ellerton, alt.

Alexis Lvov (1833)

1. God the Om - ni - po - tent! King, who or - dain - est
2. God the All - mer - ci - ful! earth hath for - sak - en
3. God the All - right - eous One! earth hath de - fied thee;
4. God the All - prov - i - dent! earth by thy chast'n - ing

Thun - der thy clar - ion, the light - ning thy sword;
Thy ways all ho - ly, and slight - ed thy word;
Yet to e - ter - ni - ty stand - eth thy word,
Yet shall to free - dom and truth be re - stored;

Show forth thy pit - y on high where thou reign - est:
Bid not thy wrath in its ter - rors a - wak - en:
False - hood and wrong shall not tar - ry be - side thee:
Through the thick dark - ness thy king - dom is hast'n - ing:

Give to us peace in our time, O Lord.
Give to us peace in our time, O Lord.
Give to us peace in our time, O Lord.
Thou wilt give peace in thy time, O Lord.

Hope of the World

DONNE SECOURS 11.10.11.10

299

Georgia Harkness (1954), alt.

Genevan Psalter (1551)
Harm. by Claude Goudimel

1. Hope of the world, O Christ of great com-pas-sion:
2. Hope of the world, God's gift from high-est heav-en,
3. Hope of the world, a-foot on dust-y high-ways,
4. Hope of the world, who by your cross did save us
5. Hope of the world, O Christ, o'er death vic-to-rious,

Speak to our fear-ful hearts by con-flict rent.
Bring-ing to hun-gry souls the bread of life:
Show-ing to wan-d'ring souls the path of light:
From death and dark de-spair, from sin and guilt:
Who by this sign did con-quer grief and pain:

Save us, your peo-ple, from con-sum-ing pas-sion,
Still let your Spir-it un-to us be giv-en,
Walk now be-side us lest the tempt-ing by-ways
We ren-der back the love your mer-cy gave us;
We would be faith-ful to your gos-pel glo-rious;

Who by our own false hopes and aims are spent.
To heal earth's wounds and end our bit-ter strife.
Lure us a-way from you to end-less night.
Take now our lives and use them as you will.
You are our Lord! And you for ev-er reign!

300 God the Spirit, Guide and Guardian

HOLY MANNA 8.7.8.7 D

Carl P. Daw, Jr. (1987)   William Moore (1825)

1. God the Spir - it, guide and guard - ian,
2. Christ our Sav - ior, sov - 'reign, shep - herd,
3. Great Cre - a - tor, life - be - stow - er,
4. Tri - une God, mys - te - rious be - ing,

Wind - sped flame and hov - 'ring dove,
Word made flesh, love cru - ci - fied,
Truth be - yond all thought's re - call,
Un - di - vid - ed and di - verse,

Breath of life and voice of proph - ets,
Teach - er, heal - er, suf - f'ring ser - vant,
Fount of wis - dom, womb of mer - cy,
Deep - er than our minds can fath - om,

Sign of bless - ing, pow'r of love: Give to those who
Friend of sin - ners, foe of pride: In your tend - ing
Giv - ing and for - giv - ing all: As you know our
Great - er than our creeds re - hearse: Help us in our

lead your peo - ple Fresh a - noint - ing of your grace;
may your serv - ants Learn and live a shep - herd's care;
strength and weak - ness, So may those the church ex - alts
var - ied call - ings Your full im - age to pro - claim,

Send them forth as bold a - pos - tles
Grant them cour - age and com - pas - sion
O - ver - see her life stead - fast - ly,
That our min - is - tries u - nit - ing

To your church in ev - 'ry place.
Shown through word and deed and prayer.
Yet not o - ver - look her faults.
May give glo - ry to your name.

301 Let There Be Peace on Earth

Sy Miller, Jill Jackson (1955)

Sy Miller, Jill Jackson (1955)
Acc. by Diana Kodner (1993)

Let there be peace on earth, and let it be-gin with
me. Let there be peace on earth, the
peace that was meant to be. With God as our
Fa - ther, broth - ers all are we.
fam - 'ly
Let me walk with my broth-er in per - fect har - mo-
us each oth - er

ny.   Let   peace   be - gin   with me;   let

this be the mo - ment now.   With   ev - 'ry

step   I   take,   let this be my sol - emn vow;   To

take   each mo - ment, and live   each mo - ment in peace   e -

ter - nal - ly!   Let   there   be

peace   on   earth,   and let it be - gin   with me.

302   # How Clear Is Our Vocation, Lord

REPTON 8.6.8.8.6.6

Fred Pratt Green (1981)   Charles Hubert Hastings Parry (1888)

1. How clear is our vo - ca - tion, Lord, When
2. But if, for - get - ful, we should find Your
3. We mark your saints, how they be - come In
4. In what you give us, Lord, to do, To -

once we heed your call: To live ac - cord - ing
yoke is hard to bear, If world - ly pres - sures
hin - dranc - es more sure, Whose joy - ful vir - tues
geth - er or a - lone, In old rou - tines or

to your word, And dai - ly learn, re -
fray the mind And love it - self can -
put to shame The cas - ual way we
ven - tures new, May we not cease to

freshed, re - stored, That you are Lord of
not un - wind Its tan - gled skein of
wear your name, And by our faults ob -
look to you— The cross you hung up -

all And will not let us fall.
care: Our in - ward life re - pair.
scure Your pow'r to cleanse and cure.
on— All you en - deav - ored done.

303   Lead on, O King Eternal

LANCASHIRE 7.6.7.6 D

Ernest Warburton Shurtleff (1887)   Henry Thomas Smart (1835)

1. Lead on, O King e - ter - nal, The day of march has come; Hence - forth in fields of con - quest Thy tents shall be our home: Through days of prep - a - ra - tion Thy grace has made us strong, And

2. Lead on, O King e - ter - nal, Till sin's fierce war shall cease, And ho - li - ness shall whis - per The sweet a - men of peace; For not with swords loud clash - ing, Nor roll of stir - ring drums, But

3. Lead on, O King e - ter - nal: We fol - low, not with fears; For glad - ness breaks like morn - ing Wher - e'er thy face ap - pears. Thy cross is lift - ed o'er us; We jour - ney in its light: The

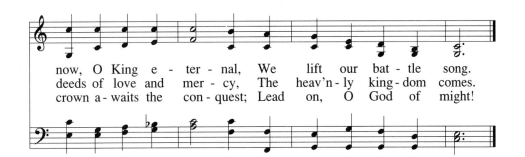

now, O King e - ter - nal, We lift our bat - tle song.
deeds of love and mer - cy, The heav'n - ly king - dom comes.
crown a - waits the con - quest; Lead on, O God of might!

304 Whatsoever You Do

WHATSOEVER YOU DO 10.10.11 with refrain

Matthew 5:3-12
Willard F. Jabusch (1966)

Willard F. Jabusch (1966)
Harm. by Robert J. Batastini (1975)

Refrain

What - so - ev - er you do to the least of my peo - ple, that you do un - to me.

Verses

1. When I was hun - gry, you gave me to eat;
2. When I was home - less, you o - pened your door;
3. When I was wea - ry, you helped me find rest;
4. When I was lit - tle, you taught me to read;
5. When in a pris - on, you came to my cell;
6. In a strange coun - try, you made me at home;
7. Hurt in a bat - tle, you bound up my wounds;
8. When I was Black, or La - ti - no, or white;
9. When I was a - ged, you both - ered to smile;
10. You saw me cov - ered with spit - tle and blood;
11. When I was laughed at, you stood by my side;

When   I   was   thirst - y,   you   gave   me   to   drink.
When   I   was   na - ked,   you   gave   me   your   coat.
When   I   was   anx - ious,   you   calmed   all   my   fears.
When   I   was   lone - ly,   you   gave   me   your   love.
When   on   a   sick - bed,   you   cared   for   my   needs.
Seek - ing   em - ploy - ment,   you   found   me   a   job.
Search - ing   for   kind - ness,   you   held   out   your   hand.
Mocked   and   in - sult - ed,   you   car - ried   my   cross.
When   I   was   rest - less,   you   lis - tened   and   cared.
You   knew   my   fea - tures, though   grim - y   with   sweat.
When   I   was   hap - py,   you   shared   in   my   joy.

D.C.

Now en - ter   in - to   the   home   of   my   Fa - ther.

305   O God of Love, O King of Peace

TALLIS' CANON LM

Henry Williams Baker (1860)   Thomas Tallis (c. 1567)

1. O God of love, O King of peace, Make
2. Whom shall we trust but you, O Lord? Where
3. Where saints and an - gels dwell a - bove, All

wars through - out the world to cease; Our vio - lent ways help
rest but on your faith - ful word? None ev - er called on
hearts are joined in ho - ly love; O bind us in that

us con - tain; Give peace, O God, give peace a - gain!
you in vain; Give peace, O God, give peace a - gain!
heav'n - ly chain; Give peace, O God, give peace a - gain!

May be sung as a two or four-voice canon.

Where Cross the Crowded Ways of Life　306

GERMANY LM

Matthew 22:9
Frank Mason North (1903)

Gardiner's *Sacred Melodies* (1815)

1. Where cross the crowd - ed ways of life,
2. In haunts of wretch - ed - ness and need,
3. From ten - der child - hood's help - less - ness,
4. The cup of wa - ter giv'n for you
5. O Mas - ter, from the moun - tain - side
6. Till all the world shall learn your love

Where sound the cries of race and clan, A -
On shad - owed thresh - olds dark with fears, From
From wom - an's grief, man's bur - dened toil, From
Still holds the fresh - ness of your grace; Yet
Make haste to heal these hearts of pain; A -
And fol - low where your feet have trod, Till,

bove the noise of self - ish strife, We
paths where hide the lures of greed, We
fam - ished souls, from sor - row's stress, Your
long these mul - ti - tudes to view The
mong these rest - less throngs a - bide; O
glo - rious from your heav'n a - bove, Shall

hear your voice, O Son of man.
catch the vi - sion of your tears.
heart has nev - er known re - coil.
sweet com - pas - sion of your face.
tread the cit - y's streets a - gain,
come the cit - y of our God!

307 Lord Christ, When First You Came to Earth

MIT FREUDEN ZART 8.7.8.7.8.8.7

Walter Russell Bowie (1928), alt.

Bohemian Brethren's *Kirchengesange* (1566)

1. Lord Christ, when first you came to earth, Up-
2. O awe-some Love, which finds no room In
3. New ad-vent of the love of Christ, Will
4. O wound-ed hands of Je-sus, build In

on a cross they bound you. And
life where sin de-nies you. And,
we a-gain re-fuse you. Till
us your new cre-a-tion: Our

mocked your sav-ing king-ship's worth By
doomed to death, shall bring to doom The
in the night of hate and war We
pride is dust, our boast-ing stilled: We

thorns with which they crowned you. And
pow'r which cru-ci-fies you, Till
per-ish as we lose you? From
wait your rev-e-la-tion. O

still   our   wrongs   may   fash - ion now   New
not   a   stone   be   left on stone,   And
an - cient doubts   our   minds re - lease   To
Love   that   tri - umphs   o - ver loss,   We

thorns to pierce   that   stead - y brow,   And
then the na - tions'   pride, o'er - thrown, Will
seek the king - dom   of your peace,   By
bring our hearts   be -   fore your cross   To

robe   of   sor -   row   round   you.
nev - er - more   de -   fy   you!
which a - lone   we   choose   you.
fin - ish your   sal -   va - tion.

308 Lord, Whose Love in Humble Service

IN BABILONE 8.7.8.7 D

Albert F. Bayly (1961)

Traditional Dutch melody
Arr. by Julius Röntgen (1906)

1. Lord, whose love in hum - ble serv - ice
2. Still your chil - dren wan - der home - less;
3. As we wor - ship, grant us vi - sion,
4. Called from wor - ship in - to serv - ice

Bore the weight of hu - man need,
Still the hun - gry cry for bread;
Till your love's re - veal - ing light,
Forth in your great name we go,

Who did on the Cross for - sak - en,
Still the cap - tives long for free - dom;
Till the height and depth and great - ness
To the child, the youth, the a - ged,

Show us mer - cy's per - fect deed;
Still in grief we mourn our dead.
Dawns up - on our hu - man sight:
Love in liv - ing deeds to show;

309 O Jesus, I Have Promised

ANGEL'S STORY 7.6.7.6 D

Luke 9:57
John Ernest Bode (c. 1866)

Arthur Henry Mann (1881)

1. O Je - sus, I have prom - ised To serve thee to the end; Be thou for ev - er near me, My mas - ter and my friend. I shall not fear the bat - tle If

2. O let me feel thee near me! The world is ev - er near; I see the sights that daz - zle, The tempt - ing sounds I hear; My foes are ev - er near me, A -

3. O let me hear thee speak - ing In ac - cents clear and still, A - bove the storms of pas - sion, The mur - murs of self - will. O speak to re - as - sure me, To

4. O Je - sus, thou hast prom - ised To all who fol - low thee That where thou art in glo - ry There shall thy ser - vant be. And Je - sus, I have prom - ised To

thou art by my side, Nor wan - der from the
round me and with - in; But Je - sus, draw thou
has - ten or con - trol; O speak, and make me
serve thee to the end; O give me grace to

path - way If thou wilt be my guide.
near - er, And shield my soul from sin.
lis - ten, Thou guard - ian of my soul.
fol - low, My mas - ter and my friend.

310 O God of Earth and Altar

LLANGLOFFAN 7.6.7.6 D

Gilbert K. Chesterton (1906)

Welsh hymn melody
Evans' *Hymnau a Thonau* (1865)

1. O God of earth and al - tar, Bow down and hear our
2. From all that ter - ror teach - es, From lies of tongue and
3. Tie in a liv - ing teth - er The prince and priest and

cry; Our earth - ly rul - ers fal - ter, Our
pen; From all the eas - y speech - es That
thrall; Bind all our lives to - geth - er, Smite

peo - ple drift and die; The walls of gold en -
com - fort cru - el men; From sale and prof - a -
us and save us all; In ire and ex - ul -

tomb us, The swords of scorn di - vide; Take
na - tion Of hon - or and the sword; From
ta - tion A - flame with faith, and free, Lift

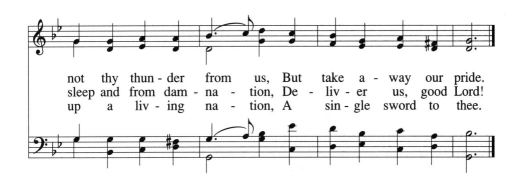

not thy thun - der from us, But take a - way our pride.
sleep and from dam - na - tion, De - liv - er us, good Lord!
up a liv - ing na - tion, A sin - gle sword to thee.

Nearer, My God, to Thee

311

BETHANY 6.4.6.4.6.6.6.4

Genesis 28:10-22
Sarah F. Adams (1841)

Lowell Mason (1856)

1. Near - er, my God, to thee, Near - er to thee!
2. Though like the wan - der - er, The sun gone down,
3. There let the way ap - pear, Steps un - to heav'n;
4. Then, with my wak - ing thoughts Bright with thy praise,
5. Or if, on joy - ful wing Cleav - ing the sky,

E'en though it be a cross That rais - eth me,
Dark - ness be o - ver me, My rest a stone;
All that thou send - est me, In mer - cy giv'n;
Out of my ston - y griefs Beth - el I'll raise;
Sun, moon, and stars for - got, Up - ward I fly,

Still all my song shall be, Near - er, my God, to thee;
Yet in my dreams I'd be Near - er, my God, to thee;
An - gels to beck - on me Near - er, my God, to thee;
So by my woes to be Near - er, my God, to thee;
Still all my song shall be, Near - er, my God, to thee;

Near - er, my God, to thee, Near - er to thee!

312   You Are Near

Psalm 139   Dan Schutte (1971)
Dan Schutte (1971)   Acc. by Sr. Theophane Hytrek, OSF

313 ## O Day of Peace

JERUSALEM LMD

Isaiah 11:6-7
Carl P. Daw, Jr. (1982)

Charles Hubert Hastings Parry (1916)
Arr. by Janet Wyatt (1977)

1. O day of peace that dim - ly shines Through all our
2. Then shall the wolf dwell with the lamb, Nor shall the

hopes and prayers and dreams, Guide us to jus - tice, truth, and
fierce de - vour the small; As beasts and cat - tle calm - ly

love, De - liv - ered from our self - ish schemes. May swords of
graze, A lit - tle child shall lead them all. Then en - e -

hate   fall from our hands,   Our hearts from en - vy find re -
mies   shall learn to love,   All crea-tures find   their true ac -

lease,   Till by God's grace   our war-ring world   Shall see Christ's
cord;   The hope of peace   shall be ful-filled,   For all the

1.

prom - ised reign of   peace.
earth shall know the

2.

Lord.

O God, Our Help in Ages Past   **314**

ST. ANNE CM

Psalm 90
Isaac Watts (1719)

Attr. to William Croft (1708)

1. O God, our help in a - ges past, Our
2. Un - der the shad - ow of your throne Your
3. Be - fore the hills in or - der stood, Or
4. A thou - sand a - ges in your sight Are
5. Time, like an ev - er - roll - ing stream, Soon
6. O God, our help in a - ges past, Our

hope for years to come, Our shel - ter from the
saints have dwelt se - cure; Suf - fi - cient is your
earth re - ceived its frame, From ev - er - last - ing
like an eve - ning gone, Short as the watch that
bears us all a - way; We fly for - got - ten,
hope for years to come, Still be our guard while

storm - y blast, And our e - ter - nal home.
arm a - lone, And our de - fense is sure.
you are God, To end - less years the same.
ends the night Be - fore the ris - ing sun.
as a dream Dies at the op - 'ning day.
troub - les last, And our e - ter - nal home.

315 God of Day and God of Darkness

BEACH SPRING 8.7.8.7 D

The Sacred Harp (1844)

Marty Haugen (1985)

Harm. by Marty Haugen (1985)

1. God of day and God of dark - ness, Now we
2. Still the na - tions curse the dark - ness, Still the
3. Show us Christ in one an - oth - er, Make us
4. You shall be the path that guides us, You the
5. Praise to you in day and dark - ness, You our

stand be - fore the night; As the shad - ows stretch and
rich op - press the poor; Still the earth is bruised and
ser - vants strong and true; Give us all your love of
light that in us burns; Shin - ing deep with - in all
source and you our end; Praise to you who love and

deep - en, Come and make our dark - ness bright. All cre -
bro - ken By the ones who still want more. Come and
jus - tice So we do what you would do. Let us
peo - ple, Yours the love that we must learn, For our
nur - ture us As a fa - ther, moth - er, friend. Grant us

316   Give to the Winds Thy Fears

FESTAL SONG SM

Psalm 37:5; Paul Gerhardt (1653)
Trans. by John Wesley (1739)

William H. Walter (1894)

1. Give to the winds thy fears; Hope and be un-dis-mayed. God hears thy sighs and counts thy tears, God shall lift up thy head.
2. Through waves and clouds and storms, God gent-ly clears thy way; Wait thou God's time; so shall this night Soon end in joy-ous day.
3. Leave to God's sov-'reign sway To choose and to com-mand; So shalt thou, won-d'ring, own that way, How wise, how strong this hand.
4. Let us in life, in death, Thy stead-fast truth de-clare, And pub-lish with our lat-est breath Thy love and guard-ian care.

Kum Ba Yah

DESMOND Irregular

African-American spiritual
Harm. by Carlton R. Young (1988)

African-American spiritual

1. Kum ba yah, my Lord, kum ba yah. Kum ba
yah, my Lord, kum ba yah. Kum ba yah, my Lord,
kum ba yah. Oh, Lord, kum ba yah!

2. Someone's praying, Lord…

3. Someone's crying, Lord…

4. Someone needs you, Lord…

5. Someone's singing, Lord…

6. Let us praise the Lord…

318   Almighty Father, Strong to Save

MELITA 8.8.8.8.8.8

St. 1&4, William Whiting (1860)
St. 2-3, Robert Nelson Spencer, alt.

John Bacchus Dykes (1861)

1. Al - might - y Fa - ther, strong to save, Whose arm hath bound the rest - less wave, Who bidd'st the might - y o - cean deep Its own ap - point - ed lim - its keep: O hear us when we cry to thee For those in per - il on the sea.

2. O Christ, the Lord of hill and plain O'er which our traf - fic runs a - main By moun - tain pass or val - ley low; Wher - ev - er, Lord, thy peo - ple go, Pro - tect them by thy guard - ing hand From ev - 'ry per - il on the land.

3. O Spir - it, whom the Fa - ther sent To spread a - broad the firm - a - ment; O Wind of heav - en, by thy might Save all who dare the ea - gle's flight, And keep them by thy watch - ful care From ev - 'ry per - il in the air.

4. O Trin - i - ty of love and pow'r, Our peo - ple shield in dan - ger's hour; From rock and tem - pest, fire and foe, Pro - tect them where-so - e'er they go; Thus ev - er - more shall rise to thee Glad praise from space, air, land, and sea.

Rock of Ages, Cleft for Me 319

TOPLADY 7.7.7.7.7.7

Augustus M. Toplady (1776) Thomas Hastings (1830)

1. Rock of A - ges, cleft for me, Let me hide my - self in thee; Let the wa - ter and the blood, From thy wound - ed side which flowed, Be of sin the dou - ble cure; Save from wrath and make me pure.

2. Not the la - bors of my hands Can ful - fill thy law's de - mands; Could my zeal no res - pite know, Could my tears for ev - er flow, All for sin could not a - tone; Thou must save, and thou a - lone.

3. Noth - ing in my hand I bring, Sim - ply to the cross I cling; Na - ked, come to thee for dress; Help - less, look to thee for grace; Foul, I to the foun - tain fly; Wash me, Sav - ior, or I die.

4. While I draw this fleet - ing breath, When mine eyes shall close in death, When I soar to worlds un - known, See thee on thy judg-ment throne, Rock of A - ges, cleft for me, Let me hide my - self in thee.

320 God Is Working His Purpose Out

PURPOSE Irregular

Habakkuk 1:14
Arthur C. Ainger (1894), alt.

Martin Shaw (1931)

1. God is work - ing his pur - pose out As
2. From ut - most east to ut - most west, Wher -
3. March we forth in the strength of God, With the
4. All we can do is worth - less toil Un -

year suc - ceeds to year:
ev - er foot has trod,
ban - ner of Christ un - furled,
less God bless - es the deed;

By the
That the

God is work - ing his pur - pose out, And the
mouth of man - y mes - sen - gers Goes
light of the glo - rious gos - pel of truth May
Vain - ly we hope for the har - vest - tide Till

time is draw - ing near;
forth the voice of God;
shine through - out the world:
God gives life to the seed; Yet

Near - er and
Give ear to
Fight we the
near - er and

More Love to Thee, O Christ　　321

MORE LOVE TO THEE 6.4.6.4.6.6.4.4

Elizabeth P. Prentiss (1869)　　　　　　　　　William H. Doane (1870)

1. More love to thee, O Christ, More love to thee!
2. Once earth-ly joy I craved, Sought peace and rest;
3. Let sor-row do its work, Come grief and pain;
4. Then shall my lat - est breath Whis - per thy praise;

Hear thou the prayer I make On bend - ed knee.
Now thee a - lone I seek, Give what is best.
Sweet are thy mes - sen-gers, Sweet their re - frain,
This be the part - ing cry My heart shall raise;

This is my ear - nest plea: More love, O
This all my prayer shall be: More love, O
When they can sing with me: More love, O
This still its prayer shall be: More love, O

Christ, to thee; More love to thee, More love to thee!
Christ, to thee; More love to thee, More love to thee!
Christ, to thee; More love to thee, More love to thee!
Christ, to thee; More love to thee, More love to thee!

322   **Jesus, Remember Me**

Luke 23:42
Taizé Community (1981)   Jacques Berthier (1981)

323 O Love That Wilt Not Let Me Go

ST. MARGARET 8.8.8.8.8.6

George Matheson (1882)

Albert L. Peace (1884)

1. O   Love   that wilt not   let   me   go,
2. O   Light that fol - low'st all   my   way,
3. O   Joy   that seek - est me through pain,
4. O   Cross that lift - est up   my   head,

I   rest   my   wea - ry   soul   in   thee;
I   yield my   flick - 'ring torch to   thee;
I   can - not close my   heart to   thee;
I   dare not ask   to   fly   from thee;

I   give   thee back the   life   I   owe,
My heart re - stores its   bor - rowed ray,
I   trace the   rain - bow through the rain,
I   lay   in   dust life's glo - ry   dead,

That   in   thine o - cean depths its   flow
That   in   thy   sun - shine's blaze its   day
And   feel the   prom - ise   is   not   vain,
And   from the   ground there blos - soms red

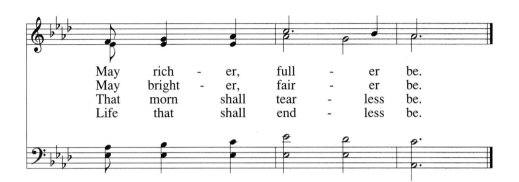

May	rich	-	er,	full	-	er	be.
May	bright	-	er,	fair	-	er	be.
That	morn		shall	tear	-	less	be.
Life	that		shall	end	-	less	be.

324   **Be Still, My Soul**

FINLANDIA 10.10.10.10.10.10

Katharina von Schlegel (1752)   Jean Sibelius (1899)
Trans. by Jane Laurie Borthwick (1855)   Arr. from *The Hymnal* (1933)

1. Be still, my soul: the Lord is on your side.
2. Be still, my soul: your God will un - der - take
3. Be still, my soul: the hour is has - t'ning on

Bear pa - tient - ly the cross of grief or pain;
To guide the fu - ture, as in a - ges past.
When we shall be for ev - er with the Lord,

Leave to your God to or - der and pro - vide;
Your hope, your con - fi - dence let noth - ing shake;
When dis - ap - point-ment, grief, and fear are gone,

In ev - 'ry change God faith-ful will re - main.
All now mys - te - rious shall be bright at last.
Sor-row for - got, love's pur - est joys re - stored.

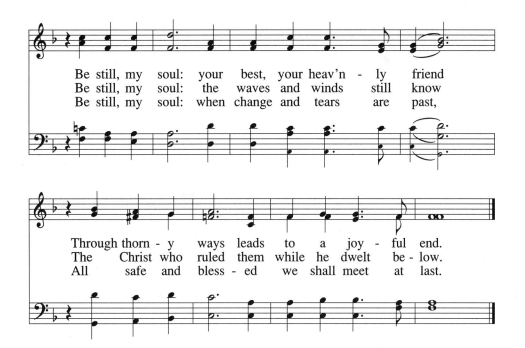

Be still, my soul: your best, your heav'n - ly friend
Be still, my soul: the waves and winds still know
Be still, my soul: when change and tears are past,

Through thorn - y ways leads to a joy - ful end.
The Christ who ruled them while he dwelt be - low.
All safe and bless - ed we shall meet at last.

325   Sweet Hour of Prayer
SWEET HOUR LMD

William Walford (1845)   William B. Bradbury (1861)

1. Sweet hour of prayer! sweet hour of prayer! That calls me from a world of care, And bids me at my Fa - ther's throne Make all my wants and wish - es known.

2. Sweet hour of prayer! sweet hour of prayer! The joys I feel, the bliss I share Of those whose anx - ious spir - its burn With strong de - sires for thy re - turn!

3. Sweet hour of prayer! sweet hour of prayer! Thy wings shall my pe - ti - tion bear To him whose truth and faith - ful - ness En - gage the wait - ing soul to bless.

In sea - sons of dis - tress and grief, My
With such I has - ten to the place Where
And since he bids me seek his face, Be -

soul has of - ten found re - lief, And
God my Sav - ior shows his face, And
lieve his word, and trust his grace, I'll

oft es - caped the tempt - er's snare By
glad - ly take my sta - tion there, And
cast on him my ev - 'ry care. And

thy re - turn, sweet hour of prayer!
wait for thee, sweet hour of prayer!
wait for thee, sweet hour of prayer!

326 Open My Eyes, That I May See

OPEN MY EYES 8.8.9.8 with refrain

Clara H. Scott (1895)

Clara H. Scott (1895)

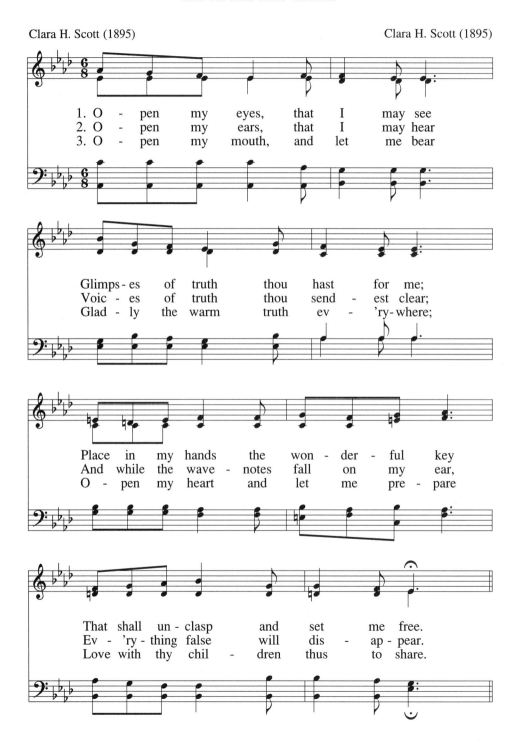

1. O - pen my eyes, that I may see
2. O - pen my ears, that I may hear
3. O - pen my mouth, and let me bear

Glimps - es of truth thou hast for me;
Voic - es of truth thou send - est clear;
Glad - ly the warm truth ev - 'ry-where;

Place in my hands the won - der - ful key
And while the wave - notes fall on my ear,
O - pen my heart and let me pre - pare

That shall un - clasp and set me free.
Ev - 'ry-thing false will dis - ap - pear.
Love with thy chil - dren thus to share.

Si - lent - ly now I wait for thee,
Si - lent - ly now I wait for thee,
Si - lent - ly now I wait for thee,

Read - y, my God, thy will to see. O - pen my eyes,
Read - y, my God, thy will to see. O - pen my ears,
Read - y, my God, thy will to see. O - pen my heart,

il - lu - mine me, Spir - it di - vine!

327   I Heard the Voice of Jesus Say

KINGSFOLD CMD

English folk melody

Horatius Bonar (1846)

Harm. by Ralph Vaughan Williams (1906)

1. I heard the voice of Je - sus say, "Come
2. I heard the voice of Je - sus say, "Be -
3. I heard the voice of Je - sus say, "I

un - to me and rest; Lay down, O wea - ry
hold, I free - ly give The liv - ing wa - ter;
am this dark world's light; Look un - to me, your

one, lay down Your head up - on my breast." I
thirst - y one, Stoop down, and drink, and live." I
morn shall rise, And all your day be bright." I

came to Je - sus as I was, So
came to Je - sus, and I drank Of
looked to Je - sus, and I found In

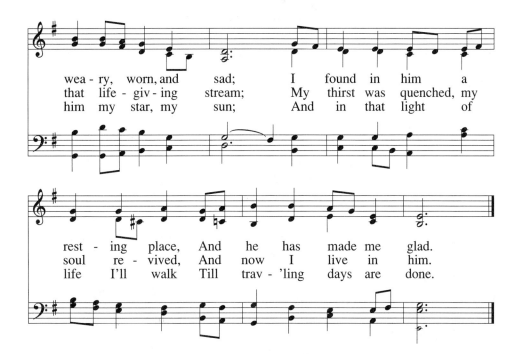

wea - ry, worn, and sad; I found in him a
that life - giv - ing stream; My thirst was quenched, my
him my star, my sun; And in that light of

rest - ing place, And he has made me glad.
soul re - vived, And now I live in him.
life I'll walk Till trav - 'ling days are done.

328 My Hope Is Built

THE SOLID ROCK LM with refrain

Edward Mote (1834)   William B. Bradbury (1863)

1. My hope is built on noth-ing less Than
2. When dark-ness veils his love-ly face, I
3. His oath, his cov-e-nant, his blood Sup-
4. When he shall come with trum-pet sound, O

Je-sus' blood and right-eous-ness. I dare not trust the
rest on his un-chang-ing grace. In ev-'ry high and
port me in the whelm-ing flood. When all a-round my
may I then in him be found! Dressed in his right-eous-

sweet-est frame, But whol-ly lean on Je-sus' name.
storm-y gale, My an-chor holds with-in the veil.
soul gives way, He then is all my hope and stay.
ness a-lone, Fault-less to stand be-fore the throne!

On Christ the sol-id rock I stand, All oth-er ground is

sink-ing sand; All oth-er ground is sink-ing sand.

Come Down, O Love Divine   329

DOWN AMPNEY 6.6.11 D

Bianco da Siena
Trans. by Richard F. Littledale (1867)

Ralph Vaughan Williams (1906)

1. Come down, O Love di - vine, Seek now this soul of
2. O let it free - ly burn, Till earth - ly pas - sions
3. And so the yearn - ing strong, With which the soul will

mine, And vis - it it with your own ar - dor glow - ing;
turn To dust and ash - es in its heat con - sum - ing;
long, Shall far out-pass the power of hu - man tell - ing;

O Com fort er, draw near, With - in my heart ap -
And let your glo - rious light Shine ev - er on my
For none can guess its grace, Till love cre - ates the

pear, And kin - dle it, your ho - ly flame be - stow - ing.
sight, And clothe me round, the while my path il - lum - ing.
place Where - in the Ho - ly Spir - it makes its dwell - ing.

330   A Mighty Fortress Is Our God

EIN' FESTE BURG 8.7.8.7.6.6.6.6.7

Martin Luther (1529)
Trans. Frederick Henry Hedge (1852)

Martin Luther (1529)
Harm. by Johann Sebastian Bach

1. A might - y for - tress is our God, A
2. Did we in our own strength con - fide, Our
3. And though this world, with dev - ils filled, Should
4. That word a - bove all earth - ly pow'rs, No

bul - wark nev - er fail - ing; Our help - er he a -
striv - ing would be los - ing; Were not the right man
threat - en to un - do us; We will not fear, for
thanks to them, a - bid - eth; The Spir - it and the

mid the flood Of mor - tal ills pre -
on our side, The man of God's own
God hath willed His truth to tri - umph
gifts are ours Through him who with us

vail - ing: For still our an - cient foe Doth
choos - ing: Dost ask who that may be? Christ
through us; The prince of dark - ness grim, We
sid - eth: Let goods and kin - dred go, This

seek to work us woe; His craft and pow'r are great, And,
Je - sus, it is he; Lord Sa - ba - oth his Name, From
trem - ble not for him; His rage we can en - dure, For
mor - tal life al - so; The bod - y they may kill: God's

armed with cru - el hate, On earth is not his e - qual.
age to age the same, And he must win the bat - tle.
lo! his doom is sure, One lit - tle word shall fell him.
truth a - bid - eth still, His king - dom is for ev - er.

331 God Is Here! As We His People

ABBOT'S LEIGH 8.7.8.7 D

Fred Pratt Green (1979)   Cyril V. Taylor (1942)

1. God is here! As we his people,
2. Here are sym - bols to re - mind us
3. Here our chil - dren find a wel- come
4. Lord of all, of church and king-dom,

Meet to of - fer praise and prayer,
Of our life - long need of grace;
In the Shep - herd's flock and fold;
In an age of change and doubt,

May we find in ful - ler meas - ure
Here are ta - ble, font and pul - pit,
Here, as bread and wine are tak - en,
Keep us faith - ful to the gos - pel,

What it is in Christ we share:
Here the cross has cen - tral place:
Christ sus - tains us as of old:
Help us work your pur - pose out:

Here,   as   in   the   world   a - round   us,
Here   in   hon - es - ty   of   preach - ing,
Here   the   ser - vants   of   the   Ser - vant
Here,   in   this   day's   ded   -   i - ca - tion,

All   our   var - ied   skills   and   arts
Here   in   si - lence   as   in   speech,
Seek   in   wor - ship   to   ex   - plore
All   we   have   to   give,   re   - ceive;

Wait   the   com - ing   of   his   Spir - it
Here   in   new - ness   and   re   - new - al
What   it   means   in   dai   - ly   liv - ing
We   who   can - not   live   with - out   you,

In   -   to   o   - pen   minds   and   hearts.
God   the   Spir - it   comes   to   each.
To   be - lieve   and   to   a   -   dore.
We   a - dore   you!   We   be   - lieve!

332　　　God Himself Is with Us

ARNSBERG 6.6.8.6.6.8.6.6.6

Gerhardt Tersteegen (1729)　　　　　　　　　Joachim Neander (1680)

1. God him - self is with us; Let us now a - dore him,
2. God him - self is with us; Hear the harps re - sound - ing!
3. Fount of ev - 'ry bless - ing, Pu - ri - fy my spir - it,

And with awe ap - pear be - fore him. God is in his
See the crowds the throne sur - round - ing! "Ho - ly, ho - ly,
Trust-ing on - ly in your mer - it. Like the ho - ly

tem - ple; All with - in keep si - lence, Pros-trate lie with
ho - ly," Hear the hymn as - cend - ing, An - gels, saints, their
an - gels Who be - hold your glo - ry, May I cease - less -

deep-est rev - 'rence. Him a - lone do we own
voic - es blend - ing! Bow your ear to us here;
ly a - dore you, And in all, great and small,

As   our God   and   Sav - ior;   Praise his   name for   ev - er.
Hear, O   Christ, the   prais - es   That   your church now   rais - es.
Seek   to   do   most near - ly   What   you   love   so   dear - ly.

333   O Day of Rest and Gladness
MENDEBRAS 7.6.7.6 D

Christopher Wordsworth (1862)

Old German melody
Arr. by Lowell Mason (1839)

1. O day of rest and glad - ness, O day of
2. On thee, at the Cre - a - tion, The light first
3. New grac - es ev - er gain - ing From this our

joy and light, O balm of care and sad - ness,
had its birth; On thee, for our sal - va - tion,
day of rest, We reach the rest re - main - ing

Most beau - ti - ful, most bright; On thee the high and
Christ rose from depths of earth; On thee our Lord, vic -
To spir - its of the blest. To Ho - ly Ghost be

low - ly, Through a - ges joined in tune, Sing ho - ly,
to - rious, The Spir - it sent from heav'n; And thus on
prais - es, To Fa - ther, and to Son; The Church her

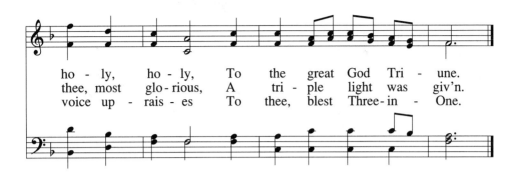

ho - ly, ho - ly, To the great God Tri - une.
thee, most glo - rious, A tri - ple light was giv'n.
voice up - rais - es To thee, blest Three- in - One.

334   We Gather Together

KREMSER 12.11.12.11

Netherlands folk hymn (1625)
Trans. by Theodore Baker (1894)

Neder-landtsch Gedenckclanck (1626)
Harm. by Edward Kremser (1877)

1. We gath - er to - geth - er to ask the Lord's bless - ing;
2. Be - side us to guide us, our God with us join - ing,
3. We all do ex - tol you our lead - er tri - um - phant,

He chas - tens and has - tens his will to make known;
Whose king - dom calls all to the love which en - dures.
And pray that you still our de - fend - er will be.

The wick - ed op - press - ing now cease from dis - tress - ing:
So from the be - gin - ning the fight we were win - ning:
Let your con - gre - ga - tion es - cape trib - u - la - tion:

Sing prais - es to his name; he for - gets not his own.
You, Lord, were at our side; all glo - ry be yours!
Your name be ev - er praised! O Lord, make us free!

Lord, Dismiss Us with Thy Blessing   **335**

SICILIAN MARINERS 8.7.8.7.8.7

The European Magazine and Review (1792)

Attr. to John Fawcett (1773)   Harm. from the *Methodist Hymn and Tune Book* (1889), alt.

1. Lord, dis - miss us with thy bless-ing; Fill our hearts with
2. Thanks we give and ad - o - ra - tion For thy Gos - pel's

joy and peace; Let us each, thy love pos - sess-ing,
joy - ful sound. May the fruits of thy sal - va - tion

Tri- umph in re - deem-ing grace. O re - fresh us,
In our hearts and lives a - bound; Ev - er faith-ful,

O re - fresh us, Trav- 'ling through this wil - der - ness.
ev - er faith - ful To the truth may we be found.

336 God Be with You Till We Meet Again

RANDOLPH 9.8.8.9

Jeremiah E. Rankin (1880)   Ralph Vaughan Williams (1906)

1. God be with you till we meet a-gain;
2. God be with you till we meet a-gain;
3. God be with you till we meet a-gain;
4. God be with you till we meet a-gain;

By his coun - sels guide, up - hold you,
'Neath his wings pro - tect - ing hide you,
When life's per - ils thick con - found you,
Keep love's ban - ner float - ing o'er you,

With his sheep se - cure - ly fold you:
Dai - ly man - na still pro - vide you:
Put his arms un - fail - ing round you:
Smite death's threat - 'ning wave be - fore you:

God be with you till we meet a-gain.
God be with you till we meet a-gain.
God be with you till we meet a-gain.
God be with you till we meet a-gain. A - men.

God Be with You Till We Meet Again　337
GOD BE WITH YOU 9.8.8.9

Jeremiah E. Rankin (1880)　　　　　　　　William G. Tomer (1880)

1. God be with you till we meet a - gain;
2. God be with you till we meet a - gain;
3. God be with you till we meet a - gain;
4. God be with you till we meet a - gain;

By his coun - sels guide, up - hold you,
'Neath his wings pro - tect - ing hide you,
When life's per - ils thick con - found you,
Keep love's ban - ner float - ing o'er you,

With his sheep se - cure - ly fold you:
Dai - ly man - na still pro - vide you:
Put his arms un - fail - ing round you:
Smite death's threat - 'ning wave be - fore you:

God be with you till we meet a - gain.
God be with you till we meet a - gain.
God be with you till we meet a - gain.
God be with you till we meet a - gain.　A - men.

338   Savior, Again to Thy Dear Name
ELLERS 10.10.10.10

John Ellerton (1866), alt.   Edward J. Hopkins (1869)

1. Sav - ior, a - gain to thy dear name we raise
2. Grant us thy peace up - on our home-ward way;
3. Grant us thy peace through - out our earth - ly life;
4. Thy peace in life, the balm of ev - 'ry pain;

With one ac - cord our part - ing hymn of praise;
With thee be - gan, with thee shall end the day.
Peace to thy church from er - ror and from strife;
Thy peace in death, the hope to rise a - gain;

Guard thou the lips from sin, the hearts from shame,
From harm and dan - ger keep thy chil - dren free,
Peace to our land, the fruit of truth and love;
Then, when thy voice shall bid our con - flict cease,

That in this house have called up - on thy name.
For dark and light are both a - like to thee.
Peace in each heart, thy Spir - it from a - bove;
Call us, O Lord, to thine e - ter - nal peace.

Father, We Praise You

339

CHRISTE SANCTORUM 11.11.11.5

Attr. to St. Gregory the Great
Trans. by Percy Dearmer (1906), alt.

La Feillees *Methode du plain-chant* (1782)

1. Fa - ther, we praise you, now the night is o - ver,
2. Mak - er of all things, fit us for your man-sions;
3. All - ho - ly Fa - ther, Son and e - qual Spir - it,

Ac - tive and watch - ful, stand we all be -
Ban - ish our weak - ness, health and whole - ness
Trin - i - ty bless - ed, send us your sal -

fore you; Sing - ing we of - fer pray'r and med - i -
send - ing; Bring us to heav - en, where your saints u -
va - tion; Yours is the glo - ry, gleam - ing and re -

ta - tion: Thus we a - dore you.
nit - ed Joy with - out end - ing.
sound - ing Through all cre - a - tion.

340 When Morning Gilds the Skies

LAUDES DOMINI 6.6.6 D

Katholisches Gesangbuch (1828)
Trans. by Edward Caswall (1854)

Joseph Barnby (1868)

1. When morn - ing gilds the skies, My heart, a-
2. To God, the Word, on high The hosts of
3. Let earth's wide cir - cle round In joy - ful
4. Be this while life is mine My can - ti -

wak - ing, cries, "May Je - sus Christ be praised!" A-
an - gels cry: "May Je - sus Christ be praised!" Let
notes re - sound: "May Je - sus Christ be praised!" Let
cle di - vine: "May Je - sus Christ be praised!" Be

like at work and prayer To Je - sus I re -
mor - tals, too, up - raise Their voice in hymns of
air, and sea, and sky, From depth to height, re -
this the e - ter - nal song, Through all the a - ges

pair: "May Je - sus Christ be praised!"
praise: "May Je - sus Christ be praised!"
ply: "May Je - sus Christ be praised!"
long: "May Je - sus Christ be praised!"

Christ, Whose Glory Fills the Skies 341

RATISBON 7.7.7.7.7.7

J. G. Werner's *Choralbuch* (1815)
Harm. by William Henry Havergal (1861)

Charles Wesley (1740)

1. Christ, whose glo-ry fills the skies, Christ, the true, the
2. Dark and cheer-less is the morn Un-ac-com-pa-
3. Vis-it then this soul of mine; Pierce the gloom of

on-ly light, Sun of Right-eous-ness, a-rise,
nied by thee; Joy-less is the day's re-turn,
sin and grief; Fill me, Ra-dian-cy di-vine,

Tri-umph o'er the shades of night; Day-spring from on
Till thy mer-cy's beams I see; Till they in-ward
Scat-ter all my un-be-lief; More and more thy-

high, be near; Day-star, in my heart ap-pear.
light im-part, Cheer my eyes and warm my heart.
self dis-play, Shin-ing to the per-fect day.

342 Awake, My Soul, and with the Sun
OLD HUNDREDTH LM

Thomas Ken (1674), alt.   Attr. to Louis Bourgeois (1551)

1. A - wake, my soul, and with the sun Thy
2. Lord, I my vows to thee re - new; Dis -
3. Di - rect, con - trol, sug - gest, this day, All
4. Praise God, from whom all bless - ings flow; Praise

dai - ly stage of du - ty run; Shake off dull sloth, and
perse my sins as morn-ing dew; Guard my first springs of
I de - sign, or do, or say; That all my pow'rs, with
him, all crea-tures here be - low; Praise him a - bove, ye

joy - ful rise To pay thy morn-ing sac - ri - fice:
thought and will, And with thy - self my spir - it fill.
all their might, In thy sole glo - ry may u - nite.
heav'n - ly host: Praise Fa - ther, Son, and Ho - ly Ghost.

Morning Has Broken

BUNESSAN 5.5.5.4 D

343

Gaelic melody
Harm. by David Evans (1927)

Eleanor Farjeon (1931)

1. Morn - ing has bro - ken Like the first
2. Sweet the rain's new fall Sun - lit from
3. Mine is the sun - light! Mine is the

morn - ing, Black-bird has spo - ken Like the first
heav - en, Like the first dew - fall On the first
morn - ing Born of the one light E - den saw

bird. Praise for the sing - ing! Praise for the
grass. Praise for the sweet - ness Of the wet
play! Praise with e - la - tion, Praise ev - 'ry

morn - ing! Praise for them, spring - ing Fresh from the Word!
gar - den, Sprung in com - plete - ness Where his feet pass.
morn - ing, God's re - cre - a - tion Of the new day!

344 Day Is Dying in the West

CHAUTAUQUA 7.7.7.7.4 with refrain

Isaiah 6:3
Mary A. Lathbury (1878)

William F. Sherwin (1877)

1. Day is dy - ing in the west;
2. Lord of life, be - neath the dome
3. While the deep - 'ning shad - ows fall,
4. When for ev - er from our sight

Heav'n is touch - ing earth with rest;
Of the u - ni - verse, thy home,
Heart of love en - fold - ing all,
Pass the stars, the day, the night,

Wait and wor - ship while the night Sets the eve - ning
Gath - er us who seek thy face To the fold of
Through the glo - ry and the grace Of the stars that
Lord of an - gels, on our eyes Let e - ter - nal

lamps a - light Through all the sky.
thy em - brace, For thou art nigh.
veil thy face, Our hearts as - cend.
morn - ing rise And shad - ows end.

Ho - ly, ho - ly, ho - ly, Lord God of Hosts!

Heav'n and earth are full of thee! Heav'n and earth are

prais - ing thee, O Lord most high!

345 Abide with Me

EVENTIDE 10.10.10.10

Henry Francis Lyte (1847)

William Henry Monk (1861)

1. A - bide with me: fast falls the e - ven - tide;
2. I need thy pres - ence ev - 'ry pass - ing hour;
3. I fear no foe, with thee at hand to bless;
4. Hold thou thy cross be - fore my clos - ing eyes;

The dark - ness deep - ens; Lord, with me a - bide:
What but thy grace can foil the tempt - er's pow'r?
Ills have no weight, and tears no bit - ter - ness.
Shine through the gloom, and point me to the skies;

When oth - er help - ers fail and com - forts flee,
Who, like thy - self, my guide and stay can be?
Where is death's sting? where, grave, thy vic - to - ry?
Heav'n's morn - ing breaks, and earth's vain shad - ows flee;

Help of the help - less, O a - bide with me.
Through cloud and sun - shine, Lord, a - bide with me.
I tri - umph still, if thou a - bide with me.
In life, in death, O Lord, a - bide with me.

O Gladsome Light

NUNC DIMITTIS 6.6.7.6.6.7

346

Ancient Greek hymn
Trans. by Robert S. Bridges (1899)

Louis Bourgeois (1547)
Harm. by Claude Goudimel (1551)

1. O glad-some light, O grace Of our Cre - a - tor's face,
2. As fades the day's last light We see the lamps of night,
3. To you of right be - longs All praise of ho - ly songs,

The e - ter - nal splen-dor wear - ing: Ce - les - tial, ho - ly blest,
Our com-mon hymn out-pour - ing, O God of might un-known,
O Son of God, Life - giv - er; You, there-fore, O Most High,

Our Sav - ior Je - sus Christ, Joy - ful in your ap-pear - ing!
You, the in - car-nate Son, And Spir - it blest a - dor - ing.
The world does glo - ri - fy And shall ex - alt for ev - er.

347   # Now the Day Is Over
MERRIAL 6.5.6.5

Sabine Baring-Gould (1865), alt.   Joseph Barnby (1868)

1. Now the day is o - ver,
2. Je - sus, give the wea - ry
3. Com - fort those who suf - fer,
4. When the morn - ing wak - ens,

Night is draw - ing nigh,   Shad - ows of the
Calm and sweet re - pose;   With thy ten - d'rest
Watch-ing late in pain;   Those who plan some
Then may I a - rise   Pure, and fresh, and

eve - ning   Steal a - cross the sky.
bless - ing   May mine eye - lids close.
e - vil   From their sin re - strain.
sin - less   In thy ho - ly eyes.

The Day You Gave Us, Lord, Is Ended   348
ST. CLEMENT 9.8.9.8

John Ellerton (1870), alt.   Clement C. Scholefield (1874)

1. The day you gave us, Lord, is end - ed, The
2. We thank you that your Church, un - sleep - ing While
3. A - cross each con - ti - nent and is - land As
4. The sun that bids us rest is wak - ing Your
5. So be it, Lord; your throne shall nev - er, Like

dark - ness falls at your be - hest; To
earth rolls on - ward in - to light, Through
dawn leads on an - oth - er day, The
friends be - neath the west - ern sky, And
earth's proud em - pires, pass a - way: Your

you our morn - ing hymns as - cend - ed, Your
all the world its watch is keep - ing, And
voice of prayer is nev - er si - lent, Nor
hour by hour fresh lips are mak - ing Your
king - dom stands, and grows for ev - er, Till

praise shall sanc - ti - fy our rest.
rests not now by day or night.
dies the strain of praise a - way.
won - drous do - ings heard on high.
all your crea - tures own your sway.

349   God, Who Made the Earth and Heaven

AR HYD Y NOS 8.4.8.4.8.8.8.4

St. 1, Reginald Heber (1827)
St. 2, 4, William Mercer (1864)
St. 3, Richard Whately (1838), alt.

Traditional Welsh melody (c. 1784)

1. God, who made the earth and heav-en, Dark - ness and light:
2. And when morn a - gain shall call us To run life's way,
3. Guard us wak-ing, guard us sleep-ing, And, when we die,
4. Ho - ly Fa - ther, throned in heav-en, All - ho - ly Son,

You the day for work have giv - en, For rest the night.
May we still, what - e'er be - fall us, Your will o - bey.
May we in your might - y keep-ing All peace-ful lie.
Ho - ly Spir - it, free - ly giv - en, Blest Three - in - One:

May your an - gel guards de - fend us, Slum - ber sweet your
From the pow'r of e - vil hide us, In the nar - row
When the last dread call shall wake us, Then, O Lord, do
Grant us grace, we now im - plore you, Till we lay our

mer - cy send us, Ho - ly dreams and
path - way guide us, Nev - er be your
not for - sake us, But to reign in
crowns be - fore you, And in wor - thier

hopes   at - tend us   All   through the night.
smile   de - nied us   All   through the day.
glo - ry take us   With   you on high.
strains a - dore you   While   a - ges run.

350   All Praise to Thee, My God, This Night

TALLIS' CANON LM

Thomas Ken (c.1674)   Thomas Tallis (c.1567)

1. All praise to thee, my God, this night, For
2. Forgive me, Lord, for thy dear Son, The
3. Teach me to live, that I may dread The
4. O may my soul on thee repose, And
5. Praise God, from whom all blessings flow; Praise

all the blessings of the light! Keep
ill that I this day have done, That
grave as little as my bed. Teach
with sweet sleep mine eyelids close, Sleep
him, all creatures here below; Praise

me, O keep me, King of kings, Be -
with the world, myself, and thee, I,
me to die, that so I may Rise
that may me more vig - 'rous make To
him a - bove, ye heav - 'nly host; Praise

neath thine own al - might - y wings.
ere I sleep, at peace may be.
glo - rious at the judg - ment day.
serve my God when I a - wake.
Fa - ther, Son, and Ho - ly Ghost.

May be sung in canon.

Sun of My Soul, Thou Savior Dear   351

HURSLEY LM

John Keble (1820)   *Katholisches Gesangbuch* (1774)

1. Sun of my soul, thou Sav - ior dear,
2. When the soft dews of kind - ly sleep
3. A - bide with me from morn till eve,
4. Watch by the sick; en - rich the poor
5. Come near and bless us when we wake,

It is not night if thou be near;
My wea - ried eye - lids gen - tly steep,
For with - out thee I can - not live;
With bless - ings from thy bound - less store;
Ere through the world our way we take,

O may no earth - born cloud a - rise
Be my last thought, how sweet to rest
A - bide with me when night is nigh,
Be ev - 'ry mourn - er's sleep to - night,
Till in the o - cean of thy love

To hide thee from thy ser - vant's eyes.
For ev - er on my Sav - ior's breast.
For with - out thee I dare not die.
Like in - fants' slum - bers, pure and light.
We lose our - selves in heav'n a - bove.

352   God of All Ages, Whose Almighty Hand
NATIONAL HYMN 10.10.10.10

Daniel C. Roberts (1876), alt.   George W. Warren (1892)

Trumpets before each stanza (optional)

1. God   of   all   a - ges,
2. Thy   love   di - vine   hath
3. From   war's   a - larms,   from
4. Re - fresh   thy   peo - ple

whose   al - might - y   hand   Leads   forth   in
led   us   in   the   past;   In   this   free
dead - ly   pes - ti - lence,   Be   thy   strong
on   their   toil - some   way,   Lead   us   from

beau - ty   all   the   star - ry   band   Of   shin - ing
land   by   thee   our   lot   is   cast;   Be   thou   our
arm   our   ev - er   sure   de - fense;   May   true   re -
night   to   nev - er   end - ing   day;   Fill   all   our

worlds   in   splen - dor   through   the   skies:
rul - er,   guard - ian,   guide,   and   stay;
lig - ion   in   our   hearts   in - crease,
lives   with   love   and   grace   di - vine;

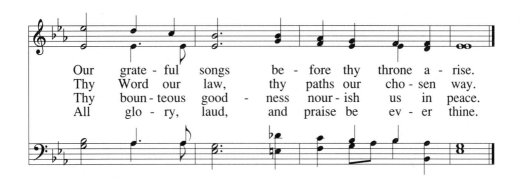

Our grate - ful songs be - fore thy throne a - rise.
Thy Word our law, thy paths our cho - sen way.
Thy boun - teous good - ness nour - ish us in peace.
All glo - ry, laud, and praise be ev - er thine.

353   Star-Spangled Banner

NATIONAL ANTHEM Irregular

Francis Scott Key   John S. Smith

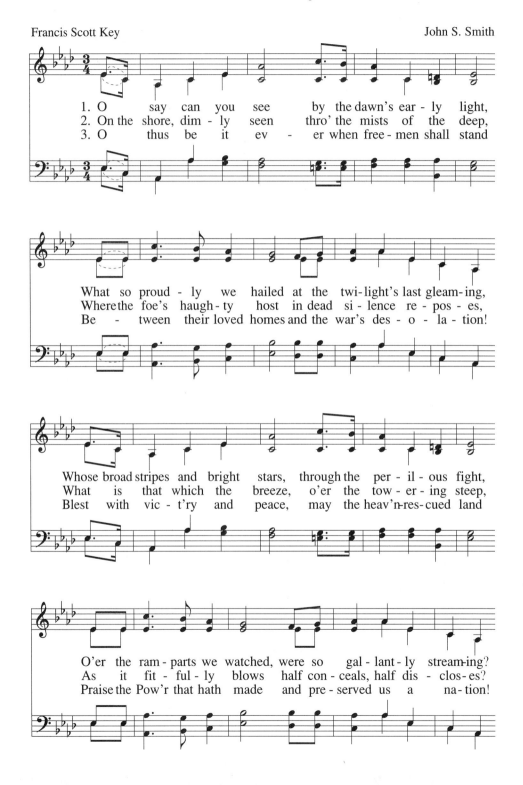

1. O say can you see by the dawn's ear - ly light,
2. On the shore, dim - ly seen thro' the mists of the deep,
3. O thus be it ev - er when free - men shall stand

What so proud - ly we hailed at the twi-light's last gleam-ing,
Where the foe's haugh - ty host in dead si - lence re - pos - es,
Be - tween their loved homes and the war's des - o - la - tion!

Whose broad stripes and bright stars, through the per - il - ous fight,
What is that which the breeze, o'er the tow - er - ing steep,
Blest with vic - t'ry and peace, may the heav'n-res-cued land

O'er the ram - parts we watched, were so gal - lant - ly stream-ing?
As it fit - ful - ly blows half con - ceals, half dis - clos-es?
Praise the Pow'r that hath made and pre - served us a na - tion!

My Country, 'Tis of Thee

354

AMERICA 6.6.4.6.6.6.6.4

Samuel F. Smith (1832)   *Thesaurus Musicus* (1744)

1. My coun-try, 'tis of thee, Sweet land of lib-er-ty, Of thee I sing; Land where my fa - thers died, Land of the pil - grim's pride, From ev - 'ry moun-tain-side Let free-dom ring!

2. My na-tive coun - try, thee, Land of the no - ble, free; Thy name I love; I love thy rocks and rills, Thy woods and tem - pled hills; My heart with rap - ture thrills, Like that a - bove.

3. Let mu - sic swell the breeze, And ring from all the trees Sweet free-dom's song; Let mor - tal tongues a - wake; Let all that breathe par - take; Let rocks their si - lence break, The sound pro - long.

4. Our fa - thers' God, to thee, Au - thor of lib - er - ty, To thee we sing; Long may our land be bright With free-dom's ho - ly light; Pro - tect us by thy might, Great God, our King.

355 Come, Ye Thankful People, Come

ST. GEORGE'S WINDSOR 7.7.7.7 D

Henry Alford (1844), alt.   George Elvey (1858)

1. Come, ye thank-ful peo-ple, come, Raise the song of
2. All the world is God's own field, Fruit un-to God's
3. For the Lord our God shall come, And shall take the
4. E-ven so, Lord, quick-ly come To your fi-nal

har-vest-home: All is safe-ly gath-ered in,
praise to yield; Wheat and tares to-geth-er sown,
har-vest home; From the field shall in that day
har-vest-home; Gath-er all your peo-ple in,

Ere the win-ter storms be-gin; God, our Mak-er,
Un-to joy or sor-row grown; First the blade, and
All of-fens-es purge a-way, Giv-ing an-gels
Free from sor-row, free from sin; There, for ev-er

does pro-vide For our wants to be sup-plied;
then the ear, Then the full corn shall ap-pear:
charge at last In the fire the tares to cast,
pu-ri-fied, In your pres-ence to a-bide:

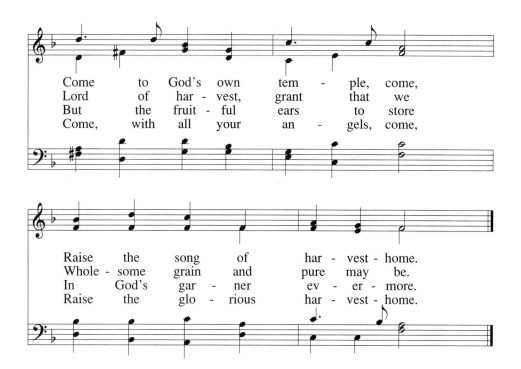

Come   to   God's   own   tem - ple,   come,
Lord   of   har - vest,   grant   that   we
But   the   fruit - ful   ears   to   store
Come,   with   all   your   an - gels,   come,

Raise   the   song   of   har - vest - home.
Whole - some   grain   and   pure   may   be.
In   God's   gar - ner   ev - er - more.
Raise   the   glo - rious   har - vest - home.

356   America the Beautiful

MATERNA CMD

Katherine L. Bates (1893)   Samuel A. Ward (1882)

1. O beau - ti - ful for spa - cious skies, For
2. O beau - ti - ful for pil - grim feet, Whose
3. O beau - ti - ful for he - roes proved In
4. O beau - ti - ful for pa - triot dream That

am - ber waves of grain, For pur - ple moun - tain
stern, im - pas - sioned stress A thor - ough - fare for
lib - er - at - ing strife, Who more than self their
sees be - yond the years Thine al - a - bas - ter

maj - es - ties A - bove the fruit - ed plain! A -
free - dom beat A - cross the wil - der - ness! A -
coun - try loved, And mer - cy more than life! A -
cit - ies gleam, Un - dimmed by hu - man tears! A -

mer - i - ca! A - mer - i - ca! God
mer - i - ca! A - mer - i - ca! God
mer - i - ca! A - mer - i - ca! May
mer - i - ca! A - mer - i - ca! God

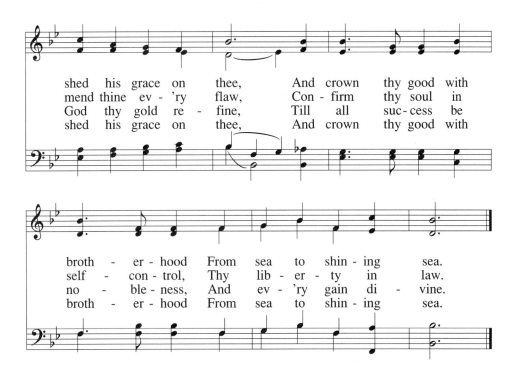

shed his grace on thee, And crown thy good with
mend thine ev - 'ry flaw, Con - firm thy soul in
God thy gold re - fine, Till all suc - cess be
shed his grace on thee, And crown thy good with

broth - er - hood From sea to shin - ing sea.
self - con - trol, Thy lib - er - ty in law.
no - ble - ness, And ev - 'ry gain di - vine.
broth - er - hood From sea to shin - ing sea.

357 Battle Hymn of the Republic

BATTLE HYMN OF THE REPUBLIC 15.15.15.6 with refrain

Julia W. Howe (1861)

Attr. to William Steffe

1. Mine eyes have seen the glo - ry of the
2. I have seen him in the watch - fires of a
3. He has sound - ed forth the trum - pet that shall
4. In the beau - ty of the lil - ies Christ was

com - ing of the Lord; He is tram - pling out the
hun - dred cir - cling camps; They have build - ed him an
nev - er call re - treat; He is sift - ing out all
born a - cross the sea, With a glo - ry in his

vin - tage where the grapes of wrath are stored; He hath
al - tar in the eve - ning dews and damps; I can
hu - man hearts be - fore his judg - ment seat; O be
bos - om that trans - fig - ures you and me; As he

loosed the fate - ful light - ning of his ter - ri - ble swift
read the right - eous sen - tence by the dim and flar - ing
swift, my soul, to an - swer him; be ju - bi - lant, my
died to make us ho - ly, let us die that all be

sword; His truth is march - ing on.
lamps; His day is march - ing on.
feet! Our God is march - ing on.
free! While God is march - ing on.

Glo - ry! Glo - ry! Hal - le - lu - jah! Glo - ry!

Glo - ry! Hal - le - lu - jah! Glo - ry! Glo - ry!

Hal - le - lu - jah! His truth is march - ing on.

358 Now Thank We All Our God

NUN DANKET ALLE GOTT 6.7.6.7.6.6.6.6

Martin Rinkart (1663)
Trans. by Catherine Winkworth (1858)

Johann Crüger (1647)
Harm. by Felix Mendelssohn (1840)

1. Now thank we all our God, With heart and hands and
2. O may this boun-teous God Through all our life be
3. All praise and thanks to God The Fa-ther now be

voic - es, Who won - drous things has done, In
near us, With ev - er joy - ful hearts And
giv - en; The Son, and him who reigns With

whom this world re - joic - es; Who from our moth-ers'
bless - ed peace to cheer us; And keep us still in
them in high - est heav - en; The one e - ter - nal

arms Has blessed us on our way With
grace, And guide us when per - plexed; And
God, Whom earth and heav'n a - dore; For

count-less gifts of love, And still is ours to - day.
free us from all ills, In this world and the next.
thus it was, is now, And shall be ev - er - more.

359 ## Sing of Mary, Meek and Lowly
PLEADING SAVIOR 8.7.8.7 D

Christian Lyre (1830)
Harm. by Richard Proulx (1986)

Roland Ford Palmer (1838)

1. Sing of Mary meek and lowly, Virgin mother
2. Sing of Jesus, son of Mary, In the home at
3. Glory be to God the Father; Glory be to

pure and mild, Sing of God's own Son most holy,
Nazareth. Toil and labor cannot weary
God the Son; Glory be to God the Spirit;

Who became her little child. Fairest child of
Love enduring unto death. Constant was the
Glory to the Three-in-One. From the heart of

fair - est moth-er, God the Lord who came to earth,
love he gave her, Though he went forth from her side,
bless - ed Mar - y, From all saints the song as - cends,

Word made flesh, our ver - y broth - er,
Forth to preach, and heal, and suf - fer,
And the church the strain re - ech - oes

Takes our na - ture by his birth.
Till on Cal - va - ry he died.
Un - to earth's re - mot - est ends.

360   **Sing We of the Blessed Mother**

OMNE DIE 8.7.8.7 D

George B. Timms (1975)   *Trier Gesängebuch* (1695)

1. Sing we of the bless-ed Moth-er Who re-ceived the an-gel's word, And o-be-dient to the sum-mons Bore in love the in-fant Lord; Sing we of the
2. Sing we, too, of Mar-y's sor-rows, Of the sword that pierced her through, When be-neath the cross of Je-sus She his weight of suf-f'ring knew, Looked up-on her
3. Sing a-gain the joys of Mar-y When she saw the ris-en Lord, And in prayer with Christ's a-pos-tles, Wait-ed on his prom-ised word: From on high the
4. Sing the great-est joy of Mar-y When on earth her work was done, And the Lord of all cre-a-tion Brought her to his heav'n-ly home: Vir-gin Moth-er,

joys of Mar-y At whose breast that child was fed
Son and Sav-ior Reign-ing from the aw - ful tree,
blaz-ing glo-ry Of the Spir-it's pres - ence came,
Mar-y bless-ed, Raised on high and crowned with grace,

Who is Son of God e - ter - nal
Saw the price of our re - demp - tion
Heav'n - ly breath of God's own be - ing,
May your Son, the world's re - deem - er,

And the ev - er - last - ing Bread.
Paid to set the sin - ner free.
To - kened in the wind and flame.
Grant us all to see his face.

361 **Immaculate Mary**

LOURDES HYMN 11.11 with refrain

St. 1, Jeremiah Cummings, alt.
St. 2-7, Brian Foley (1971)

Traditional Pyrenean melody
Grenoble (1882)

1. Im - mac - u - late Mar - y, your prais - es we sing;
2. Pre - des - tined for Christ by e - ter - nal de - cree,
3. To you by an an - gel, the Lord God made known
4. Most blest of all wom - en, you heard and be - lieved,
5. The an - gels re - joiced when you brought forth God's Son;

You reign now in splen-dor with Je - sus our King.
God willed you both vir - gin and moth - er to be.
The grace of the Spir - it, the gift of the Son.
Most blest in the fruit of your womb then con - ceived.
Your joy is the joy of all a - ges to come.

A - ve, A - ve, A - ve, Ma - ri - a.

A - ve, A - ve, Ma - ri - a.

6. Your child is the Savior, all hope lies in him:
   He gives us new life and redeems us from sin.

7. In glory for ever now close to your Son,
   All ages will praise you for all God has done.

For All the Saints

SINE NOMINE 10.10.10 with alleluias

362

Hebrews 12:1
William W. How (1864)

Ralph Vaughan Williams (1906)

1. For all the saints, who from their la - bors
2. Thou wast their rock, their for - tress, and their
3. O may thy sol - diers, faith - ful, true, and
4. O blest com - mun - ion, fel - low - ship di -
5. And when the strife is fierce, the war - fare
6. From earth's wide bounds, from o - cean's far - thest

rest, Who thee by faith be - fore the world con -
might; Thou, Lord, their cap - tain in the well - fought
bold, Fight as the saints who no - bly fought of
vine! We fee - bly strug - gle, they in glo - ry
long, Steals on the ear the dis - tant tri - umph
coast, Through gates of pearl streams in the count - less

fessed, Thy name, O Je - sus, be for ev - er blest.
fight; Thou, in the dark - ness drear, their one true light.
old, And win with them the vic - tor's crown of gold.
shine; Yet all are one in thee, for all are thine.
song, And hearts are brave a - gain, and arms are strong.
host, Sing - ing to Fa - ther, Son, and Ho - ly Ghost:

Al - le - lu - ia! Al - le - lu - ia!

363 Faith of Our Fathers

ST. CATHERINE LM with refrain

Henry F. Hemy (1864)
Frederick William Faber (1849)
Adapt. by James G. Walton (1874)

1. Faith of our fa - thers! liv - ing still
2. Our fa - thers, chained in pris - ons dark,
3. Faith of our fa - thers! faith and prayer
4. Faith of our fa - thers! we will love

In spite of dun - geon, fire and sword:
Were still in heart and con - science free:
Shall win all na - tions un - to thee;
Both friend and foe in all our strife:

O how our hearts beat high with joy,
And tru - ly blest would be our fate,
And through the truth that comes from God,
And preach thee, too, as love knows how,

When - e'er we hear that glo - rious word:
If we, like them, should die for thee.
We shall all then in - deed be free.
By kind - ly deeds and vir - tuous life.

Faith of our fa - thers, ho - ly faith!

We will be true to thee till death.

364   I Sing a Song of the Saints of God

GRAND ISLE Irregular

Lesbia Scott (1929), alt.   John Henry Hopkins (1940)

1. I sing a song of the saints of God,
2. They loved their Lord so dear, so dear, And
3. They lived not on-ly in a - ges past, There are

Pa - tient and brave and true, Who toiled and fought and
his love made them strong; And they fol - lowed the right, for
hun-dreds of thou - sands still, The world is bright with the

lived and died For the Lord they loved and knew. And
Je - sus' sake, The whole of their good lives long. And
joy - ous saints Who love to do Je - sus' will. You can

one was a doc - tor, and one was a queen, And one was a
one was a sol - dier, and one was a priest, And one was
meet them in school, or in lanes, or at sea, In church, or in

shep-herd-ess on the green: They were all of them saints of
slain by a fierce wild beast: And there's not an - y rea - son
trains, or in shops, or at tea, For the saints of God are just

God— and I mean, God help - ing, to be one too.
no, not the least, Why I should-n't be one too.
folk like me, And I mean to be one too.

365   O Holy City, Seen of John

MORNING SONG 8.6.8.6.8.6

Revelation 21
Walter Russell Bowie (1909)

Wyeth's *Repository of Sacred Music* (1813)
Harm. by Charles Winfred Douglas (1940)

1. O Ho - ly Cit - y, seen of John, Where Christ, the Lamb, does reign, With - in those four - square walls shall come No night, nor need, nor pain, And where the tears are wiped from eyes That shall not weep a - gain.

2. O shame to us who rest con - tent While lust and greed for gain In street and shop and ten - e - ment Wring gold from hu - man pain, And bit - ter lips in blind de - spair Cry, "Christ has died in vain."

3. Give us, O God, the strength to build The Cit - y that has stood Too long a dream, whose laws are love, Whose ways, the com - mon good, And where the shin - ing sun be - comes God's grace for hu - man good.

4. Al - read - y in the mind of God That Cit - y ris - es fair: Lo, how its splen - dor chal - leng - es The souls that great - ly dare: Yea, bids us seize the whole of life And build its glo - ry there.

Jerusalem the Golden

366

EWING 7.6.7.6 D

Bernard of Cluny (12th C.)
Trans. by John Mason Neale, alt.
St. 4, *Hymns Ancient and Modern* (1861)

Alexander Ewing

1. Je - ru - sa - lem the gold - en, With milk and hon - ey
2. They stand, those halls of Zi - on, All ju - bi - lant with
3. There is the throne of Da - vid; And there, from care re -
4. Oh, sweet and bless - ed coun - try, The home of God's e -

blest, Be - neath thy con - tem - pla - tion Sink heart and voice op -
song, And bright with man - y an an - gel, And all the mar - tyr
leased, The shout of them that tri - umph, The song of them that
lect! Oh, sweet and bless - ed coun - try That ea - ger hearts ex -

pressed: I know not, oh, I know not, What joys a - wait us
throng: The Prince is ev - er in them, The day - light is se -
feast; And they who with their Lead - er Have con - quered in the
pect! Je - sus, in mer - cy bring us To that dear land of

there; What ra - dian - cy of glo - ry, What bliss be - yond com - pare!
rene; The pas - tures of the bless - ed Are decked in glo - rious sheen.
fight, For ev - er and for ev - er Are clad in robes of white.
rest, Who art, with God the Fa - ther, And Spir - it, ev - er blest.

367 Glorious Things of Thee Are Spoken
AUSTRIAN HYMN 8.7.8.7 D

Psalm 87:3; Isaiah 33:20; Exodus 13:22
John Newton (1779)

Croatian folk song
Arr. by Franz Joseph Haydn (1797)

1. Glo - rious things of thee are spo - ken, Zi - on, cit - y
2. See, the streams of liv - ing wa - ters, Spring - ing from e -
3. Round each hab - i - ta - tion hov - 'ring, See the cloud and
4. Blest in - hab - i - tants of Zi - on, Washed in our Re -

of our God; God, whose word can - not be bro - ken,
ter - nal love, Well sup - ply thy sons and daugh-ters,
fire ap - pear For a glo - ry and a cov - 'ring,
deem - er's blood; Je - sus, whom our souls re - ly on,

Formed thee for his own a - bode. On the Rock of
And all fear of want re - move. Who can faint while
Show - ing that the Lord is near! Thus de - riv - ing
Makes us mon-archs, priests to God. Us, by his great

A - ges found-ed, What can shake thy sure re-pose?
such a riv - er Ev - er will their thirst as-suage?
from our ban - ner Light by night and shade by day,
love, he rais - es, Rul - ers o - ver self to reign,

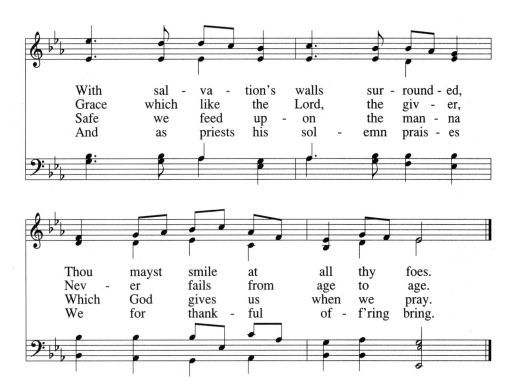

With   sal - va - tion's   walls   sur - round - ed,
Grace   which   like   the   Lord,   the   giv - er,
Safe   we   feed   up - on   the   man - na
And   as   priests his   sol - emn   prais - es

Thou   mayst   smile   at   all   thy   foes.
Nev - er   fails   from   age   to   age.
Which   God   gives   us   when we   pray.
We   for   thank - ful   of - f'ring bring.

Acknowledgements/*continued*

297 Text: © 1958, renewal 1986, Hymn Society of America. All rights reserved. Used by permission of Hope Publishing Co., Carol Stream, IL 60188. Tune: Harm. © 1906, *The English Hymnal,* Oxford University Press

299 Text: © 1954, renewal 1982, Hymn Society of America. All rights reserved. Used by permission of Hope Publishing Co., Carol Stream, IL 60188.

300 Text: © 1989, Hope Publishing Co., Carol Stream, IL 60188. All rights reserved. Used by permission.

301 Text: © 1955, 1983, Jan-Lee Music Tune: © 1955, 1983, Jan-Lee Music; acc. © 1993, GIA Publications, Inc.

302 © 1982, Hope Publishing Co., Carol Stream, IL 60188. All rights reserved. Used by permission.

304 Text: © 1966, 1979, Willard F. Jabusch. Tune: © 1966, 1979, Willard F. Jabusch; harm. © 1975, GIA Publications, Inc.

308 Text: © 1961, *Seven New Social Welfare Hymns,* Oxford University Press

310 Text: © 1906, *The English Hymnal,* Oxford University Press Tune: Harm. © 1906, *The English Hymnal,* Oxford University Press

312 © 1971, Daniel L. Schutte, administered by New Dawn Music

313 Text: © 1982, Hope Publishing Co., Carol Stream, IL 60188. All rights reserved. Used by permission. Tune: Arr. © 1977, Robertson Publications. Used by permission of Theodore Presser Co. 1 Presser Place. Brn Mawr, PA 19010-3490

315 Text: © 1985, 1994, GIA Publications, Inc. Tune: Harm. © 1985, GIA Publications, Inc.

317 Tune: Harm. © 1989, United Methodist Publishing House

318 Text: St. 2-3 © The Church Pension Fund

320 Tune: © 1931, *Enlarged Songs of Praise,* Oxford University Press

322 © 1981, Les Presses de Taizé, GIA Publications, Inc., agent

324 Tune: Harm. © 1933, 1961, Presbyterian Board of Christian Education Westminster. John Knox Press, Louisville, Kentucky

327 Tune: Harm. © 1906, *The English Hymnal,* Oxford University Press

329 Tune: © 1906,*The English Hymnal,* Oxford University Press

331 Text: © 1979, Hope Publishing Co., Tune: © 1942, renewal1970, Hope Publishing Co., Carol Stream, IL 60188. All rights reserved. Used by permission.

336 Tune: © 1906, *The English Hymnal,* Oxford University Press

339 Text: Trans. © 1906, *The English Hymnal,* Oxford University Press

343 Text: © David Higham Assoc., Ltd. Tune: Acc. © 1927, *The Church Hymnary,* Oxford University Press

359 Tune: Harm. © 1986, GIA Publications, Inc.

360 Text: © 1975, *The English Hymnal,* Oxford University Press

361 Text: © 1971, Faber Music, Ltd., London. Reprinted from NEW CATHOLIC HYMNAL

362 Tune: © 1906, *The English Hymnal,* Oxford University Press

364 Text: © 1929, Lesbia Scott, used by permission of Morehouse Publishing Co., Inc.

365 Text: © 1909, Harper and Row

Index of Composers, Authors, and Sources/ *continued*

Index of Composers, Authors, and Sources/ *continued*

Topical Index/ *continued*

Topical Index/ *continued*

Topical Index/ *continued*

Topical Index/ *continued*

Topical Index/ *continued*

Topical Index/ *continued*

Topical Index/ *continued*

306 Where Cross the Crowded Ways of Life

REPENTANCE
165 Ah, Holy Jesus
87 All Glory Be to God on High
350 All Praise to Thee, My God, This Night
261 Amazing Grace
160 Beneath the Cross of Jesus
235 Bread of the World, in Mercy Broken
158 By the Babylonian Rivers
292 Christ for the World We Sing
341 Christ Whose Glory Fills the Skies
272 Come, Thou Fount of Every Blessing
125 Comfort, Comfort O My People
265 Dear Lord and Father of Mankind
159 Forty Days and Forty Nights
109 Glory and Praise to Our God
274 God Be in My Head
90 God of the Sparrow, God of the Whale
104 God Moves in a Mysterious Way
222 God of Grace and God of Glory
298 God the Omnipotent
349 God, Who Made the Earth and Heaven
113 Great Is Thy Faithfulness
181 Hail, Thou Once Despised Jesus
299 Hope of the World
276 How Firm a Foundation
212 How Sweet the Name of Jesus
247 I Need Thee Every Hour
249 I Sought the Lord
203 Jesus, the Very Thought of Thee
239 Jesus, Thou Joy of Loving Hearts
248 Just As I Am
238 Let Us Break Bread Together
307 Lord Christ, When First You Came to Earth
161 Lord Jesus, Think on Me
271 Love Divine, All Loves Excelling
296 Make Me a Channel of Your Peace
154 My Faith Looks Up to Thee
284 My Shepherd Will Supply My Need
264 Nobody Knows the Trouble I See
347 Now the Day Is Over
204 O Christ, the Healer
259 O Happy Day, That Fixed My Choice
152 Out of the Depths I Cry
48 Psalm 22:1-18, 25-31: My God, My God, Why Have You Forsaken Me?
53 Psalm 51:1-17: Have Mercy on Me, O God
55 Psalm 90: Lord, You Have Been Our Dwelling Place
58 Psalm 103:1-18: Bless the Lord, O My Soul
60 Psalm 116: I Love the Lord
63 Psalm 130: Out of the Depths I Cry to You, O Lord
64 Psalm 139: O Lord, You Have Searched Me
319 Rock of Ages
283 Seek the Lord
98 Seek Ye First the Kingdom of God
91 Sing a New Song
107 The King of Love My Shepherd Is
103 The Lord's My Shepherd
250 There Is a Balm in Gilead
166 There Is a Green Hill Far Away
112 There's a Wideness in God's Mercy
273 'Tis the Gift to Be Simple
163 What Wondrous Love Is This
170 When I Survey the Wondrous Cross
153 Wilt Thou Forgive that Sin
230 Wonderful Words of Life

REST
217 Come, Gracious Spirit
255 Come to the Water
344 Day Is Dying in the West
362 For All the Saints
349 God, Who Made the Earth and Heaven
212 How Sweet the Name of Jesus
327 I Heard the Voice of Jesus Say

366 Jerusalem the Golden
279 Jesus, Priceless Treasure
203 Jesus, the Very Thought of Thee
239 Jesus, Thou Joy of Loving Hearts
286 Near to the Heart of God
333 O Day of Rest and Gladness
46 Psalm 16:5-11: The Lord Is My Chosen Portion
49 Psalm 23: The Lord Is My Shepherd
54 Psalm 62:5-12: For God Alone My Soul Waits in Silence
60 Psalm 116: I Love the Lord
348 The Day You Gave Us, Lord, Is Ended

SAINTS
201 All Hail the Power of Jesus' Name
363 Faith of Our Fathers
362 For All the Saints
95 For the Beauty of the Church
332 God Himself Is with Us
66 Holy God, We Praise Thy Name
70 Holy, Holy, Holy! Lord God Almighty
302 How Clear Is Our Vocation, Lord
364 I Sing a Song of the Saints of God
366 Jerusalem the Golden
305 O God of Love, O King of Peace
50 Psalm 24: The Earth Is the Lord's
96 The God of Abraham Praise
83 Ye Watchers and Ye Holy Ones

SALVATION
87 All Glory Be to God on High
164 All Glory, Laud, and Honor
213 All Praise to Thee, for Thou, O King Divine
261 Amazing Grace
179 At the Lamb's High Feast We Sing
202 At the Name of Jesus
258 Blessed Assurance, Jesus Is Mine
37 Canticle of Praise to God
42 Canticle of Simeon
43 Canticle of Zechariah
183 Christ Jesus Lay in Death's Strong Bands
185 Christ the Lord Is Risen Today
194 Fairest Lord Jesus
339 Father, We Praise You
85 From All That Dwell Below the Skies
367 Glorious Things of Thee Are Spoken
181 Hail, Thou Once Despised Jesus
200 I Love to Tell the Story
247 I Need Thee Every Hour
157 Jesus, Keep Me Near the Cross
239 Jesus, Thou Joy of Loving Hearts
248 Just As I Am
127 Let All Mortal Flesh Keep Silence
307 Lord Christ, When First You Came to Earth
156 Lord, Who throughout These Forty Days
259 O Happy Day, That Fixed My Choice
275 O Savior, in This Quiet Place
228 O Zion, Haste
50 Psalm 24: The Earth Is the Lord's
51 Psalm 27: The Lord Is My Light and My Salvation
53 Psalm 51:1-17: Have Mercy on Me, O God
54 Psalm 62:5-12: For God Alone My Soul Waits in Silence
56 Psalm 96: O Sing to the Lord
60 Psalm 116: I Love the Lord
61 Psalm 118:14-29: The Lord Is My Strength and My Power
319 Rock of Ages
256 Savior, Like a Shepherd Lead Us
118 Savior of the Nations, Come
214 Sing, My Soul, His Wondrous Love
110 Sing Praise to God Who Reigns Above
233 Thanks to God Whose Word Was Spoken
210 The King of Glory
112 There's a Wideness in God's Mercy
199 To Jesus Christ, Our Sovereign King
67 We Believe in One True God
163 What Wondrous Love Is This

SALVATION HISTORY
205 O Love, How Deep
233 Thanks to God Whose Word Was Spoken

SEASONS
77 All Beautiful the March of Days
95 For the Beauty of the Church
113 Great Is Thy Faithfulness
65 Lord of Our Growing Years
73 Now Praise the Hidden God of Love
82 Praise to God, Immortal Praise
182 Welcome, Happy Morning

SECOND COMING
202 At the Name of Jesus
357 Battle Hymn of the Republic
229 Come, Labor On
355 Come, Ye Thankful People, Come
187 Crown Him with Many Crowns
362 For All the Saints
320 God Is Working His Purpose Out
149 How Brightly Beams the Morning Star
269 I Want to Walk as a Child of the Light
252 It Is Well with My Soul
366 Jerusalem the Golden
123 Lift Up Your Heads
271 Love Divine, All Loves Excelling
328 My Hope Is Built
295 O Day of God, Draw Nigh
365 O Holy City, Seen of John
206 Of the Father's Love Begotten
135 Once in Royal David's City
188 Rejoice, the Lord Is King
91 Sing a New Song
210 The King of Glory
124 Wake, O Wake, and Sleep No Longer
253 We Remember
163 What Wondrous Love Is This

SECURITY
318 Almighty Father, Strong to Save
262 Be Thou My Vision
101 Children of the Heavenly Father
295 O Day of God, Draw Nigh
46 Psalm 16:5-11: The Lord Is My Chosen Portion
63 Psalm 130: Out of the Depths I Cry to You, O Lord
312 Yahweh, I Know You are Near

SEEKING
232 Break Thou the Bread of Life
249 I Sought the Lord
152 Out of the Depths I Cry
50 Psalm 24: The Earth Is the Lord's
63 Psalm 130: Out of the Depths I Cry to You, O Lord
283 Seek the Lord
98 Seek Ye First the Kingdom of God
189 Spirit of God, Who Dwells within my Heart
325 Sweet Hour of Prayer

SERVICE
84 All People that on Earth Do Dwell
229 Come, Labor On
265 Dear Lord and Father of Mankind
242 Gift of Finest Wheat
274 God Be in My Head
76 God, Who Stretched the Spangled Heavens
257 I Am Thine
224 In Christ There Is No East or West
288 Jesu, Jesu
308 Lord, Whose Love in Humble Service
290 Lord, You Give the Great Commission
289 O Jesus Christ, May Grateful Hymns Be Rising
281 O Master, Let Me Walk with Thee
197 There's a Spirit in the Air

SHEPHERD
165 Ah, Holy Jesus

Topical Index/ *continued*

Topical Index/ *continued*

Topical Index/ *continued*

MATTHEW

2:1-2	O Little Town of Bethlehem 132
2:1-11	We Three Kings of Orient Are 148
2:1-11	Good Christian Friends, Rejoice 142
2:1-12	Angels, from the Realms of Glory 134
2:1-12	As with Gladness Men of Old 147
2:1-12	The First Nowell 128
2:1-12	We Three Kings of Orient Are 148
2:10-11	O Come, All Ye Faithful 133
2:11	What Child Is This 136
4:1-2	Forty Days and Forty Nights 159
4:1-11	Lord, Who throughout These Forty Days 156
4:16	Comfort, Comfort, O My People 125
4:24	The King of Glory 210
4:24	Your Hands, O Lord, in Days of Old 150
5:13	Gather Us In 240
6:25-34	Lord of All Hopefulness 287
6:33	Seek Ye First the Kingdom of God 98
7:7	Seek Ye First the Kingdom of God 98
10:42	There's a Spirit in the Air 197
11:25-30	I Heard the Voice of Jesus Say 327
11:28-30	Come to the Water 255
12:21	Hope of the World 299
13:21-43	Come, Ye Thankful People, Come 355
14:14	Love Divine, All Loves Excelling 271
14:22-33	How Firm a Foundation 276
14:22-33	I Sought the Lord 249
16:13-15	Tell Me the Stories of Jesus 277
18:10-14	My Shepherd Will Supply My Need 284
18:10-14	The King of Love My Shepherd Is 107
20:1-16	For the Fruits of This Creation 93
21:1-17	All Glory, Laud, and Honor 164
21:8-9	Tell Me the Stories of Jesus 277
21:33-43	Christ Is Made the Sure Foundation 223
23:37	O Jesus Christ, May Grateful Hymns Be Rising 289
25:1-13	How Brightly Beams the Morning Star 149
25:31-46	There's a Spirit in the Air 197
25:37-45	For the Fruits of This Creation 93
26:30	When, in Our Music, God Is Glorified 81
27:27-31	O Sacred Head, Now Wounded 168
28:6-9	Christ the Lord Is Risen Today 185
28:18	Alleluia! Sing to Jesus 186
28:18	Lord, You Give the Great Commission 290

MARK

1:1-8	Comfort, Comfort, O My People 125
1:12-15	Lord, Who throughout These Forty Days 156
1:29-39	Your Hands, O Lord, in Days of Old 150
1:30-34	O Christ, the Healer 204
1:40-45	Your Hands, O Lord, in Days of Old 150
4:26-29	For the Fruits of This Creation 93
4:35-41	How Firm a Foundation 276
5:15	O Christ, the Healer 204
5:21-43	O Jesus Christ, May Grateful Hymns Be Rising 289
6:30-34	I Heard the Voice of Jesus Say 327
6:30-34	There's a Wideness in God's Mercy 112
10:13-16	Tell Me the Stories of Jesus 277
11:1-11	All Glory, Laud, and Honor 164
11:8-10	Tell Me the Stories of Jesus 277
12:28-34	God Be in My Head 274
13:2	Lord Christ, When First You Came to Earth 307
14:26	When, in Our Music, God Is Glorified 81
15:16-20	O Sacred Head, Now Wounded 168

LUKE

1:26-38	Immaculate Mary 361
1:26-38	Sing We of the Blessed Mother 360
1:26-45	Savior of the Nations, Come 118
1:46b-55	Tell Out, My Soul, the Greatness of the Lord 120
1:46b-55	Canticle of Mary 41
1:68-79	Canticle of Zechariah 43
1:78-79	O Come, O Come, Emmanuel 121
2:1-10	The First Nowell 128
2:1-18	From Heaven Above 144
2:6-7	Savior of the Nations, Come 118
2:6-14	Silent Night, Holy Night 146
2:6-18	Angels, from the Realms of Glory 134
2:6-18	God Rest You Merry, Gentlemen 138
2:6-18	Go Tell It on the Mountain 140
2:6-18	What Child Is This 136
2:6-20	Infant Holy, Infant Lowly 126

2:7	Away in a Manger 130 131
2:7	Good Christian Friends, Rejoice 142
2:7	Lo, How a Rose E'er Blooming 119
2:7	Once in Royal David's City 135
2:7	Sing of Mary, Meek and Lowly 359
2:8-14	It Came Upon the Midnight Clear 141
2:8-14	While Shepherds Watched Their Flocks 137
2:10-11	God Rest You Merry, Gentlemen 138
2:10-11	Good Christian Friends, Rejoice 142
2:10-11	Go Tell It on the Mountain 140
2:10-11	It Came Upon the Midnight Clear 141
2:10-11	O Come, All Ye Faithful 133
2:10-11,14	From Heaven Above 144
2:10-14	Immaculate Mary 361
2:13-14	All Glory Be to God on High 87
2:13-15	O Come, All Ye Faithful 133
2:13-18	Angels We Have Heard on High 139
2:14	Canticle of God's Glory 38
2:14	From Heaven Above 144
2:15	O Come, All Ye Faithful 133
2:29-32	Canticle of Simeon 42
2:40	Sing of Mary, Meek and Lowly 359
3:4,6	On Jordan's Bank 116
4:1-2	Lord, Who throughout These Forty Days 156
4:1-13	Forty Days and Forty Nights 159
6:20ff	Be Not Afraid 266
7:11-17	Your Hands, O Lord, in Days of Old 150
8:22-25	How Firm a Foundation 276
9:57	O Jesus, I Have Promised 309
11:1-13	Seek Ye First the Kingdom of God 98
13:29	In Christ There Is No East or West 224
15:3-7	The King of Love My Shepherd Is 107
15:31-32	For the Fruits of This Creation 93
18:9-14	Gather Us In 240
19:37-38	All Glory, Laud, and Honor 164
23:33,44,50-53	Were You There 169
23:42	Jesus, Remember Me 322
24:1-2	Were You There 169
24:1-12	O Sons and Daughters, Let Us Sing! 180
24:34	Christ the Lord Is Risen Today 185
24:50-53	Alleluia! Sing to Jesus 186
24:51-53	Love Divine, All Loves Excelling 271

JOHN

1:1	At the Name of Jesus 202
1:1-5	O Come, All Ye Faithful 133
1:1-18	Christ Is the World's Light 196
1:9	I Heard the Voice of Jesus Say 327
1:9	O Gladsome Light 346
1:14	O Come, All Ye Faithful 133
1:14	Of the Father's Love Begotten 206
1:15-28	On Jordan's Bank 116
1:29	Canticle of God's Glory 38
3:5	Hark! The Herald Angels Sing 143
3:16	Christ Is Made the Sure Foundation 223
3:16	What Wondrous Love Is This 163
4:5-42	I Heard the Voice of Jesus Say 327
4:14	I Heard the Voice of Jesus Say 327
4:20	Christ Is the World's Light 196
6:	Eat This Bread 244
6:	I Am the Bread of Life 207
6:34	Gift of Finest Wheat 242
6:35-58	Deck Thyself, My Soul, with Gladness 241
6:35,51	Let All Mortal Flesh Keep Silence 127
6:41-59	Alleluia! Sing to Jesus 186
6:48	Hope of the World 299
8:12	Christ Is the World's Light 196
8:12	I Heard the Voice of Jesus Say 327
8:31	Faith of Our Fathers 363
9:1-41	Amazing Grace 261
10:	My Shepherd Will Supply My Need 284
10:	The King of Love My Shepherd Is 107
10:1-29	Savior, Like a Shepherd Lead Us 256
10:1-5	Gift of Finest Wheat 242
11:25-27	I Am the Bread of Life 207
12:12-16	All Glory, Laud, and Honor 164
12:13	Tell Me the Stories of Jesus 277
12:20-33	O God beyond All Praising 78
12:46	I Want to Walk as a Child of the Light 269
13:3-5	Jesu, Jesu, Fill Us with Your Love 288

14:1-3	Father, We Praise You 339
14:8-10	Christ Is the World's Light 196
14:15-21	Come Down, O Love Divine 329
14:18	Alleluia! Sing to Jesus 186
15:1-8	How Brightly Beams the Morning Star 149
15:5	I Need Thee Every Hour 247
17:24	The God of Abraham Praise 96
19:	What Wondrous Love Is This 163
19:1-5	O Sacred Head, Now Wounded 168
19:2	When I Survey the Wondrous Cross 170 171
19:25	Immaculate Mary 361
19:25	Sing We of the Blessed Mother 360
19:34	Were You There 169
20:	That Easter Day with Joy Was Bright 173
20:	O Sons and Daughters, Let Us Sing! 180
20:11-18	Christ the Lord Is Risen Today 185
20:19-31	O Sons and Daughters, Let Us Sing! 180

ACTS

1:8	Come Down, O Love Divine 329
1:8	Alleluia! Sing to Jesus 186
2:	O Spirit of the Living God 220
10:37	On Jordan's Bank 116

ROMANS

1:28-32	O Christ, the Healer 204
4:20-21	The God of Abraham Praise 96
6:4, 9	We Know That Christ Is Raised 245
6:5-11	Christ Is Alive 177
8:14-17	In Christ There Is No East or West 224
8:15-16	At the Name of Jesus 202
8:15-17	Every Time I Feel the Spirit 216
8:18-39	There's a Wideness in God's Mercy 112
11:33-35	There's a Wideness in God's Mercy 112

1 CORINTHIANS

1:15-20	We Know That Christ Is Raised 245
1:18	Lift High the Cross 208
3:11	Christ Is Made the Sure Foundation 223
3:13-15	Come, Ye Thankful People, Come 355
5:18-20	God Is Working His Purpose Out 320
10:16	One Bread, One Body 234
10:16-17	Gift of Finest Wheat 242
11:23-26	I Come with Joy 236
11:23-29	Let Us Break Bread Together 238
12:	In Christ There Is No East or West 224
12:4	One Bread, One Body 234
12:27-31	God Is Here! As We His People 331
13:	Not for Tongues of Heaven's Angels 291
13:12	Love Divine, All Loves Excelling 271
15:10	Amazing Grace 261
15:20-28	Come, Ye Faithful, Raise the Strain 184
15:25	Christ Is the World's Light 196
15:51-54	The Strife Is O'er 175
15:55	Christ the Lord Is Risen Today 185
16:	When, in Our Music, God Is Glorified 81
17:	One Bread, One Body 234

2 CORINTHIANS

3:18	Love Divine, All Loves Excelling 271
4:5	God Is Here! As We His People 331
5:17	Love Divine, All Loves Excelling 271
9:10-14	Come, Ye Thankful People, Come 355
13:11	The God of Abraham Praise 96
13:13	May the Grace of Christ Our Savior 246

GALATIANS

2:20	I Heard the Voice of Jesus Say 327
3:23, 28	In Christ There Is No East or West 224
3:28	One Bread, One Body 234
4:4	Hark! The Herald Angels Sing 143
5:22	For the Fruits of This Creation 93
6:14	When I Survey the Wondrous Cross 170 171

EPHESIANS

1:9-11	God Is Working His Purpose Out 320
1:19-23	Holy God, We Praise Thy Name 66
2:8	Amazing Grace 261
2:11-18	Christ Is the World's Light 196
2:20-22	Christ Is Made the Sure Foundation 223

4:	O Christ, the Healer 204
4:1-6	In Christ There Is No East or West 224
4:8	The God of Abraham Praise 96
5:14	Wake, O Wake, and Sleep No Longer 124
5:27	Love Divine, All Loves Excelling 271
6:9	For the Fruits of This Creation 93
6:10-17	Stand Up, Stand Up for Jesus 270

PHILIPPIANS

2:5-7	At the Name of Jesus 202
2:5-11	All Praise to Thee, for Thou, O King Divine 213
2:8	Hark! The Herald Angels Sing 143
2:9-10	All Hail the Power of Jesus' Name 201
2:9-10	The God of Abraham Praise 96
2:11-12	At the Name of Jesus 202
3:7-11	When I Survey the Wondrous Cross 170 171
4:4-5	Rejoice, the Lord Is King 188

COLOSSIANS

1:16	Ye Watchers and Ye Holy Ones 83
1:18	Christ the Lord Is Risen Today 185
3:11	In Christ There Is No East or West 224
3:16	When, in Our Music, God Is Glorified 81

2 THESSALONIANS

2:15	God Is Here! As We His People 331

1 TIMOTHY

1:17	Immortal, Invisible, God Only Wise 74
6:12	Faith of Our Fathers 363
6:15-16	Immortal, Invisible, God Only Wise 74

2 TIMOTHY

2:19	How Firm a Foundation 276
4:3-7	Faith of Our Fathers 363

TITUS

2:14	God Is Here! As We His People 331

HEBREWS

1:3	Rejoice, the Lord Is King 188
7:12	The God of Abraham Praise 96
9:11-14	Alleluia! Sing to Jesus 186
9 & 10	The King of Glory 210
10:20	Alleluia! Sing to Jesus 186
11	Faith of Our Fathers 363
11:32-40	Faith of Our Fathers 363
12:1	For All the Saints 362
12:1	I Want to Walk as a Child of the Light 269
12:1-3	Holy God, We Praise Thy Name 66
13:5	How Firm a Foundation 276
13:6	My Shepherd Will Supply My Need 284

JAMES

1:10-17	Immortal, Invisible, God Only Wise 74
1:17	For the Beauty of the Earth 95
1:17	From All That Dwell below the Skies 85
1:17	I Sing the Almighty Power of God 97
1:17	America the Beautiful 356
2:1	In Christ There Is No East or West 224
5:13-16	O Christ, the Healer 204
5:13-16	Your Hands, O Lord, in Days of Old 150

1 PETER

1:16	Take Time to Be Holy 254
2:4-6	Christ Is Made the Sure Foundation 223
2:9-10	God Is Here! As We His People 331

2 PETER

1:4	How Firm a Foundation 276

1 JOHN

1:5	I Want to Walk as a Child of the Light 269
1:5	Canticle of Light and Darkness 44
2:9	Christ Is the World's Light 196
3:18	Faith of Our Fathers 363
4:7-17	Love Divine, All Loves Excelling 271
4:9-10	What Wondrous Love Is This 163
4:9-10	O God of Every Nation 297

REVELATION

1:8	Of the Father's Love Begotten 206
1:18	Rejoice, the Lord Is King 188
1:18	The Strife Is O'er 175
2:10	For All the Saints 362
4:	Holy, Holy, Holy! Lord God Almighty 70
4:2-11	Hail, Thou Once Despised Jesus 181
4-5	Holy God, We Praise Thy Name 66
4:6	Alleluia! Sing to Jesus 186
4:8	Come, Thou Almighty King 69
4:8	Of the Father's Love Begotten 206
4:8	The God of Abraham Praise 96
4:8-11	Holy, Holy, Holy! Lord God Almighty 70
4:10	Love Divine, All Loves Excelling 271
5:9	Alleluia! Sing to Jesus 186
5:9	At the Lamb's High Feast We Sing 179
5:9	Crown Him with Many Crowns 187
5:9	To Jesus Christ, Our Sovereign King 199
5:11-14	All Hail the Power of Jesus' Name 201
5:13	All Glory, Laud, and Honor 164
5:13	The God of Abraham Praise 96
6:9-11	All Hail the Power of Jesus' Name 201
6:9-11	Holy God, We Praise Thy Name 66
7:2-4,9-14	For All the Saints 362
7:9-12	From All That Dwell below the Skies 85
15:4	Holy, Holy, Holy! Lord God Almighty 70
19:11-16	Come, Thou Almighty King 69
19:11-16	Let All Mortal Flesh Keep Silence 127
19:12	Crown Him with Many Crowns 187
21:	O Holy City, Seen of John 365
21:9-13	Wake, O Wake, and Sleep No Longer 124
21:23	I Want to Walk as a Child of the Light 269
22:	O Holy City, Seen of John 365
22:17	I Heard the Voice of Jesus Say 327
22:17	We Know That Christ Is Raised 245

Metrical Index of Tunes /*continued*

ONE OF A KIND

4.4.7.4.4.7.4.4.4.4.7
126 W ZLOBIE LEZY

4.10.10.10.4
229 ORA LABORA

5.4.6.7.7
90 ROEDER

5.5.5.4 D
343 BUNESSAN

5.6.8.5.5.8
194 ST. ELIZABETH

6.4.6.4 D
232 BREAD OF LIFE

6.4.6.4 WITH REFRAIN
247 NEED

6.4.6.4.6.6.4.4
321 MORE LOVE TO THEE

6.4.6.4.6.6.6.4
311 BETHANY

6.5.6.5
347 MERRIAL

6.5.6.5 WITH REFRAIN
221 ST. GERTRUDE

6.6.11 D
329 DOWN AMPNEY

6.6.5.6.6.5.7.8.6
279 JESU, MEINE FREUDE

6.6.6 D
340 LAUDES DOMINI

6.6.6.6.4.4.8
211 DARWALL'S 148TH

6.6.7.6.6.7
346 NUNC DIMITTIS

6.6.7.7.7.7.5.5
142 IN DULCI JUBILO

6.6.8.4 D
96 LEONI

6.6.8.6.6.8.6.6.6
332 ARNSBERG

6.6.8.9.6.6
146 STILLE NACHT

6.7.6.7.6.6.6.6
358 NUN DANKET ALLE GOTT

7.6.7.6 D WITH REFRAIN
200 HANKEY

7.6.7.6.6.7.
119 ES IST EIN' ROS' ENTSPRUNGEN

7.6.8.6.8.6.8.6
160 ST. CHRISTOPHER

7.7.7.7 WITH ALLELUIAS
185 EASTER HYMN

7.7.7.7 D WITH REFRAIN
143 MENDELSSOHN

7.7.7.7.4 WITH REFRAIN
344 CHAUTAUQUA

7.8.7.8.7.7
66 GROSSER GOTT

8.4.8.4.5.4.5.4
277 STORIES OF JESUS

8.6.8.6.6.6
230 WORDS OF LIFE

8.6.8.6.7.6.8.6
132 ST. LOUIS

8.6.8.6.8.6 WITH REFRAIN
138 GOD REST YOU MERRY

8.6.8.8.6
265 REST

8.6.8.8.6.6
302 REPTON

8.7.8.5
282 ST. LEONARDS

8.7.8.7.4.7
233 WYLDE GREEN

8.7.8.7.6.6.6.6.7
330 EIN' FESTE BURG

8.7.8.7.7.7
135 IRBY

8.7.8.7.7.7.8.8
125 GENEVA 42

8.7.8.7.7.8.7.4
183 CHRIST LAG IN TODESBANDEN

8.8.4.4.6 WITH REFRAIN
148 KINGS OF ORIENT

8.8.7.8.8.7.4.4.4.4.8
149 WIE SCHÖN LEUCHTET

8.8.8.4
218 MEYER

8.8.8.8.6
323 ST. MARGARET

8.8.9.8 WITH REFRAIN
326 OPEN MY EYES

Metrical Index of Tunes /*continued*

Index of Tunes/ *continued*

Index of First Lines and Common Titles/ *continued*

Index of First Lines and Common Titles/ *continued*

Index of First Lines and Common Titles/ *continued*

Appendix
Psalm Tones

These tones may be photocopied for use with the psalms included in this hymnal.

Tone 1

Tone 2

Tone 5